DATE DUE

MY 9 05			
AP 27 '10			

DEMCO 38-296

split

a counterculture childhood

lisa michaels

Houghton Mifflin Company

BOSTON · NEW YORK 1998

For information about permission to reproduce
selections from this book, write to
Permissions, Houghton Mifflin Company,
215 Park Avenue South, New York,
New York 10003.

Library of Congress Cataloging-in-Publication Data
Michaels, Lisa.
Split : a counterculture childhood / Lisa Michaels
p.   cm.
ISBN 0-395-83739-1
1. Michaels, Lisa — Childhood and youth.
2. Authors, American — California — Biography.
3. Hippies — California — Biography. 4. Sub-
culture —California — History — 20th century.
5. Communal living — California — History —
20th century. 6. California — Biography. I. Title.
CT275.M51315A3   1998
979.4'05'092 [B] — dc21   98-11867 CIP

Printed in the United States of America

Book design by Robert Overholtzer

QUM 10 9 8 7 6 5 4 3 2 1

The poem "The Burden of Protest" is reprinted
with permission from *Life* magazine.
Copyright © Time Inc.

For my sisters and my brother

acknowledgments

....

My thanks to Mauricio Schabes for his easy
companionship, to Leslie Jonath and Bill Hayes,
who took time away from their own writing to
read drafts, and to Ann Lewis and Bernard
Cooper for long-distance moral support. Dawn
Seferian, Andrew Wylie, and, in particular,
Sarah Chalfant had faith in this project from the
beginning, for which I am amazed and grateful.
Carl Walesa gave the manuscript a careful
once-over. William Lung and Jin Auh helped
with countless details. To Wendy Lesser I owe
a debt that I can't repay. This book would
not have been possible without her.

split

one

A FEW YEARS AGO, when I was visiting New York, my Grandma Leila (the archivist of the family) produced a pristine copy of *Life* magazine, dated November 21, 1969: the day I turned three. Johnny Cash is on the cover, playing acoustic guitar in front of the massive wheels of a freight train, steam gusting up around his waist. He has one pointy boot poised on the edge of a railroad tie, and a silver lamé scarf glitters at his neck: "The Rough-Cut King of Country Music," the headline reads. Inside is an article on Jesse Jackson — "black hope, white hope" — and photographs of Dr. Elisabeth Kübler-Ross's first seminar on death and dying, in which a beautiful young woman talks about her leukemia while health care workers weep behind a two-way mirror. It is a sampling of the times, but that wasn't why my grandmother saved it for twenty-five years.

On the last page of the issue, under the heading "Parting Shots," is a picture of me just shy of three, carrying an unfurled Vietcong flag across a patch of trampled grass. At the top of the frame, the flag bisects the body of a man, leaving a diagonal of rumpled coat, one arm stuffed into a pocket. Long, bottle-nosed cars are parked on the street behind him, bleached white by the glare. What looks to be cold autumnal light shines through the flag — two silky panels with a star in the center — and lifts a white corona around the edges of my head. I look highly serious, hunched over to counter the weight of the long pole, wearing a short dress and little brown work boots: a pintsize protester, trudging along, head down, my chin slung forward in concentration.

The editors at *Life* wrote a poem to go with the picture, which they called "The Burden of Protest":

> Is toting a Vietcong flag
> In a war demonstration the bag
> Of a child or a parent?
> We'd say someone's errant —
> This kid should be off playing tag.

It's a smarmy piece of copy — never a good idea to take the moral high ground in a limerick. Notably, the poem took a potshot at my mother, who to the editor's mind was conspicuously absent, having loaded me up with my ideological burden and disappeared.

But my mother says she was there that day, and the picture lied: I had picked up the flag on my own. She can almost recite the doggerel from memory. "That poem was a criticism of my parenting," she said once with a laugh. "Some mothers worried about stuff going on at those rallies, but me, a nice girl from the suburbs, I was a trusting soul. I came to pick you up from your dad and there you were dancing around with that flag. Your dress — you can't see this from the picture because it's black-and-white — was red velvet, a real thick velvet, and some part of the flag was red and you looked gorgeous. They found one shot where you seem burdened, but really you were having a blast. And the photographer knew it."

The first time I saw this picture was in my father's house. I must have been eight or so. He had trimmed away the offending poem, framed the photo in mat board, and typed his own caption. I can't reconstruct his text entire, because the picture was lost in some move, but his final line sticks in my head: "Could it be that at three you caught the spirit of the worldwide movement for socialism, and shouted, 'Hey, everybody, wait for me!'"

Clearly, he had caught the spirit. I imagine that at three I measured the world on more intimate terms: my father was the sun; my mother was the moon. Years later when I looked at my father's handiwork, hung in the living room, the site of many a strategy meeting and leaflet-folding session, I felt a mixture of pride and pique. I was the treasured one, matted and reframed. But his gaze fell on me at an odd angle. That caption says much about what my father wanted me to be: a comrade, a willing enthusiast for the work to be done.

But caption or no caption, looking at that picture now takes my breath away. November 21, 1969. Two months earlier, my father carried that same flag into the Harvard Center for International Affairs — an organization that did counterinsurgency research for the government — and along with twenty of his fellow Weathermen ran through the building, dumping over filing cabinets, breaking windows, and tearing out phones. In the tumult, blows were exchanged between protesters and staff. Two months after the picture was snapped my father would be in prison. When I swung that flag across Boston Common, it was a swath of fabric to me, nothing more. I waved it over the sunlit grass in a calm between emergencies, one sock up, one down, oblivious to what was to come.

I told my mother the story of my father's caption, nearly thirty years after their divorce, and she laughed with a rueful note of recognition. Still, I was surprised that she didn't leap at the chance to peg him. Instead, her laughter wound down to a sigh: "Well, I suppose my reading is just as suspect. So Pollyannaish: the sun was shining; you were the perfect child." And it's true, out of the tangle of the past my mother preserves mostly primary colors, the quality of the light, my power and exuberance. Even though she knew that in those months my father was anxiously preparing for his trial, that she was planning to pack up and head for Mexico, that our lives were about to fly apart.

My parents met at Cornell in 1962, on a grassy slope overlooking Lake Cayuga. My father, a junior, was a fitful student; my mother was a freshman, thrilled to be taking up the scholar's life. When I asked her what she thought of him that first day, she squinted off into the distance, choosing each word carefully — "lean, intense and witty, sparkly-eyed, charming." She wore her hair shoulder length, bobbed up like a Ronette, her eyes rimmed with black liner. And the clothes? "I think we wore skirts, for crying out loud. Short skirts — above our knees." I wanted to see how they looked, what they wore, but my mother would rather describe the surroundings: the big drop down from Cornell to the lake, a narrow band of silver visible through the trees, the magnolia in the library courtyard that scented the air at that time of year.

My father invited her to see a musical at the playhouse. It was *The Fantasticks*, and at the memory of it she started into one of the songs, something I'd heard her sing when I was a child, never understanding the reverence that came over her as she sang the maudlin lyrics. "Do you remember that kind of September when days were long and oh so mellow?" It was a love story, of course, and when they came out and walked through the darkened campus, my mother and father stopped on a wooden bridge, one of many that spanned the hillside's narrow gorges. The water rushed through granite pools below them, and over the white roaring they spoke perhaps too intimately for people who had met only that afternoon. It didn't seem odd to them. "I was aware of this immense electric energy between us," my mother said.

"You don't know," my father told me once, "how stunning your mother was. I was in the Jewish fraternity, and we used to sit around with the yearbook looking at the incoming freshman girls. She was a knockout."

I came across that yearbook picture in a family album when I was still a gawky schoolgirl. It's a three-quarter profile shot, my mother's thick straight hair spilling over one shoulder and beyond the frame, her long nose and smooth forehead catching the light.

"You were so pretty!" I told her, unaware of how I bungled the compliment with the past tense.

My mother bent over me, studying the photo as if it were of some other girl, someone she knew once and with whom she had long since lost touch.

As my mother tells it, she and my father were rarely apart in that first year. She helped him with his homework, and they spent many long nights exchanging stories — the way all lovers talk in the beginning, I suppose, with the kind of eloquence that passion allows. It wasn't all directed inward. That spring, in Michigan, SDS released its Port Huron Statement, and at the same time word was beginning to filter up from the South about the protests there, tales of sit-ins and marches and lynchings. It seemed that all around them, on the lawns and in the ivy-covered brick buildings, there were signs of a general awakening.

I suppose you could say my parents were both idealists, though that word has become tinged with naiveté. I mean it in a positive sense: they both believed that human conditions could be made better, and they were willing to work to make such change come about. Over that year, they talked a lot about where they had come from — the first step toward deciding who they would become.

At the end of her freshman year, my mother went to live with her parents in Huntington, New York, and took a job at La Guardia, which her father, who worked for the Port Authority, had arranged for her. She sat alone in an office all day, doing the books for a company that serviced private aircraft. Outside on the runway, planes lifted off for Istanbul or Paris, while she tallied columns across and down: how many gallons of waste were emptied out of the Lear jets, how much fuel had been sold. The boss came in for an hour or so in the morning, then disappeared for the rest of the day, casual about his sinecure.

That glimpse into her father's world disillusioned my mother. Bob Inman bore a resemblance to Bob Hope and shared a similar humor, voted for Goldwater, and was known for his business smarts and sociability. At home, he dropped the devilish charm and turned gruff. My mother once came home with her report card — five As and one A-minus — and presented it to her father, aglow with pride. "I'll give you five dollars when you get all As," he told her, turning back to his ball game. In her final year of high school, my mother spent her evenings with him in the den, memorizing every word in the Latin dictionary, a task he fell to with a sportsman's relish. It was the last hoop she jumped through to please him, but she finished with flair —

beating out students from eight states at sight-reading Latin —
and waltzed into Cornell with a Regents scholarship.

The summer after her freshman year, my mother rode back
and forth to the airport with her father and the chief of maintenance, who chauffeured them in a Port Authority car. It was
1963, and the Long Island Expressway was being paved along
the north shore. Since the car had special plates and a rack of
lights, the maintenance chief drove around the construction
barriers and rode the empty freeway all the way to Huntington.
My mother traces her first serious thoughts of social justice to
those evening rides, as she sat in the back seat staring at her
father's balding head.

My father spent that same summer living with his mother in
Valley Stream, not far from my mother's house by car, but a
world apart in mood and history. His mother, my Grandma
Leila, grew up on New York's Lower East Side, where her father
ran a series of confection businesses. He was good at his voca-
tion — frugal and hard working — but the Depression almost
put him under. Leila's mother died when she was still a young
girl, and the stepmother who replaced her on short notice was a
hardened woman, shrewd enough to keep house and feed another woman's children in hard times, but prone to harping
on Leila's shortcomings. When my grandfather, Charles, came
along and wanted to marry, Leila was quick to the chance.

I remember my grandfather in his sixties — overweight and
wracked by emphysema — but Leila once showed me an old
photograph that made me understand his appeal. He's in an
army uniform, fists perched at the small of his back so his jacket
is held at bay. This might be the way he always stood, but it has
the look of a pose, a pose meant to call attention to his belt
bristling with a soldier's accouterments: pouches and buckles,
binoculars, a canteen. He smiles slyly from under his brows,
the glare that fills one half of the photo eliding a sliver of his
cheek, so his face looks almost lean — my father's face. Behind
him: wheel ruts and a truck driving out of the frame, its cargo
draped with a tarp. The man looks like he's up to something.

My grandfather returned from the war and began a slow

withdrawal from the family. He made a bundle selling mailing lists, lost it, made another fortune in art, squandered that. Always remaking himself. During those years he kept a lover, and later he married her. When he finally abandoned the family, and failed month after month to hand over the child-support check, Leila took a job at a department store — working long hours to keep up the mortgage payments — and tried to fill the gap in her son's affections. More than once my father has acknowledged that his fierce loyalty toward the oppressed began in his own house, in his role as his mother's champion.

Still, in spite of her hard luck, my Grandma Leila moved through life with an astonishing absence of rancor. Growing up under her stepmother's shriveling gaze, she didn't choose bitterness. She visited her stepmother until the day she died, brought food to the nursing home, and listened even then to disparaging comments leveled from the heap of sour bed sheets. And of my grandfather, who used to take her down peg by peg over the dinner table, she can still speak fairly and evenly.

Looking back, Leila's gentle nature seems a miracle to me. I think sometimes of the families branching back into the millennium behind me: my father, my father's father, my father's father's father, until they become strangers, their names and stories lost. If we could pass through these families, we might watch a kind of undulating loss and recovery of happiness, of sanity — for surely certain lives are better than others — steered by material circumstance: famine or fortune, sickness or wealth or calamity. But also by choice. By one person looking at the people who raised her and deciding what to carry and what to toss away like useless freight.

Out of these varied pasts, my mother and father came together, a testament to the attraction of opposites. The only photographs I have of their brief union were taken during that time: four black-and-white frames from a coin-operated booth. My mother is nineteen, my father twenty-one. Their faces are pressed together in front of a pleated curtain, scrubbed and gleaming in the washed-out prints. My father could have stepped straight off a balcony in *West Side Story:* his curly hair slicked back into waves, his skin olive, lips full. He is laughing in the first shot, the gap in his front teeth giving him a vulnerable air. My mother's hair sweeps away from her face and cups his cheek, the last wisp seeming to give him a cleft chin. She says they had gone out to dinner in Greenwich Village and missed the train back to Valley Stream. Grand Central Station, 1 A.M.; "God, we were so in love." And yes, it's all there in the photo: their faces full of the sharp present tense of happiness.

Not long after that, my mother brought my father home to Huntington, and her parents gave him a withering reception. Kate and Bob served an endless parade of highballs and tried to mask their disdain with tight smiles and platitudes about how some of their best friends were Jews.

My mother still can't say what proportion of crassness and wisdom made them warn her off my father, but she thinks that if they hadn't hated my father, she might not have married him. Their college romance was showing its seams. But as soon as her parents made their disapproval known, as soon as they brought their stuffiness and bigotry into the equation, she told them, "In a pig's eye. I'm marrying him."

And marry they did, in 1964, when my father had just graduated from Cornell and my mother had finished her sophomore year. My grandfather Bob, despite his rue, invited his business friends and spared no expense. At the rehearsal dinner my mother ate frogs' legs with garlic, and out of some mixture of fear and indigestion she spent the night before her wedding retching in the hotel bathroom. At the reception she and my father got separated, and she wandered through the cacophonous crowd, still faint from her sleepless night, being kissed and gripped by hundreds of near strangers.

After the wedding, my parents moved in with Grandma Leila in Valley Stream. My father took a job teaching in the Newark public schools, and my mother transferred to Sarah Lawrence to finish her bachelor's degree. The change in colleges suited her. Sarah Lawrence had no official majors; students were allowed to design their own curriculum. That freedom and rigor renewed my mother's interest in her studies, at a time when talk inside the classroom had begun to seem disconnected from the urgent mood in the streets. In the fall, eight hundred students were arrested at a sit-in at U.C. Berkeley. In the spring, Lyndon Johnson launched an all-out war on North Vietnam. My father went to teach in the ghetto and brought home stories of families barely clinging to the hem of working life.

Late in her second year at Sarah Lawrence, my mother took a poetry course with Muriel Rukeyser. The class met in a cottage set in a nook of the campus, surrounded by a flowering garden. Inside, the students sat in a circle, with the doors thrown open to the greenery, and talked about poetry and politics and daily life.

My mother thought of Muriel as a mentor and went to speak with her often, but one afternoon in particular frequents her stories. She had just found out she was pregnant, and at twenty-one, with a war on and her marriage under strain, the prospect of motherhood made her worry.

"I don't know if this is a good time to bring a person into the world," she said.

Muriel looked her in the eye. "Don't worry about the baby," she said. "Babies are powerful. They look helpless, but you'll see: the world will turn around it."

That summer, my mother graduated from Sarah Lawrence and she and my father moved to Newark to work on the Newark Community Union Project, part of a wave of student activists moving to the ghettos. NCUP ran a storefront office headquarters and held meetings that stretched into the early morning hours. My father went around ringing doorbells, visiting with people in the neighborhood, working with them to file complaints against the slumlords.

Around that time, my mother's uncle took her aside and offered her a job at his bond brokerage firm. She was a bright girl; he needed people like her. She could rent a place in Manhattan, get a nanny for the baby, and start socking it away for a house on Long Island. My mother smiled and said thanks but no thanks. She had set her sights on another career: she wanted to teach school in Harlem.

It would be a while before she fulfilled that goal, but in the meantime she and my father lived in a world her uncle would have found unfathomable. They rented a dingy one-bedroom apartment in a section of Newark that had cobblestone streets and erratic garbage collection. They didn't drink or smoke, never did drugs, never ate out, never went to the movies. Instead, they spent their days organizing rent strikes, trying to get the trash collected, and, in late 1966, backing a black liberal Republican, Earl Harris, in a bid for a council seat against a white Democrat.

In a profile of Tom Hayden in *New York* magazine (another clipping Grandma Leila saved) the writer has this to say about NCUP: "Newark Community Union Project: Romance drips all over it; the young radicals love it out there across the land." In a photo that went with the article, a group of these vanguard youth are gathered on a Newark street corner, dressed in what would now be called casual business clothes. Midway through the piece, my mother makes a cameo appearance, as "the Lost Daughter of Goldwater Parents." In the writer's description, Ann, "pretty, long hair falling to her shoulders, closes the door, heading for Earl Harris' headquarters. 'If Harris loses we're going to have a fight here. Some of the community people are carrying guns.' Her eyes are flashing. It is prom night all over again."

I read these lines to my mother not long ago, thinking she'd laugh at the patronizing tone, but instead some of that flashing resurfaced: "Prom night! Yeah, and Newark fucking exploded." She was almost hissing with the memory of those riots, which would convulse the city six months later.

But the writer, despite his glib style, did manage to capture my parents' shared conviction for political work. In the private realm, they shared less. My mother, who was tending to a newborn and keeping the house polished, was becoming disillusioned with the division of labor in the new society. My father wrote the speeches and she typed them; he was to speak at a meeting and she was to give him a ride. This had as much to do with the times as it did with the depth of my father's needs, but it seemed to my mother that even amid the radical movement some aspects of the old order remained the same. When they argued, my father went off to the headquarters and she stayed up into the middle of the night scrubbing the kitchen floor with a rag and brush.

When I was four months old, my parents' marriage came apart. My mother moved to the Lower East Side and took a job teaching school in Harlem, as she had vowed to do. My father stayed in Newark. From both of their accounts, the time after their split was one of unexpected liberation. Their divorce was to be a progressive agreement, part of the new society that was to come. They passed me off with a bottle and diaper bag wherever their schedules permitted. It seems they were better friends in those years than they had been when passion clouded the air between them. "We planned things together," my mother told me once. "We had never done that before."

Their separation meant that three days out of the week my father was fully in charge. He learned how to lull me to sleep, how to warm a bottle without scalding the milk. He laughs to recall how he would set out from my mother's apartment, holding me on one arm, the bag of creams and bottles on the other. "Ann would say, 'Don't forget to put the wet clothes in a plastic bag and the dry clothes in the bag marked "D" and the damp clothes in the bag next to the pacifier, which is on top of the pediatrician's phone number.' I would nod knowingly and start losing things the minute I left her apartment." Once, he showed up to meet my mother for the tradeoff, feeling snazzy in a new khaki suit, only to have her point out a giant blossom of urine on his pants. Still, my father says he was grateful for the chance to be a real parent: "In the evenings I would sit in a chair and read and you would crawl around, using me as a home base. I enjoyed being 'forced' to miss my political meetings for a while."

After the Newark riots, my father went to work for Students for a Democratic Society, organizing at colleges up and down the eastern seaboard. He was based in Boston, but would always manage to end up back in New York by Friday night, where he would take me for the weekend while my mother went out.

Sometimes he brought me along on the speaking circuit. We "crashed" on the floors of people's apartments, went to student meetings, and rode buses together. "We had to take a Port Authority bus from midtown Manhattan to Newark," my father wrote me once, describing that time, "and, not being able to occupy you for the whole ride, I would let you crawl around on the floor where you would proudly pick up cigarette butts and show them off to me and the passengers — who were horrified. I think that a lot of my permissiveness was an attempt to cope. I was looking for some type of parenting 'style' that would allow me to be in charge without feeling the need to control. Out of that you developed a highly self-sufficient style of your own."

While my father canvassed for SDS, my mother began to distance herself from politics. At twenty-three she had believed that if she could gain entrance to the White House, if she could get Lyndon Johnson to sit still in his grand leather chair and listen for an hour, she could make clear to him how purely wrong the whole war effort was, how cracked in its very foundation — and, in the face of her lucidity, he couldn't help but change his mind.

It was a measure of my mother's faith in her own power that she actually went to the White House in 1968 and camped on the steps with a group of her friends, insisting on a meeting with the president. They stayed for nearly two days, sleeping on the cold marble steps, with no one paying them much mind, until King Haile Selassie arrived for an official visit and the protesters linked arms across the gate. Then the Secret Service arrived and whisked them away. My mother's picture was in the *New York Times*, to my grandparents' mortification. Two Secret Service men are lifting her up by her arms, her crossed legs dangling in textbook civil-disobedience style, penny loafers on her feet. She looks, in fact, like the darling coed: pegged pants and cardigan and glossy hair flipped up at the ends. My father loved that picture. He described it to me once in startling detail, a wistfulness in his voice at my mother's former passion.

But although my mother and father were both bent on political change, it seems to me that they worked from different sources. My father identified with the oppressed. It was fury at their conditions that spurred him on, and if one method wouldn't work, he would try another. My mother was attuned to other people's suffering, but what drove her to action was the idea that reason could win out. As a young girl, she once dreamt she was appointed to solve the world's problems, and she set about fixing them one by one, until solving the last dilemma presented the solution to the first. But in waking life, the problems were more intractable, and all her smarts and energy were dwarfed by the country's ills. Gradually, my mother lost heart for the slow, backsliding muckiness of protest politics — all the evenings spent arguing with people who mostly shared her views. I suspect that some of her disavowal of mass movements was a reaction to her relationship with my father, but whatever its roots, she stopped going to meetings, gave up trying to change the government, and started looking around for a smaller sphere.

She found the beginnings of one when a group of her friends rented an old hotel on the Massachusetts seashore and convinced her to join them. We left Manhattan in the summer of 1968, when the garbage workers were on strike and the mercury was climbing into the nineties. "Every inch of air had its own vile and particular smell," my mother said later. She let go of our apartment, packed all our belongings into our VW bug, and drove up the West Side Highway, leaving those cloying streets behind.

Her fellow household members were computer programmers, psychologists — many of them old friends. "Suddenly, I was living the Sgt. Pepper life by the seashore," she said. Everyone pitched in for food and cooked together; chores were posted on a rotating wheel on the fridge, with each person taking care of a slice of the housekeeping pie. On Sunday evenings, the housemates gathered in the living room for meetings where issues were raised and occasionally resolved. Her share of the rent was about forty dollars, and since we ate rice, beans, and vegetables, and spent our days on the beach, she didn't need to work. She got a little pin money from her grandmother, and passed the summer in a pleasant haze. We would wake up late and eat oatmeal at the big farm table with whoever else was around. In the afternoons, she and her friends would gather down at the beach and stretch out a blanket. My mother would read, marvel over my dawning consciousness, then take a nap while someone dangled my feet in the surf.

When she talks about Manomet, my mother's voice goes soft and she looks out into the middle distance, conjuring the long green lawn below the house, the path through the dunes to the water. She was buoyed up by the company of her friends, by the salt breeze that slipped into our room at night, and her sense of freedom and ease seeped into me. On most days I wore nothing but sandals. Sometimes she put a diaper on me; more often I was allowed to squat where I pleased. My mother was in no hurry to potty-train me. She believed then that children were possessed of a native vitality, which would guide them toward good health and good human relations. She saw her job as one of gentle helmsmanship.

In fact, I was wild as a baby goat. I ate whole sticks of butter, bit anyone who crossed me, and pushed my mother's friend Miriam over the line one day when we sat down for breakfast together and she lifted the lid on the sugar bowl to find a turd curled up neatly inside. In the moment of shocked silence while Miriam's spoon was poised, my mother pointed out that the sugar bowl did look something like a toilet — it was round and porcelain, even if the scale was wrong — and then they howled together at my dainty replacement of the lid. But Miriam helped make it clear, if it hadn't been before: I was socializing myself for a society of one.

My mother's laissez-faire parenting style was a conscious over-turning of the prim thinking of the time, and a rebellion against the conventions of her own childhood. Once or twice during that summer, we drove down to visit my grandparents on Long Island, and slipped back into the manicured world she had come from. Grandma Kate and Grandpa Bob's brick-fronted home was set on an acre of grass and maples, with a pool and cabana out back. I moved into the luxury of that world without question, jumping out of the car and running down the brick walk to the den: my grandfather's kingdom.

I remember my grandfather in the long slide of his retirement. He spent his days sunk in a La-Z-Boy recliner, holding the remote controls to two massive console TVs set side by side at the far end of the room. He would watch two sports games at once, muting one then blaring another as the action waxed and waned. He had been laid up by a wound in his foot the size of a golf ball, which began as a small nick from a piece of glass out by the pool and, because of his diabetes, never healed. That wound stayed open for the last years of his life, gathering infections and eventually gangrene, growing wider under the surgeon's knife.

On the table beside him was a spinning pipe rack topped with a brass statue of a boy and his hound, a well-thumbed TV guide, and a box of dog biscuits, which he would dole out to his beloved Yorkshire terrier. I would sit on his lap, lean against his drum-taut belly, and breath in his scent — tobacco and Vitalis and fresh gauze. Grandma brought him drinks from the bar at the back of the room — a fully stocked arsenal, with a slate floor, a chrome top-loading fridge, and a rack of shakers and stir sticks. While Grandpa sipped his Scotch, I sat on one of the barstools and downed glass after glass of Tropicana orange juice, a treasure that never appeared in the commune fridge. On the glass shelves above the bar were rows of matte black steins with handles in the shape of naked ladies. They touched their toes to the base of the mugs, then arched backward to grab the rim with dainty hands. When you lifted a mug, your thumb fit perfectly into their cleavage.

Up a flight of stairs from the den was the formal living room, with yellow brocade slipcovers on the couches, and on the coffee table a crystal paperweight with a sword-shaped letter opener thrust into its center, a mini Excalibur. The other day, I saw an ad for this very item, a Steuben it seems, priced now at thirty-one hundred dollars. "Timeless. Elegant. American," the copy read. Back then I was warned never to touch it, as I moved fast and left a trail of small calamities in my wake.

That Huntington house, down to the last detail, gave off a feeling of plenty. And it was this smugness that my mother was fleeing: the casual presumption of wealth; my grandparents' marriage, held together through rough times by decorum; the glistening dinners of roast beef and potatoes served in front of the television; the chemically enhanced lawns. It looked like the American Dream — two TVs, one pool, twelve black beer steins with naked ladies on the side — but it was full of holes.

Once, my mother told me of the life she had imagined making with my father once they married. They would buy a house in Harlem, adopt six or seven kids, plant a garden in an abandoned lot, and teach in the public schools. A fine dream, except she never once asked my father if he shared her vision. She says she knew he would have objected, but she figured she could talk him into it.

My parents' new life — separate but congenial — seemed to be working, but it was not to last. In June 1969, at the ninth and final national convention of SDS, a splinter group put out a pamphlet calling for, among other things, the creation of a revolutionary party. My father went to the convention and heeded that call, joining the two or three hundred people across the country who dubbed themselves Weatherman, after a line from Dylan's "Subterranean Homesick Blues." They believed that a revolution was imminent, but that it required a spark, some kind of violent action, to catalyze a mass uprising. In Boston, my father joined the local action project, whose members shared an apartment and spent their days training with weights and planning protests.

I don't know what attracted my father to this movement, such a long way from his early days in Newark. I know it is a period about which he has his own misgivings, although he is quick to defend the choices he made when they are criticized from afar. I believe that he joined the Weathermen out of a conviction that revolution was required — to end poverty and racial inequality, to end the war. But it's hard to imagine the context in which he came to such a conclusion, and easy, in hindsight, to see how badly he misjudged the national mood.

After he became a Weatherman, my father began to spend less and less time looking after me. As the summer wore on, my mother became exasperated, and finally she went to the Weathermen collective to confront him. It was an apocryphal moment, and they still don't agree on what was said. It is a measure of how far apart they had drifted that their memories refuse to match up.

My mother says she pounded on the door until they let her in. My father's comrades were gathered round, and in front of them she said her piece. What about the model childcare arrangement? What about his responsibilities? He told her that he had bigger responsibilities and urged her to leave me with Grandma Kate and join him in the struggle. She remembers looking at my father then and feeling that she barely knew him. "I can't believe you would give up your own kid," she said. And in her memory he replied with a line that would haunt her in the years to come: I was no more his child than were all the children in Vietnam. My mother screamed at him then, told him that political righteousness was no excuse for shitty behavior, her voice full of fury and fear, I'm sure, at what this meant to her — that she would have no help in caring for me, no one to consult with, no *air*.

My father told me, years later, that part of him knew she was right, but he was already on a path and couldn't turn back. He remembered their conversation as one between people who agreed on a goal, if not the means: the war had to be stopped. He said my mother might just as easily have been in his shoes, ready to make such a sacrifice. In his memory, they spoke that day of her resentment — that he got to be in the vanguard; that she was stuck in the traditional role. One thing they both agreed upon: they loved me, and any choice that made me suffer was a difficult one. In a letter, my father once described it this way: "The watchwords of the time were urgency, militancy, combativeness, commitment, and sacrifice. I looked at you and loved you so much, and then I looked at children dying of napalm and rifle bullets inflicted by our soldiers. As a Jew I had heard so many times, 'What did the goyim do when Hitler was killing the Jews? Why didn't they stand up?' And then I heard stories of Christians who had hidden Jews at the risk of their lives, whites who had risked their lives on the Underground Railroad sheltering slaves, and it was that tradition that I felt a part of."

Three months later, he would have the chance to prove his

mettle: the protest at the Harvard Center for International Affairs, for which he was arrested and charged with assault and battery. And nine months after that he would stand trial, the story of which strikes a chill in my heart. My father represented himself, hopeful that he could avoid jail time, and was sentenced to one year, a shockingly stiff term for the time. A lawyer who had done pro bono work for other activists offered his services and encouraged my father to appeal. But the man turned out to have qualms about the Weathermen and their tactics. He did almost nothing to prepare for the trial, and had the gall to inform my father only when they reached the courtroom that there was a chance his sentence could be increased. The judge returned from chambers and doubled his term to two years.

two

MY FATHER BEGAN serving his time at Billerica in December 1969, just days after his twenty-seventh birthday. I was three years old. Shortly after he went to prison, my mother took me to see him. He had written her a letter asking for books and a new pair of tennis shoes; he was playing a lot of pickup basketball in the yard to keep his head clear. On the ride out to the prison, I clutched a box of black Converse high-tops in my lap, half queasy with excitement, practicing the things I would tell him.

That visit has the etched clarity and foggy blanks of a fever dream. I remember pulling into the broad parking lot and stepping out to face a gray building punctured by a grid of tiny windows. Mother lifted her hand against the glare, then pointed to a figure in one of the barred openings. Was it my father? She hoisted me onto the roof of the car, and I held the shoebox over my head and shook it. The figure waved back. I'm not sure if it's right, this memory of a prison room with a view, but it's a memory my father and I share, perhaps out of the desire to have recognized each other from afar.

In the waiting room, a guard called our names in flat tones, then led us down a series of long corridors, countless hydraulic doors peeling back and shutting behind us, until we arrived at the visiting room. Once we were inside, something softened in the guard's face. "Sit right here, missy," he said. Mother lifted me into a plastic chair and my feet jutted straight out, so I stared at the toes of my tennis shoes, printed with directives in blocky capital letters: LEFT, RIGHT.

I sat still until a door on the far wall opened and a flood of men filed in. Out of the mass of bulky shapes, my father stepped forward. He grinned and reached for me across the tabletop, and despite the no-touching rule, the guards said nothing. When he took my hand, every manic bit of news I had rehearsed in the car deserted me. I was stunned by the dry warmth of his skin, his white teeth, the way he cleared his throat before speaking.

My father read out loud from a children's book that my mother had brought, his voice roving from bass to falsetto as he acted out the dialogue. I told him what I had eaten for lunch, and in the silence that followed I remembered the tennis shoes, flushed with relief to have something to give him. "Look what we got you," I said, and then tore the box open myself. I beamed while he admired them. "All Stars!" he said. "I'm gonna tear up the court."

It is my father who often recalls my worldliness in that visiting room. At the end of the hour, the guard rested one hand on his gun and called the time. Extended visits were reserved for ass-kissers, and my father refused to kowtow to the guards, but apparently I turned to the stranger by the wall and flashed a saccharine smile. "Daddy," I asked, pointing at the guard, "is that the nice man you told me about?" The guard squinched his face at me, in what passed for kindness in that place, then made a slow turn to the window and gave us a few extra minutes.

What I recall is the pressure of those visits. I sat there, straining for something to tell him, until my chest hummed and my head felt light. Then the guard said, "Time's up," and we shuffled to our feet.

In the clamor of chair legs and murmured goodbyes, we could speak again. "Hey, what do you want for Christmas?" my father asked. I stopped in the doorway and stared at his dark bulk. I wanted *him*. But his voice was filled with a sudden expansiveness, and I knew I should ask for something he could give.

"Something purple," I told him. I was partial, for some reason, to that color.

I still have a letter my father wrote me that night from his cell:

"It may take a long time, but I'll try to get you a purple thing. Here's a pretend one for now." Below it is a necklace with a carefully sketched purple star.

This was the first of many letters he wrote me, each with a drawing in colored pencil. "Darling Lisa — Hello, Hello, Hello. I am very happy tonight. I got a guitar yesterday and am learning to play it. I am on a diet so I won't be fat at all — not even a little bit." Then half the page taken up by an abstract drawing: a grid filled with tangled clots of scribbling, a black anvil shape, a downward arrow, the symbol for infinity. "I call this picture, Being in Jail: JAIL. I love you darling, Your Father."

Those notes were full of rhymes and playfulness: portraits of me with green hair, or of himself with the head of a man and the body of a conga drum. In places, his loneliness leaked through. "I will try to keep writing you," said one letter, "but it's hard when you don't write me back." I was pricked by guilt when I read these pleas, then quickly forgot them. At first his absence was a plangent note, always sounding in the background, but it became muffled as the months passed. In time, I had trouble recalling his face.

My mother made several visits to the prison, but gradually she began to cut ties. Whatever she had said in the heat of the moment when they quarreled at the Weatherman collective, her long view of the matter was clear: my father had cut out at a crucial time. She was on her own now and felt no obligation to wait for him. We moved to a third-floor walk-up in Cambridge, and my mother took a job waitressing at a restaurant from three to midnight. In the pictures from that time she is all cheekbones and arched brows. She wore narrow skirts and tied her hair back in a chignon. I wonder if she took pleasure in her beauty, in her youthful ease, or if even back then she paid more attention to things outside herself. Her stories are of the night crew, their easy camaraderie, and in particular the cook, whom she took a special shine to.

The restaurant attracted a hip clientele, and my mother reveled in the place: tables full of young bohemians, every night a different parade of faces. One evening, Rod Steiger stopped in and took a seat at one of my mother's tables. He wore gray slacks and a Brooks Brothers shirt, open at the neck. He'd just finished *The Pawnbroker*. When my mother pulled out her pen and pad, he ordered three lamb chops, which weren't on the menu, and gave her an attentive once-over. "He was a little jowly," my mother said. "But he had character; he drew me in." Steiger asked her questions: where she was going, where she had been. When he found out she had lived in Newark, he asked where, exactly, and they discovered that she had lived only blocks from his childhood turf. She refilled his glass; he recalled the sweet parts of the old neighborhood: the cobbled streets, the rows of trees that buffered the houses.

After he'd paid the bill and stepped out, Steiger's chauffeur slipped back into the restaurant and handed my mother forty dollars and a note. She still has it, tucked in the attic somewhere, a half sheet of stationery bearing the star's breezy overture: "Buy yourself a dress and someday we'll have a quiet drink."

When my mother told the story back in the kitchen, the cook howled and slapped the metal countertop. "No shit! What'd you say?"

"I put the forty dollars down on the table and told him to tell Mr. Steiger I couldn't be bought," my mother said.

The tales that filter back from those days often feature my mother's resilience and pluck. It wasn't until I once accused her of being a stranger to sorrow that my mother acknowledged the bleakness of that time. When her waitressing shift ended at 2 A.M., she picked me up from the baby-sitter — a gentle black woman named Celine, who fretted over my mother — and carried me home through the darkened streets to an empty house. When we both came down with stomach flu, and vomited for two days, there was no one to make tea or tend to us. We moved from bed to couch to floor, leaving a trail of soiled sheets. My mother had invented a myth — our poor but happy time — to spare me the fact of her loneliness. Still, I have my own memories of her darker moods, which pressed on me like the heavy air before a storm. They filter back as wordless stills, which I can't be sure I haven't imagined: my mother braced at the sink on a rainy evening, her shoulders shaking. Or of me standing at the edge of her bed while she slept, stroking the cold ends of her hair.

Not long after we moved to Cambridge, my mother took in a foster child, Vito Deviliti, a walleyed boy with hair as stiff as straw. He was fifteen; I was four. His name in rough Latin, Mother told me once with a laugh, meant "life of the little devil." She may have given up hope of changing the national scene, but not her desire to give back — "to spit out the silver spoon," as she once phrased it. In Newark, she had thought in terms of a neighborhood; now she narrowed her efforts to this one troubled boy. Maybe, just maybe, she could set a single life to rights.

One afternoon, I was playing with blocks in the kitchen when Vito padded in and fixed on me for the first time. "Hey, kid," he said, standing with arms akimbo. "C'mere." When I went to him, he hoisted me up above him until his head loomed above his feet. I shrieked with delight. I knew this game. Vito grinned and tossed me into the air. I laughed on the way up, then choked a little on the way down. When he caught me, his fingers dug into my ribs. I think Vito liked the look on my face — the mixture of terror and glee. The next time he threw me up higher, and waited a little longer to catch me under the arms. The sun cast a wedge of glare over his face, so his eyes narrowed and his teeth lit up. Another toss, still higher. My hair lifted away from my scalp like a delicate wig, then I fell and my stomach vaulted into my throat.

"Want me to do it again?" he asked. His voice had a menacing edge and yet it fascinated me, like a strange dog or the cool blue flame of the stove.

"Yes," I said.

He held me out at arm's length.

"Do it again."

Vito flashed a jagged smile and threw me toward the ceiling. His arms were folded by the time I hit the linoleum.

My wailing woke Mother, who had been sleeping in the next room. She came out, still groggy, and tried to sort out our stories. I was on the floor, gasping. "He — dropped — me."

Vito gave me a withering look. "She was laughing," he said. "She liked it."

On days like that, I watched my mother's whole body go slack. It's no wonder that, living alone with a toddler and a ward of the state, she became tenacious about order. The apartment floors would disappear under toys and clothes and mildewed towels, and then suddenly she'd spring into motion. A look of gentle determination stole over her face as she emptied the cabinets of spices and oils and wiped them down with an ammonia-soaked sponge. She got grave pleasure from a translucent windowpane, and would go from room to room rubbing the glass with balled-up newspapers dipped in vinegar. Bach's Magnificat in D was her housekeeping anthem, and those dazzling voices are forever married in my mind with a manic sweep toward order, with the vision of my mother as she scrubbed the fronts of drawers, brushed cobwebs from the ceiling, scoured the black scum from the bathtub tiles and rinsed it away.

I followed her around, happy as long as she was in my sight, seized with dread if I looked up to find her missing. I hadn't always clung to her so. When I was ten months old, Mother set me down on the grass in Central Park and I crawled off without a backward glance, past couples lounging on blankets, through the middle of a Frisbee game. She followed me, curious to see how far I would venture, but in those days my tether was longer than hers. I reached a walkway full of dogs and roller skaters, and she had to scoop me up. My mother loves to tell that story — the little mensch, the fearless one. But sometime after my father left, I lost the faith. I began to watch her, as if watching had the power to keep someone near.

My mother says I needn't have worried: "You were inextricably tied up with me by then. Our fates were linked." When the apartment was clean and she had room to think, she sat down to spin out her plans. We would move to Mexico and buy a house: stucco with tile floors and a cactus garden. She would become a potter, maybe teach English. I would run around in embroidered dresses, turning brown in the tropical sun.

Back then, the journey was the thing. We wouldn't fly to

Oaxaca. We would meander our way into a new life. Mother heard about a postal-service auction, the last stop for the government's fleet, and went down to bid on a used mail truck. For two hundred dollars, she drove off with a standard blue-and-white van, stripped of its red stripe and insignia so she couldn't impersonate a mail carrier. Mother parked it outside of our walk-up and gave me a tour. With a little tune-up, she said, it would get us south of the border. The cab had one high leather seat, a side-view mirror the size of a dinner plate, and a button gearshift, which looked fairly space-age at the time. A sliding door led back into a cold metal vault, bare but for a few mail shelves. "This is going to be our cozy rolling home," she said, her voice pinging off the walls.

When she wasn't at the restaurant, Mother worked to make the mail truck roadworthy. She was worried about a few rust spots on the side panel, so she spent a weekend driving around Cambridge in search of something to patch them with. On a narrow side street she spotted a promising sign: "Earth Guild. We Have Everything."

The store was a kind of counterculture supermarket, stocked with incense, bolts of cotton, paraffin, books on homesteading, yarn and looms. My mother made her way to the counter and asked the cashier if they had any sheet metal.

"What to do you want it for?" the woman asked. It was a slow day in the store. Had there been a line of customers, impatient for beeswax and clay, our lives might have taken a different turn.

"I need to patch a hole in the side of my mail truck," my mother said.

"Well," the woman offered, "we don't have sheet metal, but we have Jim, and he has a mail truck, too." She yelled toward the back room, and out loped a lanky man in square-toed Frye boots, smiling an easy smile.

Jim went out to the curb and looked over the rust spots. He and Mother talked about their vans, how much they'd paid at auction, where they were headed. Jim also had his eyes on Mexico. And at the very moment my mother dropped by, he had been building a kiln in the back of the store for the Earth

Guild's pottery studio. It seems she had stumbled on a man who could help her turn her schemes into brick and wood. By the time they finished talking, the sun was low in the sky and they had a date to change their oil together.

Jim wore hand-painted ties, listened to the Stones, and collected op art, but he still had the good manners of the Auburn fraternity boy he had once been. He had joined the ROTC in college, which helped pay his way through school, and when he graduated he owed two years to the navy. After basic training, they offered him two choices: he could be a pilot, or use his B.A. in architecture for a noncombat position. Jim loved planes and had always dreamed of learning to fly, but he saw where Vietnam was headed and opted out of flight school. The navy stationed him in Taiwan, where he maintained the cooling system on a communications way station. When he was discharged, he hopped jets home, taking over two years to reach the States. He stopped in Cambodia, Thailand, and India, read Krishnamurti, dabbled in meditation, bought Persian rugs. His route was marked by palaces and ruins, and he took pictures of nearly every architectural detail in his path, from onion dome to Roman arch. When he arrived home, the naval lieutenant j.g. moved into a commune in Harvard Square, whose members dubbed themselves the Grateful Union.

Not long after Jim and my mom hooked up, Vito took our mail truck on a wild-haired ride — his legs were barely long enough to work the pedals — and crashed it into a pole. He fled on foot and was missing for days. The truck had to be sold for scrap metal. When Vito turned up, Mother told him she considered their social contract broken, and the boy was sent back to the foster agency. With only one mail truck between them, Mother and Jim made plans to head across the country together.

Jim's truck was considerably cozier than my mother's. A platform bed stretched across the width of the van, and a hinged half-moon table folded down from one wall. We ate sitting cross-legged on the mattress. The walls were lined with bookshelves, fitted with bungee cords to hold the volumes in place. On a shelf just behind the cab was our kitchen: a two-burner propane cooking stove, a tiny cutting board, and a ten-gallon water jug. Jim covered the metal floor with Persian rugs and hung a few ornaments on the walls: a plaque with the Chinese characters for peace, prosperity, and happiness; a yellow wicker sun.

Before we set out, Jim bought a small wood stove and bolted it to the floor near the back. The smokestack jutted out the side of the truck, the hole weather-sealed with the fringe from a tin pie plate. One of Jim's friends from the Grateful Union wired a stereo system into the van, and Mother sewed heavy denim curtains that attached to the front windows with Velcro, so we could have privacy at night. Most of the cab was taken up by the engine, which was housed by a flat-topped metal shell. Jim cut a piece of foam in the shape of the engine cover and had me lie down to try out my new bed. A perfect fit. I was about the size, in those days, of a sack of mail.

In the spring of 1970, we packed up our essential belongings and set out toward Key West, stopping at every fruit stand and roadside attraction. When the road was smooth, Jim would put an LP on the record player — Richie Havens's *Mixed Bag* or Fred Neil — and those soulful voices carried us down the highway: "I want to go where the sun keeps shining, through the pouring rain. I want to go where the weather suits my clothes."

We were on traveling time, lazy and slow. We had no schedule or destination, no errands or household chores; certainly no one was expecting us. When the sun beat against the windshield, Mother peeled back the curtains with a toothy rip and drove to the nearest beach. She sat on a blanket and practiced her guitar, leaning over her fretting hand and singing in a reedy, off-key voice. Jim and I fished from the pier with our bamboo poles, and while he trailed his line in the water, he talked to me about the virtues of patience. Jim was a man who, if you bought him his favorite candy bar, would thank you and tuck it into his shirt pocket for a while. "Anticipation is the biggest part of pleasure," he used to say. To him, fishing was something of a spiritual exercise.

The thrill of traveling sustained me for a while, but it was a difficult age to be rootless. I played with other kids for a day or two at a campground or a city park, and then we drove on. After a day on the road, mother tucked me in on my foam pad, warmed from below by the engine's heat. I drifted off to the tick of the cooling engine. Once, when we were parked on a dark residential street, I woke to the knock of a policeman, asking us to move along.

And move along we did, down the eastern seaboard and through the Carolinas, Georgia, and into Florida, where we stopped in to visit a distant acquaintance, Mrs. Virginia Clark, who lived along the Saint Johns River, south of Jacksonville. We drove down the sandy roads through acres of pine forest to her house, perched on a wide lawn sloping down to the river. Mrs. Clark was nearly one hundred, ran a turpentine plantation, and seemed not to know that slavery had been abolished. She was an avid bird watcher, and had built perches in the forest where we would sit in the evenings, watching herons fly upriver. She still baked in a wood-fired oven, and upon our arrival she threw in an armful of logs and taught my mother the secret of a perfectly flaky pie crust. We spent a few weeks parked under a huge willow in her yard, helping Mrs. Clark check the tree taps.

When we drove out of Florida and into the Deep South, Jim took on the easy stride of a man returned to his native soil. We stopped at a string of Civil War battle sites — rolling meadows with nothing to hint at the carnage that had taken place there except a few antique cannons and commemorative plaques. These were places Jim's daddy had taken him as a boy, and when he rolled out their names — Chattanooga, Appomattox, Shiloh — and ran his hands over the blackened gunnery, stories started to well up out of him. His father had been a Nabisco cracker salesman, and for every dollar he made he saved fifty cents. "That man taught me the value of a buck," Jim said with a shake of his head.

When he was sixteen, Jim told me, he had saved up enough from his paper route to buy himself a broken-down Austin Healey, and he took the engine apart on the garage floor, laying each piece out carefully on a tarp, until he had an exploded model of the car. All summer, he worked from the manual, polishing and replacing each part, until he rolled it out into the driveway and the engine turned over and purred.

That place was full of good memories for him, but he was no

longer the clean-cut boy who had taken to those roads in his
sports car. We stood out in the South, in a way we hadn't in
Boston. On an interstate in Tennessee, we were slowed by a
police roadblock. Up ahead, station wagons and family sedans
were waved through, but when we came to the front of the line,
the patrolman motioned us onto the grassy center divider. Just
the sight of a man in uniform made my breath go shallow. I
posed daintily on the engine hood, my hands folded and ankles
crossed, while a policeman pulled the van apart. Other officers
milled around the grass, their radios squawking. They were
looking for drugs, of course, but at the time I had no idea what
they wanted from us.

The search seemed to take hours. A patrolman made Jim
empty out every jar in our toiletry bag, frustrated that he found
no sign of illicit substances. Finally, he seized on a bottle of
aspirin with a faded label and threatened to take it to a lab. Jim
knew we had nothing to hide and was unflappable. He told
him, in his polite Southern drawl, that he understood the officer's concern and that he was welcome to test the stuff if it
would set him at ease. The cop stared him down, then shrugged
and let us drive on.

It was midsummer when we made our way through the South-
west. Even with both sliding doors open, the van heated up like
a toaster oven. We drove over the Sierras at about fifteen miles
an hour, nursing the water pump, stopping often to savor the
mountains — jagged granite laced with snow. We were following the route of the great wagon trains, and barely making
better time.

Once we reached California, we headed toward the Santa
Cruz mountains to look up an old friend. Franny London and
Mother had met in Boston back in 1969, and had lived together
for a while after my father and mother split up. Back then,
Franny wore slim leather skirts and high heels, and drove her
convertible along the bank of the Charles River, turning heads.
She came from old money and didn't need to work a day in her
life, but not long after my mother took off in the mail truck,
Franny traded her pumps for rope sandals, quit bleaching her

hair, and moved out to Santa Cruz to start a knife-making business with her lover. Apparently, in those halcyon days, you could make a living selling antler-handled bowie knives.

We rumbled down Franny's rain-gutted driveway, passing a vegetable patch in a sun-filled clearing, and pulled into the shade of a redwood grove. She and her lover lived in a yellow slant-roofed house, set under the trees like a wedge of cheese. I was bowled over by the place: the mulchy sweetness of tree bark and needles, the green light, and the quiet — broken only by the patter of the creek, which wound down the narrow canyon, its banks undercut and riotous with ferns. I had come a long way from the brick walk-ups and steaming manholes of our city days.

My mother jumped out of the truck and threw her arms around her old friend. Even in the dim light Franny was radiant: long, honey-colored hair and a liquid grace. She led us into her living room, an enormous space with windows giving onto the creek. Old couches and tapestry-covered pillows surrounded a potbelly stove, and against one wall was a long table covered with heaps of leather. The windowsill was lined with jars of stain and sealant, X-Acto knives and wire brushes gathered in coffee cans.

Franny made us licorice tea and set me up at the workbench. "You can make your mother a change purse," she said, handing me a scrap of cowhide. She showed me how to decorate the surface, using stamps that looked like dental tools. On the ends were stars and sunbursts, comets and half-moons. You set the design in place and then whacked the handle with a rubber mallet. I pounded a whole galaxy into my scrap, while Franny and my mother caught up on things.

"God, was I uptight back then," I heard Franny tell my mother, recalling their Cambridge days. "Remember how I flipped out if somebody borrowed my coffee cup? The woods have really mellowed me."

The next morning, I went into Franny's room. The walls were covered with mandalas and Mexican weavings. The top of her dresser was covered with jars of what looked to me like vitamins, but which I now know must have been spirulina and bee jelly and brewer's yeast. I curled up in her covers and watched as Franny dangled a crystal over the jar lids, closing her eyes and humming to herself.

"What are you doing?" I asked.

"The crystal taps into my body's needs," she told me. "If I feel it vibrate over one of these, then I know that's what I need to take."

My mother didn't truck with the spiritual, but Franny's allure was her ability to immerse herself in something and at once give off the air that she found her own immersion amusing. She talked of reflexology and chakras, but seemed to keep some of the irony of the Boston society girl she had once been.

Now Franny, who credited my mother with having cut through some of her rich-girl puffery when they had been roommates, made my mother buoyant. Their watchwords were *Why not?* And in the face of that simple question, nothing seemed out of bounds. Not skinny-dipping, or eating pie for breakfast, or refusing to comb your hair until it matted into a burr at the back of your head. Once I caught their mood, I flew all sorts of test balloons. In the mail truck, tucked into a wooden chest, was a floor-length chiffon dress that I had worn as the flower girl in my aunt's wedding back east. I could tell from the way Grandma Kate had fussed over me on the wedding day, telling me not to sit anywhere dusty, that it was a dress reserved for special occasions. Now I asked my mother if I could wear it into the woods.

I still recall the exhilaration I felt running wild in that dress. I dashed into a clearing where a shaft of light cut down through the redwoods, stopped short by the sunlight on my sleeves. When I squatted down, the dress puffed around me like a pincushion, so I practiced that a few times: jumping up to catch air under my skirt, then curtsying and saying, "Yes, my lady." I hadn't found myself nearly so fetching at the wedding, when my tights had cut into my belly and my white patent-leather shoes made me skid unexpectedly across the church floor. I ran back to the house, where mother and Franny sat chewing on candied ginger, their feet propped up on the porch rail. They laughed at the sight of me, my tangled hair and dirty feet, the hem of that custom-fitted dress already ripped into a muddy fringe.

Life was cheap at Franny's place on Zayante Road, but we had been traveling for more than a year, and our funds were starting to run thin. I was nearly five and about to start kindergarten. Mother and Jim were ready to spend the last of their savings on a piece of land — "our pie in the sky," as Jim called it. Mother browsed through Franny's copy of *Mother Earth News* and saw a classified ad that looked promising: "Wonderful mountain parcel with springs and a good road." She located the town, population two thousand, which was marked with the tiniest speck the map allowed, and we drove up through San Francisco into the coastal mountains headed for that dot.

The parcel that lured us north was at the shoulder of a mountain, set above a narrow valley. *Road* was a generous term for the rutted dirt track that snaked up the hillside. The mail truck barely made it. Our books strained at their bungee cords. The kettle flew off the wood stove and hit the back door. At the top of the grade, the owner waited in his pickup truck to show us around. He was a wiry old man in overalls and a feed cap. As for the land, there wasn't much to show: only acres and acres of dry grass, with a few live oaks scattered here and there. Below us, the irrigated fields and vineyards spread out like a patchwork quilt. We could see the town's main drag, which we had passed on the way up, the post office and butcher shop and country store lined up like sugar cubes. We wouldn't be walking to the corner for a quart of milk.

"The ad mentioned springs," Jim ventured. "It seems pretty dry around here."

"You worried about water? No problem," the man said. He tipped his hat toward one of the oaks. "You see that tree there? It uses four hundred gallons of water a day, just to stay alive. You chop one of those down, put a draw right there, and you'll have four hundred gallons of pristine drinking water."

"Is that so?" Jim said. He was too polite to call anybody a liar. He kicked the dust and gave the tree a careful once-over. "Well, we're just city folks, so maybe we should go talk to people a bit more before we settle on a parcel."

Down at the general store, he and my mother ran the story by the shopkeeper. "That place is bone-dry," he told them. "Nate's been waiting for some city slickers to fall for the view."

Despite our brush with dust-bowl homesteading, Mother and Jim decided that the town was worth sticking to, so they looked around for a place to stay. A few doors down from the store, we came upon a cluster of paint-blistered bungalows with ivy growing through the walls. Up on one roof, a sign lettered around the rim of a wagon wheel said "Madge's Wheel-In Motel," the word *motel* drooping down as if Madge had painted it herself when she was three sheets to the wind. There was a big dirt parking lot in front, and a few scruffy kids played in front of the doorways. Mother and Jim decided to ask if we could rent a room. Parking the mail truck on someone's land was unlikely to make a good impression on our future neighbors.

We made our way to the main building, where a dead neon "Office" sign pointed up a flight of darkened stairs. Through the slats in a fence beside the entrance, I caught a glimpse of a small pool, surrounded by decaying lawn furniture. A little trap door with the word *snacks* scrawled over it was set low in a stucco wall. I liked the look of the place right away. And it has become fixed in my mind, our first visit overlaid with the many summer days I would spend there, clinging to the sides of the pool, dog-paddling around the dead wasps, listening to Donny and Marie piped from a tinny loudspeaker.

We knocked on a door at the top of the stairs, and Madge swung it wide with a grand "How do?" She was a buxom gravel-voiced lady with a peroxide-blond hive above her forehead and a Lucky Strike stuck in her fist like a sixth finger. Her apartment was surprisingly airy, with white carpeting and glass shelves packed with Hummel figurines and crystal paperweights. Mother and Jim asked about a room, saying they planned to stay awhile. Madge looked them over: "I don't got a room, but I got a piece of property for sale down the street."

Back down in the driveway, Madge hopped on the running board of the mail truck and directed us down Spring Street, hanging on to the rear-view mirror with one hand. "It's just a stone's throw," she yelled as we passed a post office, two churches, and a filling station with old white pumps as smooth as tombstones. She had us pull up at a clapboard house on the corner. Beside it was a duplex with cracked stucco siding and tiny sagging porches. There were a handful of ramshackle sheds on the property and a few rusted cars in the driveway. The yard was nothing but thistle and dry grass.

"Well, this is it," Madge said. "It ain't much."

Mother and Jim took a look around inside the buildings. Later, Mother would say that you had to call the people who lived there homeless. Only two out of the four toilets worked. The ceiling plaster bloomed with stains. Mother and Jim dickered with Madge a little, and agreed to buy the place for eighteen thousand dollars. The down payment, which they had carefully guarded during their travels, was the last bit of largess from my great-grandmother, the widow of a wildly successful bonds lawyer.

Our new address was 12000 Spring Street. Apparently the town's founders had been anticipating an explosive growth period that never arrived. Just past our house, the only sidewalk in town ceased abruptly, the last slab jutting out toward the cow pastures and orchards down Old Dam Road. We would hold down the end of the main drag on about an acre of good river-valley soil gone hard from neglect.

All the apartments were full when we took title to the place, so we lived in the mail truck for a while. Mom and Jim told the Riders, who lived in the back half of the big house, that they would have to move out, but there was no hurry. We were happy to live in the truck until they found a suitable place.

The front half of the big house was rented by an elderly woodcutter named Floyd Root, who sat around in his undershirt drinking gin. In the evenings, he had a lot of visitors: Indians from the reservation up in Covelo, old logging buddies. Floyd lived amid heaps of moldering newspapers, dirty underwear, and assorted chain saws, but his guests would pull up a stack of magazines and make themselves easy, playing cards into the night.

When Floyd heard that we were living in the truck until the Riders resettled, he called my mother to his porch. "They don't have to move," he told her.

My mother explained that we were in no rush to force them out.

"There's no need," he said, giving her a rheumy-eyed stare. "I'm going to die soon, and then there will be a place for you folks."

Mother brushed this off, but his flat tone spooked her.

A week later, Floyd invited his friends over and made great ceremony of giving away his saws and gap-tongued logging boots. The next morning, Jim saw Floyd's papers untouched on the porch and, after knocking didn't rouse him, went in to find the man lying cold in his bed, three empty gin bottles lined up neatly on the floor.

It took us a week of scrubbing to make that place fit to live in. There was standing water in the sink that the neighbor told us hadn't been drained for six months. Mother snaked the drain, lined the musty drawers with butcher paper, and sewed batik curtains for the windows. In the bedroom, the wallpaper hung in thick tatters, a yellowed flowery print laced with ribbons. We pulled that down and found a layer of cheesecloth tacked beneath it, and when that was stripped away, solid foot-wide redwood planks, rough-planed from trees that must have been over five hundred years old.

I was given Floyd's bedroom. Mother and Jim slept in the living room on a platform bed that doubled as a couch. I was not yet five, and it was summer, so I had to go to bed before the sun went down, which felt like exile from the world of light. While the air outside turned gold, I would press my face against the screen and watch the older neighborhood kids playing kickball in the street. One evening, not long after we had moved into the house, Mother and Jim came to tuck me in, and the two of them lingered for a while. Mother sat on the edge of my bed and sang to me. Jim stood in the middle of the room with his hands in his pockets, looking out the western window at the torn-up yard, the bristle of cattails in the ditch, and the corrugated roof of Earl's welding garage across the street,

where he went every afternoon to buy glass bottles of Coke
from the vending machine.

The novelty of the two of them tucking me in together in
my very own bedroom set me humming with pleasure, and I
wanted to say something in honor of this, but I didn't dare
break their reverie. Even as I lay there, mute with happiness, I
was conscious of the fragility of the scene: two parents, one
child, pausing for a few moments together under one roof at the
day's end.

We soon got to know our neighbors, who through Floyd's gen-
tlemanly exit were allowed to remain in the back half of the
house. Jackie Rider was full-blooded Choctaw, with unnerving
composure and striking beauty that she didn't make much of:
hair as shiny as obsidian, high cheekbones, and almond eyes.
She padded around the house barefoot and wore faded Levi's
that hugged her narrow hips. Jackie was in nursing school,
and worked a night-shift job. Her husband, Roger — whom my
parents called Roger Dodger — was blond and bearded and
worked as a lumberjack. Roger often spent his evenings at the
bar down by Hunter's Store, where men stopped by during
deer season to load up on beer and bullets, their four-wheel-
drives spattered with mud, their gun racks full.

The Riders had two kids, a son named Jacob and a daughter,
Alison, who was my age. She and I became instant friends. In
the scorching afternoons, we would walk down to Madge's
Motel and pay ten cents to swim in the pool. When Madge
wasn't upstairs sleeping off a bender, she would lean her head
out of the snack door and peddle stale Fritos and orange pop.
We'd spend change filched from our mothers' purses on red
licorice, splash around the shallow end, and then dry ourselves
facedown on the hot concrete until our bodies were dented by
pebbles. On Saturdays, Alison and I would walk farther down
Spring Street and lean into the smoky bar, listening for Roger's
voice amid the clack of pool balls and high laughter. After a few
beers he was a soft touch for candy money.

Once in a while, Alison and I would get in a nasty spat and
run to opposite ends of the house. It was hard, though, to hold

a grudge in such close quarters. Our bathrooms were divided by a flimsy wall, and when we were on good terms we shouted conversations through the plasterboard until our mothers told us it was not allowed. Since we had to play in the same yard, we developed a ritual for mending our rifts. When boredom got the better of fury, one of us would signal to the other with a knock on the bathroom wall. Then we'd pace the narrow concrete sidewalk beside the house, stand back to back, and take turns saying we were sorry. This system worked because we each had to travel the same distance, and we didn't have to look at each other while we ate what Jim called "humble pie."

Once, after we had made up and were leaning against the garden fence, Alison told me that her father had suggested a better way to finish the conflict: she should walk the path as planned, wait until I turned around, and then hit me in the side of the head with a roundhouse. Alison was a scrappy little thing, but she was smart. By ignoring his advice, she had proven her loyalty, but at the same time she put me on notice that she had official permission to clean my clock.

I regarded Roger with a certain suspicion after that, but not long after we moved in, he lived up to his nickname and disappeared. Jackie had her nursing degree by then, and was pulling night shift in the emergency room. The kids were left mostly to their own devices. Alison found Jacob a nuisance and tried to keep him at bay, but she cooked him breakfast every morning while her mother slept in, and dinner every night after her mother left for work. I was in awe of her easy competence with the gas stove; she would stand on a chair and grill slice after slice of perfectly browned French toast. Walking in her mother's shoes actually sustained her for a while — she had a grownup's common sense, which I noticed and paid its due — but eventually it exhausted her. Late at night, after dinner was eaten and the dishes washed, she would curl up on the couch with her dirty flannel blanket, one hand tucked deep in her armpit, the other curled at her mouth. That thumb, wrinkled from spit, forced her front teeth out over the years into a hungry overbite.

Jacob was molasses eyed and docile. He often wore a look

that I can still see now: so full of uncomplicated faith in whatever was befalling him, I couldn't decide if I wanted to take him under my wing or do him some senseless harm. He was stocky, but his hair was fine and curled at his neck. His little hands, when I held them, were damp in the creases. I remember thinking no one should be that sweet, and of course he didn't stay that way. He grew to over six feet, stopped talking to us, and spent his days shooting squirrels with a BB gun. But when he was little, Jake circled us like a dark moon. Because he didn't say much and never objected to our ministrations, he became the prized son in our daytime games of house. I would trade Alison a pack of gum for the right to be his mother, because he would actually eat small portions of the mud pies I baked. He sat on the dirt pile, a tin pan in his lap, and chewed methodically, delicately spitting pebbles into his palm and placing them at the edge of his plate like fish bones.

When Jackie was home, I often read her silence as annoyance at my presence, always aware that I was the child of the rent collector. Alison once dared me to sneak us a piece of bacon from the oven, while her mother sat reading in the next room. She squatted next to me grinning encouragement while I eased open the oven door and picked out a slice, then ran and told her mother what I'd done. Jackie ordered me home, steely fury in her eyes, and I saw it like a headline as I raced around to my mother's kitchen: Landlords' Kid Steals the Bacon!

My other yard mates, the Chapmans, lived in the stucco house beside ours. Like the Riders, they were another fatherless family, Mr. Chapman having run off years before. Mrs. Chapman, or Tillie, as everyone called her, was an enormous woman who lived in a housedress and thongs and never went out except to go to church. She had three kids. Daniel, the oldest, hulked about in discomfort at their diminished situation. He worked nights even while in high school, and since we all acknowledged he would not be long with us, he became a kind of vaporous presence. Tillie's two daughters, Charlene and Jill, spent their summer afternoons out on the rickety picnic table in the yard. Charlene, the older one, was curvy and slow moving. Her hair fell like a brown pelt down her back, full of lights. Jill was wound tighter. She had catlike reflexes, buck teeth, and a quick laugh. After school I would find them side by side on the picnic bench, combing their feathered hair and pressing their eyelashes back so they stood up for a few seconds like black tiaras.

Tillie would not let them wear mascara, but she would let them do just about anything else. On their birthdays, she banished them from the house and spent a whole day in the kitchen, emerging around sundown with her face spackled a moist rose, holding a tinfoiled board high above her head. Down on the picnic table came her creation: a cake with a bas-relief bunny rabbit fleeced with coconut, lifting one paw above a patch of candy corn. The frosting was vivid with food coloring. (She kept those tear-shaped vials lined up in her spice rack, as handy as sugar or salt.) We all sighed with admiration, and Tillie beamed and cut us each a huge slab. Beautiful as it looked, the cake left a bitter clog on the tongue.

These creations were only an elevated version of the Chapmans' staple fare: sugar and starch. Even though my mother plied Tillie with vegetables from her garden, I never saw a green or living thing pass through that family's lips. The girls often took their dinners outside and ate under the shade of the old walnut tree. Dinner might be tuna casserole topped with crumbled potato chips, or one slice of bologna on a hamburger bun, held together by a deep slick of mayonnaise. I sat on the end of the picnic table, slavering over those sandwiches, until Jill said I looked like an urchin and shooed me off. The day my mother let me buy the ingredients at the corner store and make one for myself stands out as a moment of singular gustatory pleasure: the sweet tang of white bread and fat and processed meat.

I realized then that I had been snowed by my mother, who had convinced me that powdered vitamin C mixed with water was a fitting dessert. One glass made the glands at the back of my jaw ache, but I begged for that stuff, and didn't even ask for honey to cut the sting. That was before Charlene and Jill gave me an education of the palate. When we played house they fed me spoonfuls of "baby food" from their mother's Tupperware cups: powdered sugar and cocoa mix, which dissolved slowly on my tongue like sweet ashes. Once they'd gotten hold of me, I couldn't look at our home-cooked meals in the same way. Mother grew most of our food in the garden — broccoli and kale, corn and green peppers — and served it up with steak and lamb chops and liver. And she made our bread — dark, of course, and studded with grains of whole wheat — and bought our milk from the local dairy. We'd take glass gallon jars down to Conway's Farm and wade through the cow shit and into a room with a huge silver tank where the milk flowed from a tap. Back home, Mother set the jar on a chair in the kitchen for a few hours, then dipped a length of rubber tubing into the risen cream and siphoned it off into a bowl. It all seems the picture of prairie virtue now, but at the time I wished for macaroni and cheese, cabinets full of potato chips and cookies, breakfasts of Lucky Charms.

three

I N THE SUMMER of 1971, when I was nearly five, my father was released from prison. (He had been given six
months off his sentence for good behavior.) Friends of his
were living on a commune in Oregon, and they invited him to
spend some time there sorting himself out. He came west, as
soon as he was free, and picked me up from my mother's
house.

We took a bus up to Eugene, and a friend from the commune
gave us a lift out to the property — acres of dry grass and scrub
oak. The commune members were roughing it — no running
water, no electricity, just a few dilapidated houses at the end of
a long dirt road.

My father's attempt to unwind in the woods was a disaster.
The sudden move from a cell to the wilds seemed to leave him
nervous and unsettled. The first day, he tried to play the hip
nudist and got a terrible sunburn. Then he drank some "fresh"
spring water and spent three days heaving in the outhouse. I
stayed indoors with him while he recovered, making him tell
me stories. "Me and nature never got along," he said.

But as the days drifted on, we settled into the place. My
father taught me to use a BB gun in the field beside the commune's main house. Arms around me from behind, he cheered
when we shot the faded beer cans off the stump. "Sock it to
me," he said, holding out his enormous olive-colored palm. We
ate homemade bread and black beans, and swam naked in the
creek flowing through the property.

One afternoon we wandered into one of the many rough-framed buildings on the property to take shelter from the heat. Cinder-block and knotty-pine bookshelves lined the walls. A sink and countertop unit pulled out of a remodeled kitchen shored up one wall. There was no running water; spider webs stretched from the tap. On the drain board sat a propane stove, and beneath it, on the floor, were jugs of cooking fuel and water.

My father moved to the open door, raised his arms up to the door frame, and stretched like a cat. He was there in body — a body honed by hours in the weight room, on the courts playing ball with the other prisoners — but in another way he was fitfully absent. He circled the room slowly, traced a pattern in the countertop's dust — not pent-up, but aimless, as if he had lost something and didn't know where to search. I squatted near the sink, playing with a set of plastic measuring cups, and watched him closely. He moved through the doorway — for a moment framed by light, a dark cutout of a man — then passed out of view.

The dry air made me thirsty, and I decided to have a tea party. I went outside to see if my father wanted to play, and found him sprawled under a large oak tree near the door. He was staring up at the leaves, his hands spread open in the air above him, and didn't answer at first.

"Do you want some tea?"

He raised his head, and his eyes slowly focused, placing me. "No thanks, honey."

I went back into the shack and filled two of the cups from a jug on the floor. I pretended to have a partner for my tea and chatted with him awhile before drinking from my cup, thumb and forefinger on the short handle, my pinkie raised high.

From the first sip I could tell something was wrong. The water burned my tongue, and when I opened my mouth to scream, all the air in the room was gone. I spat out what I could and yelled, feeling a white heat unfurl down my throat. My father dashed in, smelled my breath and the spilled gas, and scooped me up from the floor. He ran with me toward the spring, and over his shoulder I watched the shack jiggling smaller and smaller in the field. It seemed lonely, canted off to one side on its foundation, like a child's drawing of a house. The dry summer hay swayed like the sea, and I heard his breathing, ragged as surf.

When we reached the spring, a bearded man was there filling a green wine bottle. Water spilled down a rock face into a pool bounded by ferns and moss. My father gasped out the story and together they hovered over me, making me drink from the bottle again and again. "That's good," they said. "You're doing really good." My father stroked my hair. And though I was full and wanted to stop, I tipped my head back and drank for him.

That night we stayed in the main house. My lips and throat were chapped and burning. I began to have visions. A crowd of ghosts led by a goateed figure marched with torches through the room. I told this to the grownups and they seemed alarmed. Some of the other people staying at the house lit extra kerosene lanterns to soothe me, but I could still see the figures. The leader looked furious, driven, his whole body straining forward toward some unknown mission.

My father moved with me to a bedroom upstairs and held me in a worn corduroy armchair, talking softly, telling me stories of what we would do together when it was light. The vagueness I felt in him during the day had disappeared. He was dense, focused, his legs pressed long against the sides of the chair, his arms around me heavy and still. I sat in his lap, leaning into the rise and fall of his chest. In my last moments of delirium, I closed my eyes and saw his body supporting me like a chair, the long, still bones, and under him the real chair, fabric stretched over wood, and all of this twenty feet above the ground on the upper floor of the house, held up by the beams and foundation, and beyond that the quiet fields, silver under the moon, alive with animals, the punctured cans lying still by the stump. I saw us perched in the center of this, neither safe nor doomed, and in this unbounded space I fell asleep.

When he dropped me off after the commune visit, my father never mentioned the business with the gasoline — worried, I'm sure, that my mother wouldn't let him see me again. And since he didn't mention it, neither did I.

But if I felt at times undersupervised, it was this same freedom that stands out as one of the pleasures of my childhood.
On the weekends, Mother let me ride my bike down Spring
Street and didn't expect me back until dinnertime. The whole
town knew me and would haul me home if I was in trouble.
One Saturday, when Alison and I tried to shoplift from the
corner store, we found out what a fishbowl we lived in. We had
already succeeded in filching penny candy on a few occasions,
and we were ready to try for bulkier goods. While Alison asked
a question of Mr. Shepherd at the register, I pulled a package of
beef jerky from a peg below the counter and tucked it under my
shirt. My gait went stiff as I headed for the door, my shoulders
curled forward to hide the package. Somehow, I managed to
slip by unnoticed. It never occurred to me that Mr. Shepherd
might follow me out. I crossed the sill and stood there in the
sunlight feeling invincible, already planning my next theft,
when a hand clamped down on my shoulder and wheeled me
around. I'll never forget the look on his face. Not anger, but a
tight-faced weariness.

"Do you have something of mine?" he asked.

His. I had never thought of it that way. I had been stealing
from the store, not Mr. Shepherd, who called me honey and
smoothed the front of his immaculate butcher's apron while he
talked. He had helped my mother and Jim, that first day in the
valley, avoid a real-estate pratfall that would have landed me
out on a dry mountainside without a friend in sight.

I pulled the jerky out from under my shirt and held the
package up by one corner. The meat looked like tree bark in its
shrink-wrap casing — nothing worth eating.

"Go on home," Mr. Shepherd said. Home had never sounded
so good. I hopped on my bike and raced down the sidewalk,
trying to rid myself of the vision of Mr. Shepherd's pinched
face. But then I saw Mr. Shepherd pass by in his Bronco, headed
toward my house. His arms were ramrod straight on the wheel,
and he didn't so much as glance in my direction. I stood up on
my pedals and rode faster, hoping to arrive in time to give my
version of the story. But when I tore up the driveway and threw
my bike down in the gravel, Mr. Shepherd had come and gone.

My mother was waiting for me on the porch, her face unreadable. She led me out into the yard, as if the fresh air would make
things easier on us.

"I don't know why I did it," I told her. My mind was a
desert. Each blade of grass stood up in blank green toothiness
before me. I watched an ant climb up the delicate groove in one
blade, stop, turn, look down, head upward again. I forgot why
we were sitting there, cross-legged, facing each other with our
heads bowed like monks. Slowly, I reeled my mind in: trouble, I
was in trouble, Mr. Shepherd, beef jerky, that black peppery
tang.

"I was hungry," I said.

This was a lie, but it served me. My mother had been on an
errand while Alison and I pulled our heist, and the idea of
leaving me without snack money gnawed at her conscience.

"It's not okay to steal," my mother said. I would have to pay
Mr. Shepherd for the dried meat and would be barred from the
store for a month. Then my mother paused for a moment. "I'm
sorry I didn't leave you something to eat." I began to believe
my own lie: I was famished, my mother went off and left me
without food. But then, deep in my rapture of innocence, I
looked up at her face. She looked like she had a toothache: her
cheeks were pulled in and her eyes narrowed. And though she
tried to mask it, her guilt shriveled me. I bent forward and
leaned into the hutch of her legs, breathing in dirt and the fresh
scent of denim, and made a vow to give up my wickedness.

In the games with Charlene and Jill, I was always the baby, but
after a while I tired of this and began to visit the house of our
nearest neighbors, who had two girls younger than me, Mare
and Pippy. On their side of the fence I was the oldest, the one in
charge. I don't remember the girls' family name, though that
doesn't surprise me now: surnames were the province of parents, and the mother and father in that house were too vague
for names. They appeared once in a while at the porch rail to
call the girls to dinner, like diplomats demanding extradition
from a country they couldn't enter and in whose territories they
had little sway.

I began to go over to see Mare and Pippy often after school. The fence wires were bent wide from my passage, and I beat a narrow track in the grass. In the stretch of ground between our woodshed and the fence was a patch of mint, whose corrugated green leaves made a pleasing rasp on the tongue. I loved that it grew wild; amid the careful plots of vegetables my mother tended, this was my secret crop. I would harvest great handfuls of leaves for a pot of tea, and days later I'd discover the wilted, lint-covered mass in my pocket.

In the days to come, I would begin to feel that the things that lured me to play with those girls were less than wholesome, and so the taste of mint became married to a vague guilt, and the path through the grass became a visual record of habit — the proverbial rut — made deeper by a score of instances in which I fretted briefly — it wouldn't have looked like fretting from the outside, only a girl wandering aimlessly about her yard — and then went over anyway.

We played on a quarter-acre of dirt dominated by an old weeping willow, whose branches draped to the ground. The dusty, grassless circle under the tree was our house, furnished with two cracked kitchen chairs and top-loading washer and dryer that had been left there to rust. In that house, I was the mother; the oldest girl, Mare, was the father; and Pippy, the toddler — still in diapers, fat and placid — was our child.

As a mother, I demanded a strict discipline. First, we swept the house with switches, pushing the minnow-shaped leaves to the edge of the yard. Then I swung the baby up to the dryer and pulled her dirty socks off. Her bare feet were so tender — puffy wedges of flesh no bigger than butter cookies, the flat bottoms netted with tiny wrinkles. I made a great show of being haggard and overworked for the baby's benefit, brushing the bangs out of my eyes with the back of a hand, tossing the little socks into the agitator and punching the buttons on the washer with theatrical irritation. Mare played father to my mother with perfect aplomb. She came home from work, parting the willow leaves to enter the house with her arms akimbo, and demanded dinner.

"You cook it!" I shouted, my hip cocked out to hold the baby.

"I've been here all day cleaning and taking care of Pippy." The baby watched this drama in silence, her sweaty hand clutching my T-shirt, her sturdy legs wrapped around my side. The cooking scene quickly lost interest, and since we had no pots and pans to rattle, we would lean against the washer and dryer and roll cigarettes out of binder paper, smoking while Pippy crawled in the dust.

Where did we get this information? That cigarettes make grownups lazy and inattentive, their heads tipped back, their wrists cocked deftly to flick the ash. Neither of my parents smoked; I almost never watched TV. My mother had never spoken the kind of wooden lines I passed off on Mare. I was playing at a kind of iron-ruled family quite apart from my own. And under our hackneyed dialogue, the same dialogue used in back yards across the continent, we were carrying out a delicate test of loyalty and humiliation, of how much we would allow ourselves of the cruelty that lived in our small veiled hearts.

I don't know how the game changed; it was slowly, over a period of weeks, that we turned on the baby.

"She has been bad," I would tell Mare when she came home from work. "I can't get anything done with her around."

We conferred calmly about her punishment. Sometimes we would carry her outside the shelter of the tree. We called this "grounding," and pretended to go on about our chores. The baby didn't seem to understand this business. She wandered out by the fence, stuffing acorns in her mouth, until we let her back in.

One day when Pippy tried to eat one of our cigarette butts, I scooped her up and carried her out into the blazing sun. "Don't put anything in your mouth that isn't food," I said, and plopped her down in the dust, her sandaled feet jutting out in front of her. She was naked, except for her diaper, and I remember her hands splayed out beside her watermelon stomach in a gesture of surprise, and then the long inbreath she took in preparation for a wail. That warm-up was a fearsome thing. Her mouth gaped and her eyes welled up, and for whole seconds there was no sound. I cast a worried glance at the curtained side windows of the real house, where Pippy's mother might soon appear. "It's okay, it's okay, it's okay. Please don't cry." I lifted the baby up by her armpits, leaning back to counter her weight. Her body was as heavy and limp as a sack of lead shot. She draped herself over me and made fierce little gasps. I might have given up then on the whole punishment routine, but as soon as she was calmed, I put her down in the same spot.

"You're still grounded, Pippy," I told her solemnly. Then I swished back through the branches and told Mare that we couldn't get soft on her or Pippy would get spoiled and we'd have only ourselves to blame.

Pippy didn't understand what was the matter. She crawled over to the cascading greenery of the tree and pulled herself up on its flimsy branches. I stood in her path, with my hands on my hips. She moved left, then right, as if chance had put me in her way, then pushed through with her fat hands, leaning into my body with the leaves tangled between us.

"No," she said firmly, not quite mad yet.

"That's it," I remember saying. (I had heard that somewhere, the thing parents said when they'd hit their limit.) I parted the branches, whirled the baby around, and swatted her on her bottom. I got grim satisfaction from the smack of my palm on her plastic diaper — satisfaction and a misplaced righteousness, since the baby hadn't done a thing. In an instant, Mare was beside us. She elbowed me aside and took Pippy in her arms.

"You have to go home now," she said to me, and though there was a squeak in her voice, there was also a surprising firmness. I backed out of the yard and dipped through the fence, past the straggly patch of mint, holding in my mind the expression on Mare's face. It looked like the face of love to me — steadfast and protective and tender.

Years later, my mother would say, with a tightness in her voice, that I didn't seem quite happy in those early years at 12000 Spring Street: "I wasn't aware of how precarious our life seemed to you." When she had looked at me, running naked across the lawn at the Manomet commune, she felt fierce about protecting my freedom. "You see, peril to me was the closing down of the world like a coffin. Living according to a script. Still, I always tried to make a cozy place for you to sleep."

And it's true; my mother did her best to shield me. It may well have been my own temperament that made me alert to danger. At seven or eight, I was convinced that I would die in childhood and seized on any evidence that my body was in decline. Once, in the deep claw-foot tub in Floyd's old house, I peered through the lapping water and saw dark streaks running up my legs — signs, I decided, in a snap diagnosis, of leukemia. I sat in the cooling bath gripped by a mixture of terror and relief — terror at the grueling treatments ahead of me, and relief that the ax had finally fallen and my illness had a name. When my mother came in and found me wide-eyed and shivering, she took a washcloth and some soap and showed the streaks to be engine grease, left over from Jim's shower after work on the mail truck. She called me a nervous goose, and we laughed together as she wrapped me in a towel and tucked me into bed. But once she left, my dread returned. My mother swore that things always turned out for the best, and I wanted to believe her, but my life thus far hadn't borne this out. She couldn't promise me that I wouldn't die; I knew no one could promise me that. And if she didn't believe we were all at risk, then I would have to keep watch on my own.

Everything that had blown up in my parents' breakup, in the years on the road, was starting to fall back into place. The property at 12000 Spring Street was turning lush under my mother's hands: she rototilled half of the scruffy lawn and planted rows of corn, mounds of zucchini and melons, tufts of silvery artichokes against the fence. She learned plumbing, how to lay insulation and hammer shingles on the steep roof, her firm mouth bristling with nails. She dug trenches to lay water line, pinned her hair under a cap and reworked the building, bone to eave.

When I saw the zeal with which she threw herself into these labors, I asked for my own plot. Mother rototilled a square of dirt next to an old shed and helped me turn the earth with a pitchfork. "You want to break down the big clods and toss out the rocks," she said, "so the ground is rich and crumbly." We planted the fastest-growing varieties we could find (she knew that a budding gardener needed quick rewards): radishes, carrots, curly lettuce. When the seeds were in, I fenced off my plot with stakes and string, wary of trespassers. By some feudal instinct, I claimed the shed too, since it abutted my garden, and I think I got more pleasure from that spider trap than from the plants popping up in the blistering sun. The shed had mystery. It was built of rough planks, and chinks of light shone through the cracks, casting a stenciled pattern on the packed-dirt floor. There were a couple of shelves, a stack of buckets, and a few hoes and rakes tipped into one corner. I sat there in the dusty coolness, figuring how I might get my hands on a few furnishings: an old leather armchair for the corner, a small bookcase.

My mother was reading me fantasy then — the Narnia chronicles, *A Wrinkle in Time* — and I had faith that if I focused my powers I could make walls melt, learn the language of toads, dissolve into someone else's bloodstream and travel the chutes and tunnels of their veins. The shed was to be the laboratory for these investigations. One day, I coaxed Alison from her house and convinced her to mix a potion with me. We pulled out a steel washtub from the laundry room, dragged in a hose, and filled the tub nearly to the brim. Then we mined our medicine chests: I snuck past my mother with a shirt full of pills — aspirin and antacid, some leftover antibiotics. I skipped across the linoleum, holding my shirt hem up like a cancan dancer clutches her skirts — tra la la. That should have aroused her suspicions. Alison brought out a carton of White King D, her mother's detergent, and a fistful of black walnuts from the yard. We stirred all this into a murky whirl, the walnuts bobbing up like bad omens, said a few desultory spells, and waited for transformation.

I still remember the sickening feeling that rose in my throat when I realized we weren't going to be swept into the fourth dimension. We were stuck in that shack, which didn't even have a door we could close on our mess. Suds had sloshed out of the tub and turned the floor into creamy mud. I could hear my mother humming nearby as she shucked corn for dinner. In a minute she would appear in the doorway and find the empty aspirin bottles, the two of us, frozen, our stir sticks in a few gallons of poisonous sludge. We were tight on money in those days, so my dread centered on our wastefulness. A whole bottle of aspirin! Half a box of Jackie's good detergent! The Riders were probably on welfare at the time; Roger had already split the scene. I remembered my exile over the snatched strip of bacon and winced at the thought of Jackie's cold fury.

Alison and I moved as if we were of one mind. We threw down the sticks and dragged the bucket to the doorway, tipping the contents into my vegetable patch. I hastily hooked up the hose and sprayed the bubbles into the soil. Mother couldn't understand why my radishes sickened and died overnight: perhaps I had overwatered them, or it was too shady under the walnut tree.

My mother tore that shed down one day: tied a rope to the side, hooked it to the fender of the mail truck, and pulled it over. By the time I came home, the wood was in the scrap pile and all that was left was a tamped square of dirt. I practically wept, as if all the misdeeds I had done in there had been disrobed in one quick yank.

In the fall I was enrolled in the elementary school down the street. When it came time to fill out the registration form, Mother asked me what I wanted her to put down as my middle name. I didn't have a legal one. She had left the space blank on my birth certificate, figuring that I might like to have some say in my naming — her first nod toward my freedom. Back east, at three, I had asked to be called Lisa Cheeseburger. Now I took a good look at the girls in calico dresses lined up with their mothers in the gymnasium and changed my mind. "Let's put Lisa Leigh," I whispered. I thought it had a nice ring. Later, I would change it to Lisa Marie, a name borrowed from a character on *Hee Haw*.

I was thrilled to start school, but against the backdrop of thirty other kids, I soon saw myself in a different light. What my mother loved in me — my animation and fierce will — didn't play so well in kindergarten, and so I was tamed, slowly,

by the other children. They came from families as rooted as we
had been footloose. Their fathers were ranchers and loggers
who had lived in the valley for generations. Their mothers
stayed home. They knew about 4-H, rodeo, threshers, and quilt-
ing. They hadn't heard of Biafra, tie-dye, spirulina, or the
Stones.

I went home that first day and asked my mother not to pick
me up from school in the mail truck; I would rather walk the
mile down Spring Street.

In the first days of school, I worked hard to befriend a cute
little girl named Christine, trying to woo her with stories of our
life on the road. "My mother used to let me run beside the mail
truck all day," I told her. "I'd go off into the woods and explore
while they were driving, and then at night I'd meet them at a
campsite."

Christine gave me a dubious look. I was either a liar or a very
strange girl. "What did you eat all day?" she asked.

"Oh, we had drop points where my mother brought me
lunch," I told her, trying to sound offhand.

I had so few clues as to what was worth bragging about that I
ended up adding to my reputation for oddity. But I took it as a
good sign that Christine let me sit beside her on the rag-coil rug
while Mrs. Dillard read *See Spot Run*. I wanted to be as good
and clean as the fictional Jane, who wore a triangular dress and
spoke in short declarative sentences. I wanted it so badly my
mouth began to water. I swallowed, and swallowed again, then
looked over at Christine in a moment of queasy confusion and
projected a stream of vomit into her lap. The day had a feeling
of ruin about it. I didn't quibble when my mother pulled up in
the mail truck and drove me home.

At times like that, my mother didn't fawn over me. When
she felt downhearted, she went through the motions of happiness — smiled, took up some vigorous activity — until her
mood caught up with her actions. Sickness, second cousin to
melancholy, got the same brusque treatment. That afternoon,
she pulled a lawn chair into the garden and talked to me while
she hoed between rows of asparagus. I was limp with relief to
be taken away from the classroom, from the wearing work of

fitting into a group of kids who'd played together since they could toddle. The sun was strong on the blanket over my lap. Mother shook dirt from the roots of stubborn crabgrass, and didn't stop for me. She kept working, as if to say, These hard days are common as garden weeds; you take the sun to your back and till them under.

My father was a ghost presence in those days. After the commune visit, I didn't see him for nearly a year. I kept him alive by telling stories — to Alison, to Charlene and Jill. It was all mythology: tales of what he let me do, tales of what he gave me. He would give me a dollar — all I had to do was ask. We pretty much ate pizza every day. I could go to bed as late as I liked.

"If he's so crazy about you, how come he never comes around?" Alison asked me once, her voice like a rusty razor blade. She never bothered to tell stories about Roger. I think she knew he wasn't coming back.

It would be years before I would understand how much my father had wanted to be the figure from my fantasies — showing up to sweep me away. But after he was released from prison, my mother kept him at bay. She worried about his judgment, and after years of our quiet family life with Jim, it made her nervous to let me go again.

Once, during that time of infrequent visits, I caught a glimpse of a tall, dark-haired man in the grocery store, and a longing so fierce rushed through my body that I was halfway to his side before I caught my mistake. In that half-second or so, I had invented the story of his appearance: he had come to take me on an impromptu picnic and had stopped in to pick up some food. Then the stranger turned and revealed a face that was thicker, paler, older than the one I had searched for. I stood among the pyramids of peppers and potatoes, watching the mist machines kick up a white froth over the produce bins, until my mother came and found me.

When we had been in California for a year, my mother let me fly back to Boston to visit my father. On the day of my departure, she and I piled into the mail truck and drove down to San Francisco. As we rumbled through the city streets, Mother sighed over the Victorian houses, their gingerbread trim, but I sat up front on my old bed and watched for a chink of light between the façades. I had become used to the wide sky in the valley. This looked to me like a place with no breathing room.

I know it tested my mother's nerve to see me off alone, but she didn't show her fear, and so I had none. Once I was on board, the stewardesses treated me like a queen. They took me on a tour of the cockpit, then sat me up front and gave me playing cards and plastic wings. I thought stewardesses were paragons of womanliness, with their fixed hairdos, long frosted nails, and diamond rings. My mother wore Levi's and flannel shirts, brushed her long chestnut hair and tied it back in a bandanna. Our medicine cabinet held soap and hydrogen peroxide, dental floss and razors, but not a single tube of lipstick or bottle of perfume. When the stewardess leaned over to buckle my seat belt before takeoff, I was bewitched by the floral scent wafting out of her polyester uniform.

This was in the fatted-calf days of the airlines, when the upper deck of a 747 was a cocktail lounge. After the seat-belt sign went off, I wandered up to the bar and twirled in one of the modular lounge chairs while the bartender plied me with Shirley Temples. I was taking a real liking to airline travel. I had shown up in a hippie van and had been lifted into the sanitized world of prepackaged meals and tiny resilient pillows.

I remember nothing of Boston or that visit with my father, but the flights — the coming and going — are etched in my memory. When my father bought me a ticket on the other end, he could afford only a youth fare, which required that I travel with an adult. Since he was staying on the ground in Boston, we searched the line at the boarding gate for someone who would pose as my parent. He gave me veto rights: no, not that one; no, she looks mean. I might have seemed like a little princess, weeding out the unsuitable escorts, but I felt a deep self-consciousness as the line snaked into the plane and my choices dwindled. Someone would have to take a shine to me, and in that judging light I felt scruffy and uncombed.

We got right down to the wire. The flight attendant called out the last rows, and my father and I moved forward, scanning the crowd. A family with three kids passed by, all dressed in matching sportswear and laden with carry-on bags and stuffed animals. I would gladly have slipped in with their happy bustle, but my father didn't bother asking if they cared to shepherd a fourth child. Next came a businessman, his garment bag slung over one shoulder, his head sunk in the paper as he inched forward. My father gave me a questioning look, but I shook my head. I knew a man like that wouldn't have me. I might spill juice on his slacks; I would talk too much. I began a panicked dance from foot to foot, afraid of getting caught and being hauled off the plane, worried that I would never make it home to my mother. They made the final boarding call, and the two of us stood there hand in hand, momentarily paralyzed, when a woman came running for the plane, her trench coat flapping. My father nearly jumped on her — Ellen! It was someone he knew. Sure, she would sit with me. A quick kiss goodbye and we ran down the ramp, my father waving, smaller and smaller, at the gate.

"Thank god she came along," my father told me years later. "Your flight got grounded in Chicago by a snowstorm, and you had to spend the night in a hotel. Your mother called me in a rage when you didn't get off on the other end. She thought I'd kidnapped you."

I remember nothing of this — not the storm or the grounding or the hotel. Only my father waving goodbye. I wonder if this was a blank made by banality or terror. I can imagine myself at five following that woman anywhere, curling up under the hotel bedspread and watching TV, letting her brush my teeth, say, or tuck my hair behind my ear before sleep. Or I might have been stiff with anxiety, knowing that I was stranded between parents, in a whiteout in the middle of nowhere, sleeping next to a stranger. That sense of disconnection, of floating in the free space between my mother and father, was one that would come to feel natural.

Not long after that visit, Jim came home one day and announced that he had found a job. He'd be working for the Irrigation District, known around town as "the Ditch." Although he had trained as an architect, Jim didn't have high ambitions. His last drafting project, completed for a firm back in Boston, had been a multistory office building, slated for construction in the woods near Walden Pond. That job broke his heart. Jim believed in karma, instant and otherwise, so he looked around for work whose net effect on the universe seemed to be close to neutral. The ditch job fit the bill. People needed water, and the burden of maintaining the ditches needed to be shared. There was no profit involved; the fees were used to maintain the gates and sluiceways.

Jim's new job required some calculation of cubic feet over time, and a willingness to work at all hours of the night. The ditch boss, a gentle hulking man named Wayne, thought Jim was priceless because he wrote down the figures in tight drafts-man's numerals, never missed a day of work, and charmed the most codgerly of the town's ranchers with his good-old-boy ways. Jim would lean on a fence post and listen to them go on about cattle blight or sugar levels in their grapes, and then he'd shake his head and offer a Southern nicety. "Well, I'll be," he'd say, or "Man alive!"

Both Mother and Jim said that part of their pleasure in the country life was in the range of people around them: Mamie Watson, who had lived for eighty years in the same tin-roofed house and remembered when the Pomo Indians still lived in camps along the river; Jack Lease, an ex–NFL linebacker hob-bled by old injuries, who had come back to his hometown to sell fish out of the back of his station wagon. Sprinkled among these native sons and daughters were people like themselves, back-to-the-landers who had come to the valley in search of respite from city life. One of their favorites was Alan Sarkissian, who lived in a little apartment across the street from us. Mother, who took a visceral delight in other people's intelligence, de-clared Alan a genius. He designed and built a vacuum cleaner so powerful it could suck the hairs off a dog. He made his own telescopes, played Bach's Goldberg Variations so beautifully it gave you goosebumps, and baked his own bread. When Ali Akbar Kahn's sitar broke, he sent it to Alan for repair.

I had expressed interest in making music, so my mother bought me a recorder. Alison went to a Waldorf school, and they had a whole classroom hour devoted to tweeting on those plastic flutes. They also spent a lot of time building birdhouses, singing along to Peter, Paul, and Mary, and making god's eyes out of twigs and yarn. By the second grade, Alison had still barely heard of arithmetic.

I was bucking to be transferred to Mountain Meadow, but Mother kept holding out, and I think the recorder was a consolation prize. As soon as I unwrapped it, I took it over to Alan's house to show off, glad for an excuse to pester him. He greeted me with a gruff nod and let me lounge around his kitchen sounding out "Frère Jacques" and "Three Blind Mice." Alan's kitchen prefigured industrial chic. There was a table saw right next to the stove (both were kept meticulously clean, not a wood shaving or grease smear in sight), and the old coffee cans on the counter were full of cracked walnuts and raisins and washers sorted carefully by size.

I worked my way around the room, trying to breathe into the center of each note, the way the instruction pamphlet had described. Alan looked pained. "Hey, listen to this," he said, going quickly to his record collection and pulling an album gingerly from its sleeve. Before he set the needle down, he blew the LP clean with a tiny rubber bellows.

I stopped my serenade. I had hoped Alan would be so bowled over by my talents that he'd let me play his sarod. It sat on a velvet cloth in the living room — a trapezoid of polished, inlaid wood with two layers of strings, which you struck with delicately balanced cherrywood hammers. I slipped the recorder casually into my back pocket, as if I had tired of it.

Alan looked down as the record started, his head cocked to one side in anticipation. First, a few bright guitar chords, then Joni Mitchell came on, her voice swooping through the register. I sat down on his living-room floor with my nose in the liner notes. Alan smiled and went back to sanding a piece of wood, now and then sighting down its length in the light from the kitchen window.

That December, Jackie, Alison, and Jacob moved out and took a bigger place up Spring Street. While their half of the house was vacant, Mother and Jim tore up the rickety porch and laid new

two-by-fours, then got really zealous and ripped up the old
water line to the street. They were out there digging a ditch on
New Year's Eve — never the types to risk their necks out on the
road on such a night, or, god forbid, spend any money — when
a smiling fellow with a bushy mustache walked up.

"Looks like a piece of work there," he said.

"Yeah, well, we're trying to polish this off before the holidays
are over," Jim said, leaning on his pick and sticking out his
tongue in mock exhaustion.

"Let me give it a whirl," the man offered, and he slung the
pick for a while, as they asked him this and that. His name was
Grant, and he worked for Louisiana Pacific, which we should
have guessed from his uniform: jeans, plaid shirt, steel-toed
Redwing boots with fringe fanning out below the laces.

"What brought you by here?" Mother finally asked him.

"I heard you had an apartment for rent," Grant said, "and I
wanted to apply for it."

Apply for it. Mother and Jim chuckled at that one. The other
folks who had come by to see the place had pulled up on
Harleys and asked if we minded them running a little bike-
repair business out of the house. This, my mother said years
later, really meant they would be selling dope and revving their
bikes in the driveway at all hours of the night. Grant, on the
other hand, had just dug a good two feet of water line by way of
introduction. He moved into the apartment the next day.

I had a bit of a crush on Grant. He had full, chipmunk cheeks
and big white teeth and always treated me with polite affection.
Though I was six and he was thirty-five, I held out hope that he
didn't see our age difference as insurmountable. My parents
often sent me around the house to invite him over for dinner,
and he would always stand on his porch for a moment, protest-
ing gently, his hands tucked into his back pockets.

Once he was seated with a plateful of food, I jockeyed over
next to him and spent the meal watching his hands — long-
fingered and clean, with oval nails — while he and my parents
exchanged gossip. Grant had heard that the head of the board
of supervisors, who took a hard line against sex education in
the classroom, was running around with a seventeen-year-old
girl from the high school. Jim mumbled something about a

wealthy rancher who stole water in the middle of the night, then had the gall to stand in his wet fields in the morning and protest his innocence.

"What do you think about Mizz Crumb's paint job?" Grant asked my parents with a gleam in his eye. R. Crumb, the cartoonist, had a place on a ridge above the valley. His wife, Dana, carted their kids around in a Dodge station wagon with "Mother Trucker and Sons" painted in white script over the driver's door, and "Kiss My Ass and It's Yours" arched over the tailgate.

"The PTA put the screws to her while you were gone," Mother told him. "So she covered up 'and It's Yours' with primer paint."

After dinner, Grant coaxed Jim into pulling out his slides of Asia. "Well, jeez," Jim said, rummaging around in the trunk at the foot of the bed for a few trays, "y'all have already seen these a few times," unable to conceal his pleasure at being asked.

He set up the slide projector on a bookshelf in the living room, and while it was warming up, he made himself a martini in a cracked coffee cup — nearly pure gin, only a dash of vermouth, and a few Safeway olives — a drink he had come to love in his navy days. Once the slides were loaded, he dimmed the lights and stood with one leg up on a kitchen chair, sipping his drink and clicking his way through antiquity. The geometric complexes of Angkor Wat lifted out of the jungle, the courtyards filled with grass as bright as putting greens. His photographs were crisp and plain, so that the camera and the man behind it were nearly forgotten: a gold reclining Buddha as long as a railroad car, the temples at Khajuraho, Gaudí's Barcelona apartments.

Jim's narration was mostly marked by appreciative silence. I tried to get the clicker away from him, so we didn't have to savor each one. The buildings were impressive, but I was more interested in the people: the laughing Cambodian monks, the Thai farmer zipping down a dirt road on his motorcycle with a drunken pig strapped to the handlebars. Jim clicked quickly past these shots, as if they were of anecdotal interest, then past a close-up of subway tokens and keys against a geometric backdrop, and past a blurry slide of an Asian woman caught obliquely in a mirror.

"Now let's go back to that one," Mother said, laughing in the dark. "Tell us a little about her."

Jim smiled and kept mum, clicking forward to the next palace. "I've got to have a few secrets left when we're sitting on the porch swing," he said.

Those nights filter back with a velvety laziness. A belly full of pie. Grant stretched out in one of Floyd's corduroy chairs. Our windows clicking on and off against the black valley air, as we pulled those faraway streets through the wall.

At school, I soon learned how other families spent their nights. Half the recess chatter involved recounting the previous evening's television shows — a whole world I knew nothing about. We must have been one of the few families in the valley that didn't own a TV. I tried to play along, but at certain points I couldn't hide my ignorance. My schoolmate Christine once asked me about a classic *Brady Bunch* episode, and when I said I hadn't seen it she refused to let the subject go: "You must have seen it. The one where Bobby gets his first kiss and rockets go off?" She pressed on, and finally I blurted out the truth: "We don't have a TV. My mother doesn't *believe* in television." A profound hush fell over the group around us, a line of prissy girls smocked up at their easels. I watched their faces shift through pity, incomprehension, and at last a slowly hardening scorn.

Once I realized I was out of the loop, I savored any chance to soak up some of this precious medium. When my mother was called in to substitute teach in a neighboring town, I took the bus home with Harry Peck, a boy in my class, whose mother baby-sat me for a few hours in the afternoons. I loved this arrangement, because the Pecks had a television. Unfortunately, Mrs. Peck also had a lot of rules, principal of which was "Go play outside." Outside was the tree house, which I had fallen out of early on and refused to revisit; a patch of neatly clipped lawn; and a gravel driveway. Inside was shag carpeting, candied nuts in a bowl, and a large color TV. I spent a lot of time on the porch, pressing my face against the window screens. Sometimes Harry's mother relented and, after making us take our shoes off so as not to soil the carpet, let us watch cartoons.

I lay on my stomach, slack jawed, oblivious to anything but those nineteen inches of glowing screen. Harry and his little brother quit watching the TV and started counting the number of times I blinked in a minute (barely enough to keep my corneas damp) and trying to rouse me with nasty remarks, to which — they told me later, incredulous — I made no response.

When my mother came to pick me up I could barely hide my annoyance. I perfected a glacial donning of my socks and shoes — "All right, I'm hurrying!" — which I could make last for most of a *Tom and Jerry* episode, while my mother was forced to make polite conversation with Mrs. Peck.

The hours that other families spent curled up in front of the TV, my family spent reading. At home, we often wouldn't say a word all through dinner, each of us engrossed in a book or magazine tucked under the edge of our plate. I never thought this strange, until Christine, in a moment of rare generosity, invited me over to her house for dinner. No one, I noticed, was reading, but the family displayed a host of other odd customs. My friend kept one hand limp in her lap during the meal, as if it were useless, and she chewed with her lips sealed, breathing through her nose. From the saying of grace to Christine's polite request to be excused at the meal's end, I studied the goings-on with the curiosity of a traveler in a strange land. When I got home, I asked Mother and Jim to put the books away and teach me some table manners. "How about one night a week we do it the fancy way?" I asked them. They thought this was a hoot, but they obliged me. Jim pulled my chair out with elaborate courtesy, snapping a napkin open and laying it in my lap with a flourish. I made them talk me through the use of multiple utensils, and both of them dredged up a few arcane rules from their childhood dining rooms, laughing at being asked to remember petty matters of etiquette they had been so glad to shuck off.

*

When I was in my teens, I looked back at our surroundings in those early years and thought they seemed deprived. But at the time everything served. The living room was furnished with Floyd's old armchairs. Cigarette burns dotted the arms; I stuck my fingers through the brocade and pulled the stuffing out. Our bookshelves were slapped together out of two-by-tens; we drank out of old Mason jars and cracked coffee cups. My mother saved a ledger from those years, with our expenses tallied in her schoolteacher's open hand. In one month: nine dollars spent on frivolity, which included postage stamps.

If my mother remembers only our sunlit afternoons, I have returned with a similar selectivity to the difficult times. Loneliness was a kind of self-consciousness. Perhaps the etched quality of my darker childhood memories was produced by this sharper attention, and by my return to these periods over time, setting the mind's needle in the same groove and letting it run. I had cause, not long ago, to question my grim vision, when Grandma Leila gave me a box of old family photographs. Some my mother had entrusted to her before we set out west, others had been posted from the valley before they lost touch. In square after white-bordered square I am smiling, antic, at times that I remember as full of disruption.

In one snapshot from our first months at the house, Alison and I stand on the half-dead lawn under the walnut trees. I am wearing a pink wool A-line dress, which I loved for its one remarkable accent: three sets of brass buttons descending down the front, with a length of cheap gold chain strung between each pair. I am coy for the camera, one hand cocked on my hip. Alison is bent forward, both hands on her knees, trying to look winning, her overbite clamped down on her lower lip. Behind us is my bed, a metal frame, which Mother had dragged into the yard and spray-painted pink to match the new pink comforter she had ordered from Sears. In the background: dried-up hedge, the cagework of the bare bed, piles of scrap lumber, and a mangy dog gnawing its leg. When I was in high school, and mooning for a suburban tract home, I could barely stand to look at that picture. The yard seemed pitiful. And the sight of my five-year-old self, happy with so little, filled me with shame.

But if I scrape down through the teenage heartbreak, I see that I was delighted then by a coat of paint and a cheap comforter, by my mother's transformative powers. The pity in thinking we lived in scarcity is laid over this memory like a fake veneer. That bed made me feel lucky. I danced around the yard, watching as the dull metal turned rose.

four

I WAS GETTING my footing it seems, newly dubbed Lisa Marie, making a few friends at school, and mooning over my second-grade teacher, Miss Shelpie, who wore her raven's-wing hair in a bouffant and who turned up one Monday with a ruddy glow and the announcement that from now on we were to call her Mrs. Kelber. Mrs. K. was doing a fairly good Jackie Kennedy imitation, out there in a drab schoolroom in the middle of a lazy farming town. She wore capri pants and kept her desk immaculate — paper clips laid neatly in their well, pencils needle-sharp — and didn't so much teach as she did model, in front of the freshly swabbed blackboard, the form and bearing of a proper grown-up person.

After lunch, she led us through a relaxation exercise: "Heads down, arms limp . . . let them go limp . . . cheeks right down on the desk." Mrs. K. walked the rows in her wedgie heels — of course I peeked — and counted backward from one hundred. One day, when she had reached the single digits, she knelt beside me and lifted my wrist, taking from my damp fingers a small hair fastener. Then ever so gently she let go of my hand and watched to see if it would drop, if I had given up the last bit of muscle tension under the soothing patter of her voice. I tried to flatten my face to the desk with convincing torpor, but when she let go, my wrist floated down to the wood — a balletic gesture of lassitude — and gave me away.

"Really, honey, you can relax," Mrs. Kelber whispered.

As it turned out, I would get only a small taste of Mrs. K.'s gentling presence. A few months into the school year, I would move to Oregon. Gardening and substitute teaching had kept my mother occupied for a while, but she was only a few units shy of a teaching credential and itching for a classroom to call her own. The University of Oregon was the nearest school to offer the courses she needed. As it turned out, some old friends from Cambridge were living in Eugene, and offered to let us stay with them. We would be gone for six months, and though Mother tried to make this sound brief, I know it was hard for her to leave our sleepy town, and most of all to leave her husband. (Sometime thereabouts she and Jim went to the courthouse and made it official — no fanfare, no fuss, since they'd been calling themselves married since they arrived in the valley.) I don't think my mother ever considered leaving me with Jim; the graft was too new. He stayed in the valley, tending ditch and patching up the apartments.

Joyce and Albert Curly, my mother's friends, had moved from Boston to the outskirts of Eugene, part of the wave that had carried my parents west. Albert was an architect; each Christmas, in lieu of the typical foil card, he sent out an elaborate pen-and-ink rendering of the family dwelling, reproduced on stiff white paper. These cards had come to us at 12000 Spring Street, and for years I believed the Curlys lived in a castle — flying buttresses, a moat, stone parapets, the whole medieval works. On the cards, the Curly family would be marching across the drawbridge, knees lifted high, playing trumpet and flute, their faces thrown up toward the sun. Each year, a new banner unfurled from a turret, bearing a Christmas greeting along its length in Albert's matchstick printing.

On the drive up to Eugene, Mother told me stories about the Curlys' son, Ivan, whom I apparently adored in our days back in Boston. Soon I was convinced I remembered him, and imagined us cavorting around the castle grounds, fishing for trout in the moat.

When we rumbled into the Curlys' driveway, my spirits sank. We crossed not a moat but a small creek, spanned by a split-log bridge. Up ahead was the house, an unassuming two-story wood-frame set back from the road. Joyce came out to embrace my mother, and Ivan followed, hanging back like a perfect stranger when we were introduced. Together, they showed us around the place. There would be no palace suite. The Curlys were already pressed for room. Mother and I would sleep in the mail truck at night and would use the house to cook and take showers. Mother tried to put a bright face on things, but I could tell she was worried we were straining her old friends' hospitality.

Soon after we arrived, I was enrolled at Ivan's school. Mother walked me to the doorway of my new classroom, and there, in the face of all those strange children, I took stock of myself. I was wearing a fringed poncho and saddle shoes; my hair hung rattily over my shoulders (I kicked up a fuss when anyone tried to brush it). My front teeth were gone. Under my arm I clutched a cigar box covered with red velvet, which held my folded store of writing paper.

Mrs. Rhone, the teacher, assigned me to sit next to a boy with fat cheeks and a bristle cut.

"Don't you have a binder?" he asked as I sat down, pulling back at arm's length as if the lack of one were contagious.

On the drive home from school, I asked Albert if he could get me a binder. He had a front pocket full of mechanical pencils, and I figured he was my best hope for office supplies. "Sure thing," he promised, writing a note to himself on a sheaf of papers moldering on the dash. Albert had a halo of frizzy black hair and addressed himself to a patch of air above my head. Despite his drafting skills and his dream of living in a castle, he didn't seem to spend much time improving on the real house — shoring up the sagging front porch, say, or doing a thorough cleaning. Albert, I would learn over the months of our stay, was good for highly specific tasks. He could dig a sliver out of your foot without letting you once feel the needle. He made excellent Halloween costumes. Other than that, he moved in a private fog.

The binder, of course, never materialized, and I suffered minor humiliations during any class exercise that required us to use lined paper. Sometime during that first week, Mrs. Rhone asked us each to write a paragraph describing our bedroom. I thought about the back of the mail truck: the fold-down bed where Mother and I slept, the ping of rain on the metal roof, the spidery lines of black caulking on the skylight, and the wink of stars beyond. There was much I loved about these familiars, but I was getting the idea it wasn't wise to share them. Instead, I took a note from Albert and conjured myself a bedroom out of Sears, Roebuck: twin beds with ruffled shams, a two-story dollhouse, a chest of toys at the foot of the bed. When I'd imagined the room down to the style of night-light, I slid my hand into the desk and pulled a sheet from its velvety compartment, working under the lid to smooth the crease.

"Whatcha doing in there?" my seatmate asked, leaning his face close to mine. He flipped my desk open. "Look! Hippie girl keeps her paper in a box!" He turned to the kids beside us for appreciation.

My cheeks flushed hot. That box was a gift from my mother. She bought a cigar box from a tobacconist in Cambridge and covered it inside and out with old dress velvet. It had come west in the mail truck, gathering a pattern of watermarks and grease, the lid slowly sagging inward. Battered as it was, I loved that thing. Now it caused me a turmoil of loyalty. To join in the shrill laughter, to make a show of throwing the box out, would betray my mother's thoughtfulness, and yet part of me blamed her for sending me into the world without the proper equipment.

In the end, I did nothing. I waited for the kids to shut up and never mentioned the teasing to my mother. She looked pale to me, and tired. Her days were spent under some old boor whose first concern was how to keep students tame and quiet. She wasn't learning anything, I heard her tell Joyce; she was biding her time. If she could stand it, so could I.

I came out of the blocks badly at Twin Oaks, and I never recovered my stride. Mrs. Rhone moved me all over the room in search of a friendly zone, but the class had closed ranks. Finally, she gave up. "I don't know where else to put you," she told me, holding her palms up in front of her, as if to prove that she had nothing to offer. What bothered me, more than the knowledge that she couldn't save me, was the note of reproach that crept into her voice. She hadn't just given up; she held me responsible. I looked in her face and saw a shadow of the hardened fright I saw in my classmates.

In hindsight, I feel for Mrs. Rhone. In her very own classroom, her private domain, I made her feel powerless. She held the pointer and could glare us into silence, but over the deeper workings of the classroom she had no say. The more she favored me, the more it worked to my disadvantage, and once she saw this she withdrew behind tented eyebrows and a stiff smile. When Mrs. Rhone swiveled in front of the class, going on about Pilgrims or fractions or parts of speech, her eyes passed right over me. I kept my head down and my hand in my desk, smoothing it back and forth over the cool velvet.

By the end of the first week at Twin Oaks, I was overcome by fatigue. After school, I went into the Curlys' house and climbed the ladder to the loft above the living room. Joyce had filled the room with oversize pillows, and I lay in their soothing jumble and stared out the round attic window at the crown of the plum tree outside.

Once, I had wandered out barefoot under the tree, thinking that I might climb up to the sweetest plums, which grew on the high limbs, out of arm's reach. But when I neared the trunk, rotten fruit mashed up between my toes. I froze there, unwilling to take another step, and after a while I became absorbed in the view: the grassy slope from the house to the creek, where a serrated line of saplings clung to the bank, and the sheer face of the cliff on the far side, stiff as a cardboard cutout. The wind picked up and beat the grass into long silvery waves, and one minute it seemed to me that the grass was moving under invisible fingers, and then suddenly there seemed to be no wind, only the grass rippling of its own volition, a carpet of green cilia waving away.

I stood there for a long time with my arms outstretched before I realized what I was waiting for: someone to lift me up over those land mines in the grass and carry me to the porch. At seven, I still had the occasional faith that my wishes would go

out into the world and summon aid. When I saw that no one
was coming, I turned and picked my way back to the house,
tiptoeing gingerly on the balls of my feet, wincing when I hit
another windfall plum, my hands out and shoulders up like
some ghoul in a cheap horror film.

My friend Ivan was an odd boy, skinny and gentle, with a
narrow face and a high-pitched voice. Normally he was very
calm and had his head bent over a Tintin comic, but certain
things distressed him: cats dead by the side of the road, having
his hair cut. When he cried, the tendons stood out in his neck
like fiddle strings.

On the playground at Twin Oaks, he and I pretended not to
recognize each other, but at home we were inseparable. We
ducked into the woods behind the house, scanning nervously
for the mountain lions that Ivan said roamed there in great
packs. Or we played with his cast, the remnant of a broken arm
he'd sustained the previous summer. He'd made the orthope-
dist glue the thing back together, named it Casty, and played
medieval war games with it, smiting dragons and the like.

Once, Ivan and I made a bed-sheet and broomstick flag and
marched back and forth across the bridge crying, "Ethiopia!"
which roused our mothers to the porch. This was less a protest
than a howl of delight. We had captured the passion but little of
the meaning of the rallies we had been to back east. Ivan and I
kept up our march for a good half-hour, kicking up a trail of
dust along the driveway, chanting those strange and pleasing
syllables, our voices echoing up the canyon.

It was in the same spirit of rebellion that one night, when the
Curlys were having a party, Ivan and I gathered up all the
cigarettes in the house and flushed them down the toilet. It took
quite a few tanks to wash them down, and eventually someone
knocked on the door and asked what we were up to. We were
too proud of our efforts to lock anybody out. A few bloated
cigarettes circled in the bowl. Our mothers appeared in the
doorway, looking mortified. Ivan pointed to the pile of crumpled wrappers. "Cigarettes give you cancer," he said.

We thought they would thank us. We thought they would

gather around and applaud us for pointing out the error of their ways. Instead, our allowances were docked for a few months, and we had to go around and hand-deliver restitution to the guests.

I came to dread the school week, rising early in the dark mail truck and sprinting through the rain into the house, where Mother made me oatmeal. I watched her back as she filled the pan at the sink. The kitchen was quiet, Ivan and Joyce and Albert still asleep in their rooms. The burner made a low flap and lit my mother's hands with a blue light. While she stirred, I willed her with every muscle and tendon to ask me how I was feeling. I tried to beg her with my face: ask me. She brought me a steaming bowl and sat down.

Suddenly, I see those months as my mother might have lived them. Twenty-eight years old, trying for my sake not to show her loneliness, waking on those rainy mornings in the mail truck and missing her husband's bulk beside her. She would rise to pick out my clothes and make the oatmeal, to stir in someone else's chilled kitchen, thinking of what?

I felt her moods the way you feel along a wall in the dark: all texture and no edges. She dropped me off at school in the morning and then she was gone — gone from the world — until she drove up again at the curb to meet me. And gone, too, when she turned over at night to sleep in the wrack of her own dreams.

But the past keeps changing, and over time something has shifted in that dawn-smudged kitchen of twenty years ago. I have made us companions in our solitude. When I think of us now, I imagine us sitting together over steaming bowls of oatmeal, both of us waiting for the light to rise.

I came home from Twin Oaks looking glum often enough that in the end my mother didn't need to ask. She decided to try me out at the Montessori school across town. Ivan had gone there a few years before, but the fees had finally squeezed the Curlys' slender budget too tightly, and he had returned to public school. Now Joyce decided that we might as well go together.

Our first day at Montessori, Ivan and I were assigned to the same class. I was grateful to have him near me as our mothers walked us to the classroom. He looked half terrified, and his weakness was a comfort; it meant I didn't need to feign toughness.

The school building was shaped like a stop sign, with the rooms fanning off a central hub. The inside walls were glass, and through them I could see kids gathered around low tables, doing art projects. It seemed like a nice enough place. But when our mothers steered us through the classroom door, Ivan took one look at the teacher and began to cry.

"I don't want to be in *his* class," he wailed, trying to scoot past Joyce toward the door. He must have recognized the teacher from his previous stint at the school.

"This is your class, Ive. You've got to settle down," Joyce said. Joyce was always reasonable. She had long, tapered fingers and never raised her voice. But Ivan was beyond reason; he was hysterical. He pushed against his mother's stomach, crying, "No, no, no!" He lost traction on the floor and slid to his knees, curled over like a supplicant. The teacher stood perfectly still, watching this display.

At last Joyce relented, shrugging an apology at the class. Ivan was led out, sniffling, and taken to another classroom. No one offered to rescue me, and I didn't have the nerve to pitch a fit myself. I took my seat and faced my new teacher, a dour man with muttonchops and slicked-back hair, who inspired fits of terror on sight.

From then on, I would see Ivan only in the lunchroom. We ate at long tables covered with waxed Formica, which caught the foggy light slipping in through the dormer windows. Montessori was supposed to be gentler than public school, but the teachers kept a strict discipline during mealtime. We bent our heads quietly, and my teacher, Mr. Frick, who I soon learned was also the school principal, walked along the center aisle with a ruler to slap the hands of chatterers. After lunch, food-service workers passed out dishes of sliced carrots. This was dessert. In time, I came to appreciate the carrot's humble sweetness. I pressed my sliver against the roof of my mouth, savoring it, trying to see how long it would last.

In the afternoons, we studied science. Mr. Frick held up a cotton plant. "Who can tell me about the boll weevil?" he asked the class. "Lisa?"

I had never seen a cotton plant, but at this point I was becoming familiar with bewilderment — that feeling that I'd been dropped into a conversation midstream. Life seemed to be always in media res. If I was to catch up, I figured I had better start bluffing.

"The ball weaver makes the cotton into yarn," I said, trying for a note of confidence.

Mr. Frick looked like he'd been slapped. He knew I was a mediocre student, but it hadn't occurred to him that I might be a smart aleck. When I saw him give me that shrewd, appraising look, I knew I had gotten it wrong, badly wrong. So much for pluck. Mr. Frick took a deep breath and assumed an expression I would come to know well: *with patience and strength I will suffer the little idiots.* He never called on me again.

Once I was pegged as a slow learner, my fortunes improved. I was sent to work with Shelly, the tutor, who became a beacon of light in my day. Shelly spoke gently, the way people talk to horses, and she put her hand on my back sometimes when I asked a question. For the hour that she went over borrowing and long division, my shoulders would slowly come down from around my ears.

One morning, when the autumn cloud cover broke unexpectedly, Mr. Frick told us we would hold P.E. outside. "You're all looking a touch pale," he said. It took me a moment to recognize the rictus that split his face. Mr. Frick was smiling. "How about we jump rope?"

A cheer went up in the classroom.

When the bell rang, we filed out to the damp parking lot. Mr. Frick followed, lugging a canvas sack, which he untied, pulling out a long rope. "Chuck, Peter, why don't you each take an end?"

I waited for the shorter, individual ropes to emerge from the sack, but they never appeared. The boys got the long rope swinging, and the rest of the class made a line, waiting to jump in. I had no intention of trying this game for the first time, but I got jostled into place, and the line forced me forward. The rope made a vehement thwack on the wet asphalt, which got louder and louder, and then the girl in front of me peeled off, and I was up.

"Go!" said the girl behind me. I held my hands out, mimicking the approach and retreat of the rope, while the kids behind me shouted, "Now! Now!" I was paralyzed, rooted to the spot.

"You can go ahead," I said to the girl behind me. I melted back into the line, farther and farther, and then slipped between two parked cars and squatted down, hoping Mr. Frick had missed my exit. I would have found it pleasant to daydream back there if I hadn't been worried that I'd be discovered and hauled out. For most of the hour I played with my hair in the shine of a hubcap, prepared to say, if anyone found me, that I was looking for something I'd lost.

When I told my mother about the business with the jump rope, she dipped into our small savings and bought me a pair of white vinyl zip-up boots, a little cheer-me-up surprise. These boots were a special pride to me. I wore them nearly every day, with denim skirts, with shorts, until they released a ripe, sour smell when unzipped. I was even wearing them during P.E. on the day I finally learned how to jump rope. We were indoors this time. There was nowhere to hide. I came to the front of the line and the girls cried, "Now!" and before I could think, their voices jerked me forward. I leapt into the blur and caught the rhythm, amazed that my feet weren't swept out from under me. But no sooner had I got the hang of it than those treadless vanity boots shot out from under me.

That was the last thing I remembered. I came to on a cot in the nurse's office.

"What happened?" I asked the nurse, my head throbbing. She was bent over a pile of forms, a little paper hat pinned to the crown of her head.

"Minor concussion," she said, without looking up from her work. "Your mother will be here soon."

I don't remember how my mother behaved when she arrived. No doubt she was calm, as she always was about prac-

tical troubles. But the memory has disappeared — my head
likely addled by the blow.

In fact, much of those months floats back in fragments: the
acrid smell of Magic Markers at my classroom easel, the taste of
Orange Crush, which Ivan and I drank like water. Or one vivid
afternoon near the end of our stay. On the Montessori play yard
were rows of ladders — fat dowels that rose up the outside of
the cafeteria. I climbed one until I was under the eaves and then
hung there, leaning my weight back into the air. Down below,
some of the sixth-grade girls were playing charades. They
made a circle around Marcia, a curvy girl with hair the color of
burnt wood. She made the gesture for a song: opened her
mouth and fluttered her fingers to describe the rising notes.
Three words, she signaled, then sunk a fist into her gut and
threw her head back in mock agony. She fell to the ground,
writhing, her eyebrows sewn into a peak.

I was stunned by her conviction. I forgot the name of every
song I'd ever known. Everyone around me seemed suddenly
very clever, startling in their vividness, or else very natural and
at ease.

The song, I learned somehow — Marcia must have spoken —
was "Killing Me Softly." It played on the radio all that winter,
and I can still hear the weathered richness of Roberta Flack's
voice: "He was strumming my pain with his fingers, singing
my life with his words." She holds back in the early bars, sure
of her power, stringing it out lightly — a knowing, mournful
voice, coming from far off. Whenever I heard it, I thought of my
father, the soul albums he played, singing the bass line, snapping his fingers to the beat. But my father was lost somewhere,
and now Jim was gone, too. We seemed to be losing men at an
alarming rate, without fanfare or comment. I could see no end
to our wandering.

But in December, we returned to 12000 Spring Street, and there
was Jim, grinning in the driveway. He had built my mother a
chicken coop as a homecoming gift. Charlene and Jill burst
from their house and plied me with kisses, exclaiming at how I
had grown.

Soon after I got back into the swing of things, a letter arrived from my father, inviting me to take a trip with him to Mexico. "How would you like to ride a burro?" he wrote. My father has odd handwriting — a lefty's back-leaning scrawl, vowels like small stones, stems of consonants sprouting up wildly. But in those early notes he printed carefully, hoping I might read them to myself. At the bottom of each letter was a starburst, where he had let the felt tip pause.

I was thrilled by the idea of Mexico, though I would have gone to Siberia if he asked. I read the letter several times, then took out a pencil and printed a careful "yes" at the end of his questions, trying, I suppose, to turn a note into a conversation.

"You're lucky you have a garden," he wrote, "cause I think if I were a plant I would rather live in a garden than in a pot — don't you?" *Yes.*

"Do you like to eat tacos?" *Yes.*

I don't remember the flight to Mexico. By then I was a veteran of concourses and planes; they made little impression. I remember only the streets of Mexico City, delivered as in a dream. The air was dense and burned the inside of my nose, but I was smitten by the hubbub and the old buildings. The cars looked strange; the signs made no sense; but my father was beside me, brisk with excitement, and he seemed to know what to do. Put that man on a traffic-jammed street corner and he thrums with purpose, quickened by the jostling of the crowd. He hoisted me up on his shoulders in front of the airport and hailed the only free taxi in sight.

We headed for the railroad station to catch a train to Cuernavaca, where my father planned to take a Spanish course. There were ragged children playing outside the ticket windows, and vendors selling fruit spiced with chili, salt, and lime. I made him buy me a cucumber, peeled and salted in a cone of newsprint. While the train rocked us out of the city, I sat on our berth, eating the salty slivers and watching him. Over the years we spent apart, my father had become reduced to an icon. I had run my few vivid memories over and over in my mind until I had worn away the details, the grit. This real father, squarely across from me, was twice as potent as my memories.

He looked like a man from a Camel cigarette ad — tan, with a full head of black curly hair and a mustache, a silver hoop glinting in one ear. It was safe to say I was starstruck.

Our train came to a stop in Cuernavaca, and I took an instant liking to the city: the grid of cobbled streets and narrow sidewalks; the tile-capped walls spilling bougainvillea. We carried our bags past whitewashed churches and a shady plaza, and within hours my father found us a room, rented from a family in a quiet neighborhood at the edge of town. The house was on a peaceful, tree-lined street. We passed through a scrolled gate and rang the bell. A stocky, smiling woman swung open the door and introduced herself as Señora Gonzalez, ushering us into an airy entryway. Our room faced the street and had high narrow windows. There were fresh sheets on the bed. For a few extra pesos, we would be welcome to eat with the family. I heard children playing and followed the sounds through a dining room, past a table set with embroidered place mats, tiny bowls of sugar and salt. In the back yard was a girl my age, swinging a toddler by his arms. Beyond them was a swimming pool, dry and filled with dead leaves. When the girl saw me, she dropped the baby and ran over, chattering in Spanish. Yalili, her name was Yalili, she made me understand, slinging an arm around my shoulder. I was already drafting a letter to my mother: "Mexico is a very friendly country. I have made a new friend." As Yalili talked, I slipped into a babyish swoon, borne along by the rills of meaningless sound and her cool, tending hands.

In the mornings, we gathered for eggs and tortillas at the long table, while the señora bustled in and out of the kitchen with steaming plates. Then I would play in the back yard with the Gonzalez kids while my father went to language class. He had bought me an Instamatic camera for the trip, and I spent an afternoon wandering around the house composing arty photos: a close-up of a mucky sewage grate, a blurry shot of the empty corridor of trees outside the front gate. I even asked the gardener to take my picture, and after miming the shutter action, I posed in front of the house. That photo is at odds with the waif

I felt myself to be: a snapshot of a wiry tomboy in a horizontal-striped shirt, legs planted wide, arms akimbo.

My father and I quickly slipped into our old groove. We were easy together, quick to laugh. He told bad jokes, held my hands while I walked up the planks of his legs and flipped over. But I soon found he was more fragile than he looked, full of moodiness and childhood terrors. In the afternoon, we walked into town to the public pool, and I discovered he was afraid of the water. My mother had taught me to swim at her parents' house on Long Island. I dove for rings, did somersaults until I burst up gasping, practiced walking on the bottom, and stayed in until my fingers were pickled. I was startled to see how ill at ease my father looked when wet: dark hair plastered down on his forehead, his eyes red from chlorine. He mowed down the lane with a thrashing stroke, hit the wall, and popped up looking bewildered. When someone splashed him, he flinched. "My daughter the otter," he said, a surprising wistfulness in his voice. The next time we went to the pool, his trick knee acted up and he retired to a nearby lawn chair, where he basked in the sun.

On our way home from the pool one day we passed a health clinic. A line of women waited outside with babies and bundles. Older kids spun tops in the gutter.

"Hey, I have a joke for you," my father said. He pursed his lips and paused for effect. "A guy has to go to a doctor's appointment; he's got something wrong with his stomach. He kisses his wife, and as he's going out the door, she says, 'Listen, honey, don't get into any fights, okay?' because she knows he has a little problem with his temper, which is probably why his stomach hurts — he probably has an ulcer."

He looked over at me to see if I was following. "Two hours later, he comes back with a broken nose. 'Vinnie, what happened?' his wife says, running up to him. 'Did you get mugged?' 'No, the doctor was a jerk,' Vinnie says. 'He was messing with me, and we starting duking.' 'Whaddaya mean?' she says. 'What'd he say to you?' "

My father stopped in the street to deliver the punch line, palms and shoulders up, playing Vinnie as a lug from the

Bronx. "He said, 'Piss in a cup.' And I said, 'Shit in my hat.' And the fight started."

I laughed for a while, then cleared my throat. "You know, Jim calls those kind of jokes *bathroom humor.*"

"Really?" My father looked at me, skeptical at first, then sober as he considered this news.

We went on for a few paces in silence, both of us circling back to the man in the joke, who got in trouble for taking things too literally. I saw a grin steal over my father's face, saw him work to conceal it, and then we both gave up and burst out laughing again.

It was during that trip that my father taught me to sing oldies from his high school days in Valley Stream: "In the Still of the Night," "A Casual Look." He sang bass — the *do-wahs* and *dup-de-doops* — snapped his fingers, and walked with a syncopated swoop. I tried to carry the melody, seizing up around the high notes, adding extra vibrato to match his. Now and then we hit a sweet patch and rendered up something better than our two halves. Mood had a lot to do with it. We would fill up an alley, or the back seat of a cab, feeling half famous by the time the last phrase faded.

One morning we walked into town to buy a pair of sandals at the market. It was still cool, and we were nearly alone on the cobbled street. I walked on the narrow sidewalk, brushing my hand against the stucco wall, which changed colors to signal the end of one house and the beginning of another. My father walked in the street, holding my hand, and after going on for a while in silence, he started into "Lean on Me," stair-stepping notes meant to be sung over a blazing garbage can. "Some . . . times in our lives, we all have pain, we all have sorrow."

I looked at his face, becoming once again familiar to me, and my heart squeezed up. In the quiet of that strange and lovely street, in a country where no one knew us, those lines sunk deep and hit their mark. The song was about suffering, about people flying together over great distances when trouble struck. I took it as acknowledgment of all that had passed between us.

I should have let the feeling hold, but I was seven — jumpy and desperate to have everything at once. I didn't quite trust these moments of pleasure. "After this can we sing 'A Casual Look'?" I asked, interrupting his singing.

My father's face crumpled. "I'm singing *this* one now."

I had forgotten how easily he bruised. "I'm sorry," I said. "Please, start again."

He sulked a little, not wanting to look too eager.

"Come on," I said, swinging his hand from side to side. "Start again. You know I love that song."

Some might say it wasn't good for me to get such a glimpse of my father's fragility, but in a strange way I took strength from it. When he wavered, I had to hold firm, and that firmness made me feel sturdy. I could see that he wounded too easily, and because I loved him, I liked to think of myself as the custodian of his feelings.

He picked up the song again, and soon we were in the marketplace, weaving through the tables of meat and vegetables and woven belts. The blue plastic tarps overhead flexed in the breeze, bathing the stalls in a marine light. We found a woman selling sandals. Her husband, in the corner, cut the soles from scraps of truck tire.

"*Quiero zapatos para mi niña,*" my father said, putting a palm on my back. His Spanish was getting better, and with his olive skin and black hair he was sometimes taken for a local.

The woman pulled out a pair, biting through the thread that held them and slapping the soles together. They were stiff as dried meat, and none of them seemed to fit right. "Try these," my father said, picking out a different design. I have never met a man who liked to shop as much as my father. He was willing to immerse himself in the merits of that strap, that heel, and rarely showed signs of impatience. Perhaps it was the mark of a man raised by women: he believed in the importance of style.

Before long, the saleswoman was ringed by a litter of shoes, her face betraying a bit of pique. Her husband, seeing my quandary, pulled up a dusty pair from beneath his workbench and motioned for me to slip them on: the perfect sandals. I paraded around, turning my ankles to the side to admire.

"Those are great," my father told me as we walked through

the maze of aisles and back out to the street. "They show off
your beautiful feet."

Truth told, my feet were goofy looking — long crooked toes
and no arches. They looked exactly like his. ("You'd be tall," Jim
loved to tell me, "if you didn't have so much tucked under.")
But that day I was convinced of their loveliness, walking home
through the streets with my father. I thought everyone turned
to appreciate them, their eyes drawn by the squeak of new
leather.

Halfway through our two-week trip, my father met a woman at
language school, and they fell in love. Even I had to admit that
Leslie was beautiful. She had wheat-gold hair and even features and square teeth that turned slightly in front. Her bearing
hinted at a world of refinement that she had since renounced.
She spoke in whole, tailored sentences and moved with an easy
poise.

What drew the two of them together, besides passion, was
politics. Leslie was a lefty, too — a feminist, a Marxist — and
she lived in Berkeley, the West Coast pole of the student movement. Soon more details emerged: like my stepfather, Jim, she
was trained as an architect, and, like him, she had grown up in
the South. Later, we would learn that Jim had studied architecture in college under Leslie's father. Silly, one might say. Mere
coincidence. But these connections made my mother and father
seem more like each other, for even then I understood, though I
could never have put it into words, that people craved their
opposites. My parents had been of a piece and then cleft apart,
and now it seemed that they needed these other types — more
reserved, more ordered and steady — to make them whole.

We went with Leslie to the pool for our afternoon swim, and
while she and my father talked on the lawn I treaded water in
the shallow end, taking note of every gesture between them.
She laughed and fingered his earring. He rubbed sunscreen on
her shoulders.

A few days after they met, my father took her on a date and
left me for the evening with Yalili and baby Arturo. Señora
Gonzalez made me a pile of hot tortillas, and I sat on the floor

in their living room watching cartoons, chewing relentlessly, and growing crankier by the minute. I hated the Spanish voice-over, the attention it required to decipher the goings-on. Arturo danced in front of the TV screen, singing along with some ditty for laundry soap, bouncing on his sturdy toddler's legs. I wanted to clobber him.

When my father and Leslie finally came in, late at night, they lingered for a moment in the entryway. I heard their laughter and rushed out to meet them, hoping to hurry her out the door. But when I turned the corner and saw them together, I stopped in my tracks. They were holding hands, looking into each other's eyes, a palpable crackle in the air around them. In an instant I knew what this meant: there would be no getting rid of her.

Once I saw where my father's loyalties lay, I clung to Leslie like a desperate flunky — fingering the thick lapis lazuli necklace my father had bought her that night, fingering her fine-textured skin. We sat in the bedroom and they told me about their evening — the margaritas and mariachi band — so caught up in their happiness they didn't notice my envy. My father had the two of us pose for a photo, and when Leslie put her arm around me and smoothed a hand through my hair, I gave in to her a little. Being alone with my father was like walking a tightrope — thrilling but exhausting. She had broken up our act, but maybe she would temper us. When my father said, "Cheese!" I sagged against her and smiled for the camera.

When the date on our return tickets neared, my father told me he had decided to stay on with Leslie in Mexico. I would have to travel home to California by myself. Looking back, I can't blame them. They were at the beginning of a twenty-year love affair, and soon they'd return home to opposite coasts. At the time, I felt banished.

My father escorted me back to the capital, a trip that survives in my memory with the shadowy lighting of a nervous dream. We took a night bus, and I stayed awake as we rumbled along rutted highways, above dark canyons, and around hairpin turns. My father was beside me, but I took no comfort from his presence. Someone might have looked at my cinched-up face and seen the anxiety of a girl losing her father to another woman. Most of us get it over with early. But my father, though he dated some, had been single from the beginning of memory. Now, for the first time, I had to share his affections. I had no idea of the depths of what unnerved me.

When the bus pulled into Mexico City in the middle of the night, I didn't recognize the streets I had loved in the daytime. Boys swigged gasoline from gallon jugs and blew fire for the cars stopped at the light. Bags of oranges, which I mistook at first for bundled infants, were pushed up to the grimy bus windows.

We made our way to a hotel near the airport and were shown to a musty room, furnished with brocade bedspreads and heavy colonial furniture. The bellhop brought us glasses and a carafe of water, which my father told me not to drink. I was thirsty and worried that I would pour a glass out of instinct. My father was unusually quiet, thinking perhaps of the new turn his life had taken. I climbed into bed and watched headlights slice through the sheer curtains, the room tipped and strange, like a carnival fun house. Horns and shouts lifted from the street below. I dozed, then woke with a jolt. Were we late for the plane? It was still dark. My father slept heavily. For hours I stayed up, listening to the growling intake and release of his breath.

five

SIX MONTHS after they met in Mexico, my father moved from Boston to Berkeley to set up house with Leslie. Three hours by car, instead of five by plane, now separated us. I was thankful to have him nearer, but I couldn't help noting that it took her weight on my end of the continent to slide him over.

The two of them found a house to rent in the Berkeley flats. My father got a job working as a hospital orderly, and once the details of his life were settled, he called my mother to arrange a more regular visiting pattern. She wasn't having any of it. By now it had been four years since they'd parted ways on the East Coast, but my mother still had doubts about his trustworthiness.

I always thought, in those years, that it was my father's choice to stay away. I couldn't think of my mother as anything but heroine, rescuer. He was the fickle one. Then, in my early twenties, I came across a folder in my father's office labeled "Lisa Papers" and took my name as invitation. Inside, I found a letter in my mother's blocky printing. On brown rag paper, gone fragile with age, she laid out her terms. *Three weeks a year. No unnecessary phone calls.* She numbered each clause, then printed her name at the bottom. This was my mother's defense against my father: Here are my rules; don't mess with me. I could almost hear her voice lift off the page — those bare phrases, each word enunciated. These were the terms that kept him at bay.

It was the last rule that took my breath away, rule number four: *No unnecessary letters.*

Once he was on better footing, my father challenged those terms. He wrote letters, tried for a compromise, and when that failed, he and my mother both hired lawyers and prepared for court. A social worker was sent to my father's new home to judge its worthiness. Leslie insisted that they scrub the place in preparation. My father tried to downplay the importance of such bourgeois conventions as floor wax — pissed, I'm sure, at having to gussy himself up for inspection. To this day he praises Leslie's instincts: the first of many such saves. They straightened and polished and scoured the place, and in her report the social worker singled out Leslie's spotless house-keeping for special mention.

I was out in the garden with my mother one day when she asked me, with a casualness that put me on alert, how I felt about visiting my father. How much did I want to see him? Whom did I want to live with? And would I feel comfortable telling my wishes to a judge?

I said I wanted to live with her and see him a lot and that I would tell that to anyone. I never had to make such a declaration. On the courthouse steps, the lawyers finally convinced my mother and Jim that they would lose: though they could probably keep custody, the courts would surely grant my father visiting rights, and in the process everyone would be put through a rash of harrowing testimony. They all retired to a nearby coffee shop and hammered out an agreement.

My mother sat me down not long after that and explained the plan. I would spend one weekend a month with my dad, as well as half the summers, alternate Christmases and Thanks-givings, and every Easter.

I was glad at the prospect of seeing more of my father, but my first question betrayed my nerves: "You mean we'll never have Easter together again?"

I had never been particularly excited by Easter — we did the usual business of eggs and chocolate rabbits — but the fi-nality made me nostalgic. The little wire hooks we used to fish the eggs out of their dye baths, my mother's predictable hiding places — in the drainpipe, in a spray of daffodil spears — without me, without another child around, she probably wouldn't bother. I cast this, as I often did, in terms of her loss. Easier than admitting my own. What struck me most about the new arrangement: wherever I ended up, somebody had to be disappointed.

During the first months of the new agreement, my dad and Leslie drove up from Berkeley for the appointed weekends so we wouldn't spend most of our time together in transit. We passed those weekends in the neighboring town, and though I often spent time there with my mother, for the days of those visits, the streets looked strange. I felt disoriented, sitting in the movie theater, getting root-beer floats at the A&W drive-in. I sat in the same velvet seats, ordered the same foods, but I had different parents, so I felt like a different child.

That November I turned eight, and my father and Leslie drove up on a Friday night and booked a room at the Sweet Dreams Motel, a fifties-style complex with a pool, just off the highway. My mother dropped me off in the parking lot, and waved to my father from the car before gunning off.

My dad and Leslie seemed happy. They had already gone for a swim, and they gave me cool chlorine kisses and showed me our room. There was a huge package on the bed, which I begged them to let me open on the spot.

My father laughed. "Okay, okay. You can open it now. Just do some deep breathing first." He struck a pose out of a handbook of Hindu deities and rolled his eyes around. "Swami Papananda says, 'Relaaax.'"

I pummeled him. "I'm plenty relaxed! Please, can I open it?"

He gave up the guru shtick. "Go for it."

I had that box open before he said the last word. Inside was a new record player with two speakers. My mouth fell open. I knew they didn't have a lot of money in those days. To express my gratitude, I fell into a theatrical swoon, sailing backward toward the bed with one hand to my brow, and cracked my head on the turntable.

When I stood up, blood ran down the back of my shirt. It

soaked through several hand towels and stained the bedspread, and finally Leslie insisted we go to the hospital.

"It's almost stopped. I feel fine," I said, weaving around the room like a drunk.

My poor father. Such accidents are staples of childhood, but he must have worried about how my mother would react when he handed me over with a new stereo and a head wound. In the emergency room, he sat at the end of the table and held my hand while the doctor sewed through my scalp.

"I'm sorry, sweetie." His voice cracked when I cried out. "It's almost over."

That stereo felt like war booty when we went back to the motel room and played my first album: Stevie Wonder's *Songs in the Key of Life*. My father's finger-snapping was as loud as a wood block. I felt the bass line in the back of my skull. He and Leslie danced in front of the warped hotel mirror. But I think the three of us felt a little hollow, returning to that anonymous room with bloodied towels strewn over the floor.

When the next visit rolled around, my father decided to drive the three hours each way so we could spend a weekend together at their house in Berkeley — a slice of normal life. Leslie had taught him to drive soon after they moved to California. In all his years on the East Coast he had never sat behind the wheel. He was full of jitters and drove slowly, hands clenched at ten and two o'clock, easing slowly into intersections. The drives were grueling. On Friday, after a week of work at the hospital, lifting patients and swabbing down the operating rooms, he would drive seven hours round-trip to pick me up.

When I got into the car, I spent the first twenty minutes gushing, and once I'd exhausted any real news — I won the spelling bee; I wrote to Grandma Leila like you asked — I wracked my brain for something else, some yarn or accomplishment that might please him. Whatever I had to tell never felt like enough, and since I let it out in one breathless monologue, we had barely made it out of town before I was sitting in uncomfortable silence.

I don't think my father had any idea how much effort I was making. He was often lost in thought, talking out loud to himself about things he needed to do or having an argument with some imaginary opponent. As he mumbled, the car slowed imperceptibly, until something caught his attention and he hit the gas with a sudden compensatory burst. To break his reverie, I felt I had to be hilarious, not accomplished but a rising star in the elementary school galaxy. I must have come on like a freight train.

I was in the middle of one of my rants, turned toward him on the front seat, my hand braced on the dashboard for leverage, when my excitement proved too much for him. "Shhh!" he said, making a downward motion in the air as if to settle a bucking horse.

I slumped back in the seat, insulted. My skin was as thin as his.

"Go on, what were you saying?" he asked.

"Nothing."

"Come on, honey, I want to hear it. Just lower your voice a little."

I let a few minutes go by to soothe my pride, then picked up the thread of the story and was soon up to full volume, bouncing on the seat beside him, miming the action in gestures so broad the drivers sailing past us in the fast lane must have thought he rode with an epileptic.

We passed through a string of small towns: Cloverdale, Healdsburg, Petaluma. My dad made up a jingle for that one: you can pet a cow; you can pet a lamb; but you can't pet a *luma*. That put me in a better mood. We sailed down the straight stretches, singing as we had in Mexico. He gave me tips on style, how to relax my mouth and throat for a more natural tone.

I had hopes in those days of being a pop star, and once when we finished a particularly smooth rendition of "Sitting on the Dock of the Bay," I asked him to give me an honest assessment of my talent: "Dad, if Gladys Knight is a ten, what am I?"

He thought about for a minute, taking a few curves. "I'd say you're a two," he said.

I was crushed. "What are you then?"

"I'm probably a three," he said, keeping his eyes glued to the road.

Odd to see, in hindsight, how he helped himself to that extra notch. Then again, maybe he was just being brutally honest. I wasn't much of a singer. Certainly no Gladys Knight, probably not even a Pip. Perhaps he hoped to save me years of fruitless delusion. Much as my father thrived, growing up, on my Grandma Leila's adoration, he longed sometimes for a more tough-minded critic, one who would deliver the bald truth now and then. Having missed that, he offered it to me.

Often we stopped at a diner that marked our halfway point. My father parked in one of the diagonal spaces out front while I jumped out and claimed a vinyl booth. In that place, smelling of bacon and fried potatoes, a slow gladness seeped through me. The cylindrical light fixtures dangling from the ceiling were punctured like colanders and cast pinpricks of light over the tables. I ordered a stack of pancakes for dinner, mixing three kinds of syrup from the metal rack at my elbow, and my father drank cups of weak coffee and chatted with the waitress. I can still recall how he sat, leaning back in the booth, his long legs stretched out under the table, his hands encircling the thick white mug. He seemed happy, and over time and distance I can imagine the sources of this gladness: having his daughter before him after a month apart — powdered sugar on her shirt, her mouth full of pancakes, waving her fork as she talked — and the smaller relief of stepping away from the wheel for a few minutes, the workweek over, the small rituals of the weekend before him.

The house on Grant Street where we arrived for those weekend visits was spacious and sunlit, with built-in bookcases, dark molding, oak floors, and windows in every direction. The decor was classic bohemian, though of course I didn't know that then: a platform bed in the living room covered with Marimekko pillows; books everywhere, most of them Marxist texts; plants in macramé hangers. It was all bare, simple, and functional. A top-of-the-line stereo system was the only luxury in the place. Next to the thigh-high speakers sat my father's conga drums, perched on their black ring stands. Occasionally he pulled them into the center of the room and played along to selections from his record collection, which was heavy on the salsa and soul: Lou Rawls, Celia and Johnny, Mighty Clouds of Joy.

The dining room, smack in the center of the floor plan, served as an office. It seemed fitting that this was the hub of the house, for work — political work — was the hub of Leslie and my father's life together, and in this room were the tools of the trade: leaflets ("Boycott Grapes," "Overturn the Bakke Decision"), back issues of *Beijing Today*, a swivel chair, and a typewriter where my father sat at night writing.

My father was more content in that house, and in his new life with Leslie, than I'd ever seen him. He'd lost some of his lonely edge. He muttered less and seemed to lose himself in daily pleasures — making huge salads in a teak bowl the size of a bassinet, running at a nearby park, going shopping for used albums, practicing his drums. I could see that Leslie was the source of this ease, and slowly I began to warm to her. On Saturday mornings, I would climb into their bed and we'd make plans for our weekend outing.

Often we went for a stroll down Telegraph Avenue, which looked to me like a long amusement park. This was nothing like Spring Street, and the country girl in me was agape at the street life: Hare Krishnas with painted foreheads and monotonous finger cymbals; gusts of incense billowing from the head shop; tables of pottery and silver and leatherwork. There was a man who seemed never to leave his post at the corner of Telegraph and Dwight. He was trussed up artfully in a sheet and said he had a toothpick in his ear that could pick up transmissions from the CIA.

I looked at my father to see what he made of this. His loose stride, the smoothness of his forehead, said it all: he reveled in the place. "Bezerkeley," he called it, shaking his head and laughing. He may have had more serious work to do, but the carnivalesque mood in the streets seemed to suit him. Often my father sang as he walked — not loudly, but not sotto voce either: a frank, full-throated singing, as if he were alone in the square yard of space through which his voice carried. I flushed a little, but no one around us seemed to bat an eye. They passed by, lost in conversation, or gave him a smile. I couldn't help noticing my own stiffness. Now and then the truth would steal over me: you could sing in public and no one cared.

My father's lower back gave him trouble, but he had discovered that yoga helped ease the pain. He did triangle poses in the living room, Downward Facing Dog when we went to the nearby track to run laps. Once, when we were out shopping for jeans, he felt a spasm coming on, and before I knew it he had dropped to the carpet in the department store. He splayed out his arms and flipped his legs over his head. The Plow pose: it was accompanied by deep inspirations through the nose, followed by fierce outbreaths.

Mortified, I tried to melt into the nearest rack of clothes. I backed in so hard I broke through the wall of tweed and fell into the empty oval in the center of the rack. It was peaceful in there, so I stayed. I could see feet passing by below the hems, then a ruffle in the skirts as someone sampled the fabric. Sitting on a silver crossbar with Muzak tinkling down from above, I listened to the sound of my father's breath. When he was through, I stuck my head out to see if he had drawn a crowd. A few people milled nearby, none of them giving him a second glance. In 1974, stranger things were happening on the streets.

After a full weekend, the drive home was grim. It was Sunday afternoon when we set out. The route began on a four-lane highway and narrowed into a winding two-lane road, skirting boulders and following the sinuous curve of the Russian River. My father went white-knuckled when eighteen-wheelers blasted by in the opposing lane. I was aware of his hesitancy, the vulnerable look on his face as darkness fell and he squinted into the oncoming headlights. "Watch the white line, over on the side," I told him. "Don't look into the lights."

When he dropped me off at the motel (my mother met us in town, partly to save him the extra twenty minutes, partly, I imagine, to keep him as far from her real life as possible), my shoulders slid down in relief. Riding with my mother, I didn't need to be vigilant. But then I remembered that my father had to make the return trip on his own.

"Make sure to stop for some coffee along the way," I told him, leaning across the seat for a kiss, in case it was my last.

He laughed at my concern, but I could see his face soften. "Don't worry about me, honey. I'll be fine."

When the visiting pattern was still new, I thought I belonged in the ether: space junk from a marriage that barely was. If you asked me to construct my family tree, I'd build it like a model of a molecule — tiny atoms held together by valences. On one end, Mother and Jim; on the other, Dad and Leslie. I was the free electron, bouncing back and forth between clusters.

One weekend, early on, Mother and Jim drove me down to my father's house in Berkeley for the Friday night drop-off. I assumed this was for my sake — they wanted me to ease into the new arrangements — but I imagine now that they made the trip in order to take in a few city pleasures. Mainly, rural life seemed to suit them. Still, they must have missed Cambridge now and then: the bookstores and art-house movies and good coffee.

They saw me to my father's door and said terse goodbyes under the glare of the porch light. I was embarrassed to touch my mother, to be affectionate with her in front of my father. She told me to be good and to "think about the other guy," her traditional sendoff. It was a fitting reminder, I suppose, for an only child. I had to be reminded that there *was* another guy. It sounded odd, though, coming to her lips in front of my father and Leslie.

"Yeah, sure," I said, looking down, feigning impatience — perhaps even feeling it. But the minute she was gone, my throat ached and it was all I could do not to run after the truck.

My dad and Leslie understood that I was raw for the first few hours. They took me on a tour of the apartment, pointing out a new fern my father was tending (he loved plants, but had trouble figuring out what they wanted from him), a new clothes hamper in the bathroom. In preparation for my visit, my dad had stocked up on the foods I liked — orange juice, Shredded Wheat, Fig Newtons. He was touchingly earnest about this, flinging open the cabinet on enough cookies to feed a day camp.

"See, we got Figgy Newtons, your favorites," he said. There was a note of triumph in his voice, as if he were amazed at his

new domesticity. Those bready cookies with the grit in each
bite: I ate them by the package, and as soon as they were gone,
my father bought more. There would come a time when I could
barely stand to look at another Fig Newton, but I never had the
heart to let him know.

That night, we went to the movies. We had just settled in with
our sodas when, in the dimness before the curtain rose, I looked
up to see my mother and Jim in the aisle.

"Mom," I blurted out. I saw her stiffen for a moment, surprised to hear my voice. She squinted into the seats, then made
me out, and waved. There was nothing she could do but come
over and suffer through more stilted banter.

"Hey, there," my father said, looking tight.

"Well, here we are, following you around," my mother said,
giving Leslie a nod. Jim flashed a chilly smile.

"You must have read the same review we did," Leslie said,
doing her best to put them at ease.

Mother and Jim stood there for a moment, as if held by
surface tension. There were empty seats beside us, but we all
tried not to look at them.

"Well . . . I guess we'll see you on Sunday," Mother said to
me. Then they moved off down the aisle.

I had been grinning stupidly through the whole business,
and now I watched them take a seat down front, right in my
line of vision. I didn't have the heart to leave my father, but it
made my shoulders cinch up to have my mother so near, lost in
a sea of strangers. When the trailers came on, I kept an eye on
her head, rimmed by the shifting light from the screen.

The feature was *Barry Lyndon,* and for several hours I sat in
a darkened room with my four parents — the longest patch
of time I would spend with all assembled for the next twenty
years, and the strangest — while a bunch of men in ruffled
shirts rode horses and dueled and strolled through formal gardens. The movie was filled from its first frames with all kinds
of sexual innuendo, and though I missed most of the meaning,
it opened my eyes to certain things. In an early scene, Ryan
O'Neal pulls a ribbon out of a woman's squished-up bosom,
then leans toward the cleft where he has found it and wobbles

like a man with a fever. Below him, in what seemed to be miniature, I saw my mother lean her head toward Jim's in the shadows, in a way that was utterly private and opaque. They were on a date. I could barely get my mind around it. They had a life between them in my absence. At home, they shared an easy affection. Mother would slide her arms around Jim and call him her "handsome devil." He would do an "aw, shucks" number, grinning and rubbing a flat palm over her back. These gestures were playful, fond; they had no heat, and I paid them little mind. Now a door swung open in my head, and through it, at a distance, I saw them joined by private passion.

I whispered to my father that I was stepping out to the lobby for a drink and spent most of the first reel out at the snack bar, eating licorice and talking to the clerk. The carpeting in the lobby was red with black diamonds, and I passed the time by hopping from one diamond to another, mouthing a schoolyard chant under my breath: "Eenie, meenie, minie, moe. Catch a tiger by its toe." I remember this oddment, and only now does it make sense: it was a rhyme for picking teams. If someone had asked me why it popped into my head on that particular evening, I couldn't have answered.

When I snuck back in and took my seat, someone was killed in a duel, and later, Ryan O'Neal gave his stepson ten whacks with a switch, while the boy winced and cried very convincingly. I looked over at Leslie to see if she was hardened to the boy's pain.

Other scenes are seared into my head: the flippant son with limp blond hair, who is thrown from a horse and dies slowly, his head bundled up with gauze; or his mother's beautiful masklike face, topped by a towering pile of hair. Over and over the camera began on a hand or breast and swooped out to a landscape, framing the people against the background like figures in a diorama.

Years later, I saw the film on cable TV and discovered it was a farce. At eight, I took it for tragedy. The duels made me gasp and cover my eyes, and the sex was filled with ominous portents. When it proved too much, I backed out into the lobby again.

"Are you here with your parents?" the clerk asked as he handed over my third box of red whips.

I considered this for a moment. "Yes," I told him. "All four of them."

Back at school, two of my classmates and I were excused from school one afternoon a week and bused into the nearby town to the Mentally Gifted Minors Program, coyly called MGM to spare the feelings of the students in the lower percentiles. Genevieve and Scott and I met in a trailer, which was equipped with all the special learning gadgets that the rest of the district couldn't afford. We made pinhole cameras and dissected sheep's eyes, and after a few hours we were bused back.

When it became clear to our classmates that we were being singled out for special treatment — though what that treatment was, no one much knew — Harry Peck, the boy whose mother used to baby-sit me, fell into a funk. "I don't see why you get to go to this thing," he said to me. "I've lived in this valley my whole life."

I was fairly sure this wasn't one of the criteria. But to be frank, I wasn't sure what the real ones were. From the program's title, I knew someone had deemed us "gifted," but I didn't see what I had done to merit that assessment. I was an average student, often forgetting my homework, quick to raise my hand and blurt out answers, but slow to get them down on paper and turn them in. Year after year, my report cards bore the same note: Lisa isn't working up to her potential.

One day at MGM an art teacher came in and had us lie down on the rug. "Close your eyes and imagine a blue field," she said. She sounded just like a stewardess. "Now let images enter the field. What do you see?"

I was desperate to see something original and lovely, some Tolkienesque creation that would make the art teacher pleased. My head and neck went stiff with the effort. If only the school psychologist who deemed me gifted could have seen what I came up with that day: a teardrop with stick legs and whiskers. No intentional use of white space, no baroque fantasia or careful rendering, no representation of perspective or scale. Even I could see I was wasting the taxpayers' money.

When we got back to school, our classmates were bent over pages and pages of long division, the room suffused with the pinched smell of mimeograph fluid.

Alison Rider flashed me a tired smile when I came in, one cheek on her fist as she labored over her exercises. A few years before, she had transferred over from Mountain Meadow. No more learning math by baking double batches of molasses cookies. She was reading a year behind grade level and was up to her ears in catch-up work.

"What do you guys do when you're gone?" she asked me as I slid into the seat beside her.

I shrugged and feigned boredom. "Oh, stupid stuff."

On those bus rides back and forth to MGM, I soon learned that Genevieve and I had much in common, and I began going to her house for sleepovers. Her father used to sell insurance in Orange County. Then when she was six, her family packed up and moved to an A-frame on a seventy-acre parcel above town, a half mile from the nearest power line. Genevieve's room was in the loft, up high under the steeply pitched roof. Out the tiny windows were green draperies of pine. It was pleasant and warm up there, and we spent countless afternoons reading *Mad* magazine and making puppets out of clay and yarn.

The grownups were often down by the river, skinny-dipping in what my mother admired as the best swimming hole in the valley: deep, clear pools, with rocks to dive from. I was shy around the nude men, and whenever we went down there I went through a quandary: should I wear my bathing suit and come off like a prude, or strip down and spend most of the afternoon trying to bury myself in the sand? The idea back then was that grownups shouldn't communicate hang-ups about their bodies by bundling up and hiding behind doors. In fact, I had my own hang-ups. Long before adolescence, I had begun to adopt a nunlike modesty.

Since the swimming hole presented liabilities, Genevieve and I often spent our days playing "tiddlywinks," our term for a collection of tiny ceramic animals that we bought at the Rexall in town. They were sold glued to a tab of cardboard, posed in the trite attitudes of lawn sculpture, but irresistible to us because of their size: a chocolate Labrador no bigger than a thumbnail, a big-eared mouse frozen in a moment of perpetual fright.

We carried our collections around in brass-hinged wooden boxes, looking for a spot that had, from our grand aerial view, the cohesiveness of a miniature landscape: a ledge of moss with a dirt slope below that could serve as a split-level house, rafts of baby's tears that we laid carpets on, making Moroccan-style open-air palaces.

Our furnishings were cribbed from the junk drawer and from our mothers' rag bags: squares of carpet and flannel to line the rooms, dime-sized seashells for chairs. My mouse bedded down at night in a cotton-stuffed walnut shell — always, because of her given posture, an insomniac — and woke to survey her garden from the severe backless perch of a blue kitchen tile.

Early on, we brought our tiddlywinks to school — a terrific social blunder. While we set up in the nooks between tree roots at the edge of the play yard, a handful of freckle-faced boys raced by in V-formation and chucked sour cherries at our heads, restocking their ammo from a tree out by the fence. It was better, we learned, to leave fantasy at home.

Once we had set up the houses, the game fell flat. Genevieve sent her dog over and insulted my decorating. My mouse huffed at his insolence and kicked him out, but neither of us could summon much interest in the action. We only loved the arranging: the ordering, I think now, of a bonsai universe. Dialogue, trying to imagine what happened next — that was beyond us.

Genevieve's house didn't have a septic tank, and thus no indoor toilet. There was a wooden outhouse some yards off from the back door, and it was understood that we could pee wherever we pleased. This was fine during the day, but at night, when we were tucked into our sleeping bags in the loft, I dreaded my body's call. It was a long road to relief: down the narrow wooden ladder, through the shadowy clutter of the living room, and out the back door into the dark.

One night, when I had lain awake for a half-hour and

couldn't stand it any longer, I made the trek, nearly slipping off the edge of the loft, then going down the ladder facing out, which was all wrong and gave me vertigo, then cracking my shin on the sofa in the dark. By the time I reached the back door, every muscle and tendon was stiff.

I stepped out into the bracing air, and waited a moment for my eyes to adjust. It was a moonless night. Stars were scattered like sugar across the sky. Down in the valley, Alan Sarkissian was most likely peering up at them through his telescope. I waited and waited, but the darkness refused to divide into meaningful shapes. I opened my eyes wider, trying to take in what stray light was around, but there was nothing before me but blackness, shot now and then with strange noises. I thought I heard footfalls crackling the twigs, then a low moaning, which I told myself was the wind. I took a few hesitant steps, then froze, paralyzed by a nearby hoot and rustle. After standing there for a few moments in mortal terror, I began to weep, squeezing out fat tears in hopes that the beast out there, with its keen night vision, would take pity on me. I would never make it to the outhouse. I had no idea in which direction it lay, and even if I found it I wouldn't have the courage to pry back the hinged door on that box of gloom. Someone could be waiting in there for me. A hobo. A deranged mountain man.

Still, I knew I couldn't sleep until I finished my mission, so I forced myself into the dark, my hands held out in front of me. The ground rose slightly and I staggered against the slope, then struck a small bush. I still couldn't see a thing — even the house had disappeared behind me — and finally I lost my patience. What kind of family didn't have a toilet? This had gone far enough. If they ever found the evidence out there in the brush, they'd probably take it for bear scat.

I woke in the morning to Genevieve's mother calling from the bottom of the stairs, "Lisa, can you come here a second?" There was a note of irritation in her voice, which worried me, but I shuffled down the stairs, backward this time, and followed her out the door.

There, not more than five feet from the house, were my leavings, distinctly human.

Barbara pointed with her forefinger. "*This* is not okay," she said. Then she went off to get a shovel and stood by while I dug a hole and buried the stuff.

When I got home on Sunday, our scruffy old house looked like a palace. I went into the bathroom and flushed the toilet a few times, just to reassure myself. Back out on the sidewalk, it seemed that we lived in a metropolis. I counted five houses in plain view, and above them, the power poles and telephone wires, stringing us all together. There at the curb were our neighbors the Chapmans, loaded into their blue Chevy Nova, their heads bowed in prayer. They were on their way to church, but that wasn't why they were behaving so devoutly. Seven days a week Mrs. Chapman insisted the family make a small prayer for God's protection before she would start the car.

I didn't think I could stand to have to ask for a blessing before every meal, every turn of the road, every night's sleep. Still, when I studied their bent heads through the windshield I had to admit they looked at peace, packed together tightly on the white vinyl seats. Perhaps it was the glimpse of their contentment that made me game when my mother began waking me up on Sundays to take in the services at the Methodist church. She encouraged me to dress up, which was a tall order for me in those days, when I lived in Toughskin jeans and T-shirts. I came out for our first service in wooden platform shoes, a pair of knee socks silk-screened with Shaun Cassidy's face, and a white polyester tennis dress. My mother looked me over and shrugged. She wore a long paisley sheath, culled from a thrift store in Boston, and Dr. Scholl's sandals. We may have stood out among the girls in hand-sewn dresses and their mothers, who favored country florals, but the parishioners slid over in the pew and made room for us.

My mother's churchgoing was motivated chiefly by a sense of community. She hoped to get a job teaching at my elementary school, and going to church was a way to meet people — the rural equivalent of networking. She would have described this in metaphysical terms: you need to put positive energy into the system if you want positive outcomes. Jim, who would have called this good karma, had had enough churchgoing in his early Baptist days and spent his Sunday mornings at home.

At first we went sporadically, because Mother had a hard time sitting through the sermons. Reverend Pauling, a stooped, balding man, gave the Bible a close reading and seemed to focus on how the parishioners had failed, in their daily travails, to live up to the teachings of Jesus. The older women in the valley who had survived their various husbands — killed by logging accidents or by cancer after smoking Lucky Strikes and working in a cloud of backhoe dust for twenty years — were the mainstay of the church. They brought armloads of daffodils in the spring, tins of cookies in the winter months. If they did not love Reverend Pauling, he seemed to satisfy their sense of life's failed opportunities; they left the church chastened but sated, nodding their fleecy heads by the road.

Not long after we started going to church, Reverend Pauling retired and was replaced by Jerry Cliff, a bearded young man who drove into town in a battered pickup truck and turned the congregation on its ear. There is no doubt that Reverend Cliff took spiritual matters seriously; he just didn't mind the trimmings. He wore bell-bottom corduroys and Frye boots and opened his service with some rollicking acoustic guitar while the bewildered organist tried to follow along. Soon "Michael (Row the Boat Ashore)" crept into the Sunday repertoire, then "Blowin' in the Wind," and finally a tune that caused an exodus of the blue-rinse set from the congregation, called "Me Oh My, I Love That Methodist Pie," sung to the tune of another Dylan song.

My mother became a Sunday regular, going back for the daffodils, for the light sifting through stained glass onto familiar upturned faces, and for Jerry's sermons, because they seemed to pertain to the here and now. He talked about the gospel in concrete ways (sharing a few ears of ripe corn with a neighbor, say), and this dovetailed with the values hailed in Jim's copy of the *Whole Earth Catalog:* live simply so others may simply live, let's get back to the barter system — that sort of thing. If I know my mother, I imagine she must have liked the poetical rightness of one theme being sounded from different voices: Stewart Brand and this bearded preacher with the velvety voice.

Soon Jerry would become a frequent dinner guest — along with Alan Sarkissian and Grant, the logger — and after the table was cleared we would all retire to the living room, where Jim would stoke up the potbelly stove until the metal pinged and our cheeks flushed. I would lie with my head in Mother's lap while Jerry strummed and sang his secular repertoire — Sam Croce, Woody Guthrie — grittier tunes than the ones he played at the pulpit. I heard a note of sorrow in his voice when he sang, a whiff of loneliness in the empty pauses at the ends of songs.

Much as I loved Jerry, I found the sermons long and the pews hard, and soon migrated down the street toward the Evangelical church, where I joined an evening youth group. I even went so far as to take Jesus as my personal savior — helped in this by the preacher's wife, who treated the conversion of my soul as casually as a bank deposit — and spent most of my free time memorizing Scripture.

On the day when I asked my mother point-blank if she believed in God, she faltered for a moment. I registered this hesitation, because my mother always seemed to know precisely what she thought. Opinions spilled from her lips as easily as water from a tap — firm, strong, clear, the pressure of her thinking on the world. But that day in the kitchen she kept silent, and while she composed an answer, she wiped the counter with a sponge. Jim and a friend had made this counter out of two-by-four scraps, fastened them with hand-whittled pegs, and finished the patchwork of end grain to a high gloss. It was the kind of marriage of beauty and function that my mother most admired. Now she studied the expanse of rough rectangles as if they held some kind of answer.

"I think there are different Gods for different people," she said finally.

I tried to figure out what she meant by this — if she was hedging — and as I pondered I stared at a conical straw hat that hung over the refrigerator. Jim had brought it back from China; he said the people there wore them when harvesting rice. I used to wear the hat around the yard, playing peasant. The brim was so low it blocked out the horizon, leaving you with a view of the shady circle at your feet. Now, in the kitchen, trying to plumb my mother's silence, I stared at its perfect cone, and in the odd way that an object becomes tied to some scrap of feeling, that hat became linked to my notion of God — a thing that sheltered you and at the same time fettered your vision.

Suddenly I knew that my mother didn't believe in the God of my leather-clad Bible, but that she was searching for a gentle way to say this, a way that still left me room to choose.

"I'm wondering," she said, wringing out the sponge and turning toward me. "What do you believe?"

I don't remember my answer, but I remember some of what God meant to me for those brief months of my conversion. He was more than anything a tentacle extending from myself. God was a distant colony of my spirit, a cumbersome and soothing arrangement of my thoughts. I worked to make him real. That's what prayer was.

God was also a taking up of the pronoun *he* within my self-regard. *He* was *good.* This I intoned before each meal, as I had been taught, and just the naming of his goodness called up an attending wave of awe, for I was very clearly *not good* — full of laziness and vanity and rage. As Jim had pointed out, I took stock of myself in every mirror and sunlit windowpane (never mind that I didn't much like what I saw). And there was the matter of my occasional spankings and my plan to brain Mother with the skillet. I talked too much, and bossed kids when they would rather be left alone. Every winter I lost my coat before the first frost.

I knew little of goodness because my best behavior came about in a state of self-forgetfulness. One day I walked home from school and found Mother stacking wood against the west end of the house. Drawn nearer by the sunlit wall, the shining tarp, the satisfying clunk of the logs, I dropped my bag and started in beside her, adjusting the wedges here and there so the pile would hold firm. Then, suddenly, her hand was brushing my hair: "Well, you're sure nice to have around."

I stared at her then — pulled out of myself, blinking and confused as to what had earned the remark. It seemed I was good only when I didn't try to be.

*

Prayer seemed to offer a clearer road to virtue. At night I lay
back in my bed — bears and dolls arranged around me so I
couldn't stir — and thought of Jesus, his liquid eyes and un-
lined brow. Inspired by his visage, I sent a beam of earnest
feeling toward the people I loved. My mother, reading in the
next room, who played Scrabble with me when I asked — I had
been neglecting her, spending too much time playing kickball
and reading Scripture; I resolved to give her more attention.
Cathy, the girl who had brought me to Bible-study class —
suddenly I felt I could see her clearly: her awkward sweetness,
the way she curled a hand over her braces when she laughed. I
went on like that, through lists of friends and relations, feeling
half swollen with love. Then I closed my eyes and laid my
palms down on the comforter like a child in a picture book,
waiting for sleep.

There was, however, a small kink in this plan, an itch beneath
my piety. Before I found Jesus, I had rocked myself to sleep by a
means as old as Methuselah, and without the Bible ever saying
anything nearly to the point, I knew that God had a problem
with self-satisfaction.

I didn't sleep well in those days. I would pray and arrange
the animals around me like disciples, call on God for help, and
settle back into my Corpse pose. If I were going to accept Jesus
as my personal savior, I knew I would have to give up the sins
of the flesh.

On one of those nights I lay in bed staring, as I often did, at
the whorls and knots in the wood above me, waiting for my
mother to kiss me good night. She was in the kitchen making a
batch of lasagna, filling up enough tinfoil pans to feed us for a
week. She'd been at it so long, all the windows in the house
were laced with steam. I could hear her singing over the boiling
noodles. Finally she came in and lay down beside me. "Your
hands smell good," I said, holding them to my cheek to breathe
in the garlic and basil.

She leaned her head next to mine. "So do yours."

I tucked my hands deep into the covers, stricken with shame.

"It's all right," my mother said, looking me in the eye with a
steady expression. "It's a good thing."

*

My father never talked about God; he talked about power and about material conditions. Some people had their eye on the everlasting. He had his eye on justice, the reckoning of the here and now.

I asked him once what capitalism was, and he broke it down to basics. The companies make products as cheaply as they can and sell them for as much as the market will bear. They buy their raw materials from faraway countries where the people are poor and will sell them for a song, and they pay the workers the lowest wages they can get away with. What's left is called the profit margin, and they keep that for themselves.

There it was, the brutish truth of how one man makes his living off another. At one time, I might have asked the question of innocents: "Why can't the rich people share some of what they have so everyone can eat?" But I didn't ask those questions anymore. I knew the world was full of cruelty, and that in the lottery of birth I had come up with an exceedingly lucky card. I was already on to other questions. Couldn't the poor people be helped in some anesthetic way? Some way that didn't threaten my comfort?

"When the people build a movement, when they really threaten the power structure, capital throws out a few crumbs," my father said, warming to his subject. "They're like, 'Holy shit! These people are in the streets. We've got to do something.' That's how we got Social Security, the WPA, welfare — just enough to make sure people don't completely drop out the bottom."

"Okay," I said. "So capitalism isn't fair. But I don't see anything that looks better." I looked at him carefully, then looked down, nervous to tell the truth. "I wouldn't want to trade with some girl in Russia."

I was prepared for a lecture: *The people in Russia have more equality.* But my father nodded. "I know," he said. "I don't have the answers either. I'm still looking."

His candor caught me off guard. We sat for a few moments in that hollow, where the way wasn't clear. Things weren't good the way they were, but change might bring something worse. "I'm scared of a revolution," I said.

My father took my hand. His hands amazed me. No matter

how much I grew, they were always bigger than mine, and they never seemed to sweat. "I know," he said. "I get scared, too."

Over the longer visit that first summer, I got a better feel for my dad's and Leslie's daily lives. My dad worked at the hospital, and Leslie had a job at the shipyards in Alameda, but the bulk of their free time was spent doing political work. Gradually, I understood that they were labor organizers, a term that struck me as odd. Labor, in my mind, was simple work — picking walnuts out of the lawn or hauling manure. It didn't require planning so much as stamina. Organization was another thing altogether. It was lack of organization that made me forget my homework or lose my train of thought. The work of the mind was slippery, elusive, and somehow, in the end, more of a strain. Now these two ideas collided and coupled. How did you organize labor?

"We are trying to work for better conditions," my father explained. "More pay, safer factories." Mainly, as far as I could see, they went to work like everybody else. Sometimes, my father went to the plant early to pass out leaflets before his shift. But it was at night, at home, that they did most of their organizing work. My father sat in the dining room typing articles. And there were meetings, endless meetings. Comrades came over and sat around on the floor, writing on legal pads and discussing strategy. I was free to come and go as I pleased, but I found the gatherings dull, full of talk I couldn't understand.

I remember a girl I played with around that time who had communist coloring books: the fat factory bosses wore three-piece suits with watch chains; the workers were lean and muscled and clad in overalls. While our fathers had a meeting, we sat on the floor with her perfectly sharpened Crayolas and she told me what to do. The Capitalist Running Dogs were to be filled in with heavy black strokes. I was allowed to use only red and blue crayons for the "proletariat."

Since Leslie and my father were working full-time, I went to day camp at the YMCA about ten blocks from our house. When they had escorted me a few times and were sure I knew the

route, I made the daily trip to and fro by myself. A bit nervous
to be trusted with my own stewardship, I walked up University
Avenue, hailing people on street corners with a bluff "Howdy,"
which seemed to work well for Jim, and giving out change to
every panhandler I passed.

The day camp had been Leslie's idea. Months before I arrived
for my first summer, she began pressing my father to find a
place for me to pass my days. This was to be their lifelong
division of labor. Leslie would plan our lives on the grand scale,
always looking ahead. She made a calendar of the year on a
yard of tagboard and posted it in the kitchen. Rallies and political deadlines would be marked in one color. My comings and
goings would be mapped in another. She often looked out for
me in behind-the-scenes, practical ways I took for granted.

My father often got lost in the swamp of their hectic life, but
he always kept a handle on the daily things: keeping food in the
fridge, packing lunches, making sure I had money for the bus
or snacks — the kind of things that got Leslie down. They made
good partners; their strengths and weaknesses slotted together
like tongue and groove.

The two of them picked the YMCA because it was cheap
and close by, and because the kids came from all over town —
a mix of races and incomes. It was important to them that as
a family we walked the walk. My days there were pleasant
enough. We swam in the ancient tiled pool or hung around in
the rec room playing Ping-Pong. If the goal was for me to make
black friends, it didn't quite work. I got slapped across the face
early on by a girl whose cornrows hung to the middle of her
back. There wasn't much to the encounter. One minute I was
looking at her, then the next minute my cheek was stinging.
"Don't ever let me catch you looking my way again," she said,
her voice nearly clinical. I got the feeling it was mainly a formal-
ity, a way to make clear who was boss.

I soon attached myself to a Japanese girl who lived in the
Berkeley hills, and tried to mimic her easy self-possession.
Sumiko wasn't meek, but she didn't make any ripples either,
and no one even thought of messing with her.

"She cool," said the same girl who slapped me, giving Su-

miko a nod of approval as we passed by on the way to the gym.
I trailed in her wake, hoping for some coolness by proxy.

After day camp let out at the Y, I walked over to Edy's, an
old-fashioned ice-cream parlor on Shattuck Avenue. The dining
room was comfy, if a little down at the heels: carpeting tattooed
with stains, booths lined in orange vinyl. As a finishing touch,
someone had taken to the woodwork with a hammer, denting
it like medieval armor. The only fresh note in the place was
the plants, tucked into wells between the booths. My mother
would have approved. Then one day I fingered the leaves of the
creeping Charlie and discovered that they were made of plastic.

I wanted desperately to be known at Edy's as a regular, so
that the old waitresses with their hair nets and fallen arches
would see me and call out, "The usual?" They did this for the
rheumy-eyed men who arrived for egg-salad sandwiches and
bottomless cups of coffee in the afternoons, but after weeks of
my coming in every day without fail, Rose or Vera or Bea
would still amble up to my table, flip to a new page on the
order pad, and ask, "What'll it be?" They never even took a
good look at me.

Bea was my favorite. Prone to gentle, heaving sighs, she had
a mustache and an industrial-strength bra that strained through
her blouse. I found this bra oddly comforting. It closed in the
back with a three-inch strip of hooks and eyes — the minimum
hardware required to support her grandmotherly bosom.

I thought an eclectic order might get her attention. "V-8 and,
uh, cinnamon toast, please," I said, trying to make eye contact.
"Heavy on the cinnamon." Bea worked her tongue around in
her mouth as she wrote down my order, slapped a napkin, fork,
and knife on the table, and walked off. When my juice and toast
came, I asked for chili sauce and doused my V-8 with a wink as
she passed by. This failed to make an impression, so I took to
leaving huge tips — a whole fifty cents on my one-dollar order.
I don't know what I wanted from these women. A haven, perhaps, from the carnival outside. The dames at Edy's never took
the bait.

*

One Saturday, my father took me to a rally in support of affirmative action. As he explained it to me before we went, a white man named Allan Bakke had succeeded in convincing a judge that he had been unfairly denied entrance to medical school, pushed aside in favor of inferior minority candidates. There was a gathering at the U.C. Berkeley campus to protest the decision. I went up there with my father, someone handed me a sign, and before I knew it I was chanting along with the crowd: *El pueblo . . . unido . . . jamas será vencido; the people . . . united . . . will never be defeated.* It felt good to shout in the thicket of so many bodies. I even pumped my fist into the air a few times, until the gesture made me feel sheepish. But when we pooled into the parking lot at the march's end and sang the Internationale — *this is the final conquest, let every man stand in his place* — the gravity of that anthem stirred me. I stood on the hot asphalt, sweat running down my back, gently leaning into the people next to me — *arise ye prisoners of starvation, arise ye wretched of the earth.* The crowd was packed in tightly, our voices blending into one rough pitch, the sharps and flats of individual voices beveled off, so that in spite of each singer's meandering the melody held.

We would go to other rallies as the summer wore on. On the picket line, when passing cars honked their support, I felt a heady surge of righteousness. Even though I usually dragged my feet when my father suggested we go, and I suffered from moments of embarrassment when I was caught alone with my sign, I was full of self-congratulatory heroism when it looked like the public mood was in our favor.

But when the turnout was slim, or it rained, or the police walked the streets in riot gear, I shrank back to the girl dangling her feet in the prison waiting room. We were few and weak. They could crush us under their thumbs. I wanted to slip into the bland flow of passersby; I wanted to live a life that aroused no suspicion or trouble. After these grim events, I would lie in bed despairing over my lack of courage. I was afraid that if had lived in Nazi Germany, if I had been a Christian with an empty attic, I would have turned the Jews away, hissing and glancing down the street for spies.

But most of the time politics seeped into my family life in ways I barely understood. When I misbehaved at my father's house, I was never spanked or grounded. Instead we all sat down in the living room — my father, Leslie, and I — and discussed my lapses. It was all very reasonable: they didn't believe in corporal punishment; they just wanted to make me think. I had locked myself out of the house for the third day in a row, and once rescued, I had turned a tidy room into a shit storm and gone off to buy candy with stolen change. But this news of my bad behavior meant nothing to me. I sat with my arms crossed, sullen and confused by their arguments, starting to feel nostalgic about the swiftness of spankings. Now and then I would blurt out my version of things, amazed at how I lost my way in the telling, sounding peevish and unreasonable even to myself.

"We are trying to struggle with you on these things," my father said. "You need to work on taking constructive criticism." I was getting the hang of the lingo. "Struggle" was like medicine. It tasted bad going down, but was meant for your own betterment.

Dad and Leslie and I were driving through Oakland one night, all three of us in the front seat, when we passed by a porno theater. I saw my father glance over the flashing marquee, and I followed his gaze. "Live Girls!" was plastered on bills across the entrance. Underneath this banner were photos of naked women with blackout bands across their breasts. I was thinking about that title: Did other places have dead girls, or was it some kind of exhortation, encouraging the girls to get the most out of life?

My father saw me craning backward at the signs. He was quiet for a moment, then he cleared his throat: "Do you think Leslie and I would ever go to one of those places?"

I thought about this carefully. I knew it was a leading question, and I wanted to get the answer right. It seemed a little seedy around that part of town. But they were tolerant people, unashamed of their bodies. "Well, I guess you probably would." I saw my father's face fall, and so I quickly amended, "Maybe only once in a while, if someone else invited you?"

Leslie was quiet beside me.

My father's voice turned calm and instructive: "Leslie and I would never go into a place like that, honey. We don't agree with that kind of thing. It's very exploitative of women."

I think he often felt he had to make up for lost opportunities, that what a full-time parent could pass on by slow degrees, he had to compress into our brief visits. The result: these little moral lessons, which struck me mostly for their earnest tone.

"Dare to struggle, Dare to win," Leslie once wrote to me in the flyleaf of a book on Chinese revolutionary youth. It was a birthday gift (one of several, the others more traditional), a story about a girl who joins the brigades, who was stalwart and unselfish, ever noble in her aims. There were days when I didn't want to dare anything, when I chafed at the language of struggle and the moral weight hanging over our lives.

"This country is really falling apart, Lisa," my father would tell me. He would sigh then — an enormous outbreath — pull on his mustache hairs, and stare off into the distance. "It's really frightening."

I shrank from the news of apocalypse and from the dread that lifted from him like a sweat. I wondered sometimes how far down we could sink, how completely our world would unravel, since it had started bad and seemed always to be worsening.

Around that time, my father and Leslie were married quietly at city hall. They didn't tell even their closest friends, as marriage was quite outré among their comrades, but shortly after they were legally wed the three of us held a private ceremony sitting cross-legged on the grass in MacArthur Park. They let me serve as officiant, reading a selection they had chosen from *Quotations from Chairman Mao Tse-tung* — a passage, I believe, on the relations between men and women in revolutionary society. Both of them wore their work clothes — plaid shirts and jeans — and they were, as I remember, radiantly happy. We laughed together at the ad hoc sweetness of the moment: no carnations or banquets, and in place of a minister, a scrappy eight-year-old, elated by her vestment. I opened the book to the slender page-marking ribbon, and read carefully out loud. If I didn't catch

the meaning, I at least grasped the privilege they had granted
me, and I tried to pronounce clearly the words they set their
course by.

Back at the Grant Street house, on a window where the sun
would shine through it, sat a stained-glass panel: on the left
side, two birds facing each other; on the right, the same birds in
a row. A caption ran across the frame: "Love is not looking into
each other's eyes, but looking outward in the same direction."
A little sentimental, but it got at one of the truths of their marriage: they were bound together by a common purpose. They
considered themselves comrades, and when other things in that
partnership were shaken, this shared commitment held fast. It
boiled down to respect, I think. They respected each other's
thinking, and at a time when many of their radical friends were
moving to the suburbs and giving up organizing, neither one of
them had lost their sense of urgency.

My father loved that piece of stained glass. Now and then he
picked it up and got moist around the eyes, then placed it
gently back on the sill, winging the panels open so the thing
would stand firm.

Mao's little red book, which served as their marriage text,
went with me everywhere, though I have few memories of
reading it. My father had bought me a hand-tooled leather
purse from one of the crafts tables on Telegraph Avenue, and
when I sat at a booth in Edy's and performed my feminine-
fluster routine of arranging its contents, I pulled out cherry
lip balm, a pack of Kleenex (never opened), a vial of apricot-
scented oil, and the vinyl-covered book from the People's Re-
public of China.

I opened to the small sepia-toned portrait of Mao, protected
by a rice-paper overlay. He looked to me gentle and good-
humored, with a healthy shine to his cheeks and a precise rind
of shirt collar peeking above his jacket. The mole on his chin, so
large it cast a shadow, made him comfortingly homely. Leslie
had a mole that I admired very much. It was on her wrist, just
over a vein, with two or three fine hairs sprouting out of it,
and I thought it made her hands look strong and capable. I
draped one arm over the edge of the table so the veins would

stand up, and with the other hand I paged through chapters called "Self-Reliance and Arduous Struggle" and "Correcting Mistaken Ideas."

Halfway around the world, the Cultural Revolution was winding down, but I was insensible to this, lost in the tissue-thin pages. I imagine a few people must have passed me that day, a skinny kid eating cinnamon toast with her head bent over Mao's little red book, and shaken their heads in disbelief. Little did they know that I was thinking of weddings, and of the strange attraction of moles, or that I turned those delicate pages of theory because they let loose the smell of apricots.

At my father's house, it was hard to keep up with all the political factions I heard mentioned in the living room. I asked him once about Phil and Nancy, two former friends of his whom I had heard spoken of lately in tones of disgust.

"They're Trotskyites," my father said. "They've got bad politics." I saw him grapple with a way to articulate the terms of their desertion, their essential wrong-headedness, then give up. He settled for saying that he "disagreed with them on a lot of things." Still, the seriousness of his tone, the creases between his brows as he pronounced this, said everything. The name Trotskyites was forever married in my mind with a kind of shameful cleaving from the flock; it was the sound of bearded men in black coats cantering off, legs clenched to hold their loosening bowels.

At some point I noticed that shared politics was the base requirement for my father's friendships. He and Leslie would meet a new couple, and if the match was good, my father's assessment would nearly always begin, "You know, their politics are pretty good." There was always a note of wonder in his voice as he said this, as if he knew how rare were the folk who met this requirement and stumbling on them was an unexpected boon. I never knew my father to sustain a friendship that began out of, say, a mutual love of basketball or a shared taste in films. It wasn't that he wouldn't grant himself the pleasure of such associations, it was rather that they were, in the end, not a pleasure. For him, talk always circled back to political themes, and if he didn't feel safe tracking through that territory, then other topics couldn't hold his interest. Of course, he often talked sports or art or love with his comrades, but a sense of common political perspective was the root from which his friendships grew.

As I grew older, the world outside my family came into sharper focus. I remember one afternoon lying back on the pillows in the living room while one of my father's friends talked about the farm workers in the Central Valley. This was at the beginning of the grape boycott, when Cesar Chavez was letting the public know how they came by their cheap lettuce. My father's friend shook his head at the plight of the migrant workers: "The whole family's out there — kids, grandmothers. If the growers don't offer housing, they live in cardboard boxes by the side of the fields."

Those boxes stuck in my mind. Back at 12000 Spring Street, Charlene and Jill and I played house in an old refrigerator box. In the beginning the walls were smooth and stiff, but after a night left out in the dew, the cardboard warped and sagged inward. We hurled ourselves around inside, breaking the walls, rolling the box along the grass with someone balled up inside it. This was a pleasant diversion — but to live in a box? A chill spread over me, there in the sunny window seat. My comforts, rather than making me grateful, made me afraid. I did nothing to deserve them; I had come to them by chance, and chance might take them away.

"How come the people don't just say no and go work somewhere else?" I asked, suddenly furious at the men (it was always "the men") who made people work like oxen.

I could see that my father was excited by my interest: "They *are* saying no. That's what the boycott's about. That's what we're working for."

Our main form of bourgeois entertainment in those days was the movies. To my delight, there was little that Leslie and my father considered off-limits. It seemed to me that early on they decided I could judge for myself life's lights and mysteries. So we went to see *Three Days of the Condor* and *All the President's Men*, both of which I loved, though at ten I had trouble with the byzantine plots.

As soon as the opening titles rolled, I started asking questions. "Dad?" He didn't answer, so I whispered louder. "Dad, who is that guy?"

"Shhh, honey. Just watch."

I chewed my popcorn for a while in silence, trying to pay attention. "But why did he shoot the lady?"

"I don't know! I'm seeing it for the first time, too."

We would spend the ride home analyzing the plot. Leslie could put it all together, the dropped hint in the early frames that gave away the ending, the one line of dialogue that sewed up the theme. Suddenly the whole film would make sense to me, and I'd want to go see it again.

"You're amazing, Leslie," my dad would say. "You could write one of those scripts." He was often that way — drop-jawed at her smarts.

We gave every film a rating, one to ten. Leslie was the toughest critic, rarely doling out anything higher than seven. My father was more lenient. He loved any kind of movie — comedy, period piece, romance, cliffhanger. Only horror and action films were out. His scores frequently rose into the eights and nines. I was right there with him, a complete sucker for cinema, glad for any excuse to sit in the dark with a box of red licorice and watch a story unfold.

At the end of each summer, my father and Leslie and I sat down and evaluated my visit. This was a thorough exercise, a little of Mao's "criticism, self-criticism" applied to the domestic sphere. My father got out a piece of paper and ran categories across the top: Excellent, Good, Blah, Yech. I got to weigh in on everything, while he took notes: the summer program, my relationship with Leslie, Grandma Leila's visit, even my own behavior. I took to my task with relish, trying to judge reliably the highs and lows. "Daddy did best job as a father," I wrote in one review. (I don't know who could have been his competitor.) "Main weakness was being too critical. Almost never yells."

Four blouses that Leslie bought me were rated Excellent. When it came time to examine her mothering, my father took up the pen. Leslie and I were growing closer, it seemed, "more like mother and daughter. But Leslie holds Lisa responsible for being older than she is." In hindsight, it seems brave of them to have asked a ten-year-old for so many opinions.

six

WHEN SCHOOL STARTED — fourth grade — I was still a live wire in the classroom. I lived for those moments of chaos, when some fracas began in a corner and a general simmering started up: a spitball flew, someone flipped the bird at the teacher's back, a staccato of slammed desk lids built to a crescendo. I wanted things hectic, wanted disorder, all of us wheeling around the room, whooping and calling. It wasn't malicious. I would have been sobered to see anyone hurt. I only loved the way things gathered momentum. Wildness created a kind of static in the air about us, made us feel anonymous and thrilled. Each, as a culpable being, felt shielded by the flurry and noise. Under the cover of my neighbors' howls, I did a little guttural yodeling. (I'd been listening to *The Sound of Music*.) I tipped my head down under the general rumble and trilled, trying to throw my voice toward someone already tagged as a miscreant.

At the height of one of these brushfires, Harry Peck's face got red and he jumped up from his seat. "Flush Nixon down the toilet!" he yelled. We all stopped yammering and looked at him. None of the rest of us paid much attention to politics; most of the things I understood about national events were passed down whole from my father, and he had greeted the Watergate hearings that past summer with a headshake and shrug: more of the predictable corrosion of the right. He had no faith to be shattered, so the whole thing was just a lucky fluke, a curtain briefly pulled aside on the sham of national politics. But Harry seemed genuinely worked up about Nixon's tumble. His parents, like most of the Republican ranchers in the valley, had voted for the man, and no doubt they were scalded by the news of lies and corruption from an office they still held sacrosanct. Fresh from my summer in Berkeley, I noticed how far I had been from the mainstream. Harry's father and my father weren't even remotely on the same page. If they sat down for dinner, it might end in blows. I reminded myself never to drop a word about Mao Tse-tung.

Despite his bad politics, Harry was a lovely boy: blond, with nearly olive skin and a scattering of moles. I would have loved to be his girlfriend, and he was, over the course of that year, always considering me as a possible consort, and always, in the end, rejecting me. I was helpless to control this undulation in his attentions, but I took note of every minute shift in his voice, of whether he pulled his chair close to mine in class or shirked my stare. When he said something kind, or walked with me out of class and sat talking on the curb while we waited for the bus, a flutter of hope lifted in my throat, and I'd set about trying to be winning. This produced a spatter of stupid remarks and wild gestures. I grabbed his notebook, and took up kicking and chasing, which put a quick end to his interest. It was as if he forgot at times how rough I was, how boyish and hardheaded. Once he remembered, he gave me a wide berth, and when I noted his cooling interest, I went through a small rage of disappointment, and soon forgot I'd ever had a chance.

Then, on some day when I felt ugly, when I couldn't tame my cowlick and I came to school in a pair of old floods, my bare ankles throbbing, and sat in the back of class, quieted by shame — it was on those days that I'd look up on my way to gym and see that he had fallen in with me.

Once, on a day like this, he offered me a stick of gum, and we stopped together under the high bars while he pulled the pack from his windbreaker and slid the stick out carefully, so the paper sleeve stayed put. It was the slowness of this business that stunned me. At our age, boys and girls never held still beside each other, except under duress. We were constantly moving, jostling, bumping against one another like restless electrons, in the line for lunch, out on the blacktop playing four-square, prowling the yard in groups of threes and twos, shifting and dividing, then gathering up at the door when the bell rang with a harangue of motion still in our limbs, leaning out of line to see if the door had opened, dipping to tie a shoe, pushing at the nearest body. But here he was, standing alone with me on the empty playground with nothing between us but a stream of wind.

It came to me then: he liked me because I was humble. When I was humble, I was a better self. It was a relief, in some ways, to be rewarded for being unrehearsed. But my gratitude was mingled with confusion, because I knew I could never glimpse this version of myself. I could do nothing to help or enhance its appeal. It was the way I looked and seemed when I had no idea how I looked and seemed. The moment it was acknowledged, this seamlessness was broken.

My life at 12000 Spring Street didn't change much. That was the beauty of it. Still, my mother continued to find things to improve around the home front, and she made a point of enlisting my energies. "You've got to help the family wheel," she used to say. I had been reading a book of simplified Greek mythology, and when she invoked this phrase, I imagined us, clad in togas, pushing a two-ton granite disk uphill. One of my chores was to load up a wheelbarrow full of walnuts. The homesteaders who planted two black walnut trees in the front yard had left me a curse: the nuts were inedible, and the tough shells chipped the lawnmower blades.

On a Saturday, I would place the wheelbarrow under the tree and work in a circle around the trunk, ruffling my fingers through the grass until I struck one of the nuts, which were covered in a sticky black rind. They made a satisfying tink in the bottom of the wheelbarrow when I began, but I was impatient to hear the softer thud that came once I had lined the bottom, the sound of one walnut striking the clotted mass, the sound of progress.

I spent those hours musing on luck and fate. Would I want to trade places with, say, Iris Sledge, the class tyrant? Her mother

was a kind enough woman, heavyset, a nurse, with a perpetu-
ally weary air that made her well suited to child rearing: she let
all but the worst offenses slide in order to conserve energy. It
was Iris's father who struck fear in my heart. He was gaunt and
sallow, with narrow, curved shoulders and a headlong stride. I
tried not to stand in Mr. Sledge's path. That man always looked
like he was in a hurry to work someone over. I never saw him
without a cigarette glued to his lower lip, which flipped up and
down as he talked, a little ember burning at the end of his
sentences. His wallet was secured to a belt loop by a length of
chain, and more than once I had pitied the thief who would get
caught at the end of that leash.

For some reason, Mr. Sledge didn't allow Iris to have friends
over after school — I don't remember the reason for this, or if
there even was one — but he didn't often return home until
nightfall, so it was a rule that begged to be broken. One day
Iris and I took turns kicking a rock down Spring Street while
we exchanged uncharitable assessments of girls we considered
friends. When we looked up, we were standing at the end of her
driveway.

"I better go home," I said, casting a glance down the road.

"Oh, come on. He won't get here for hours." Iris was like a
force of nature. She had jet-black curls and buck teeth and was
the queen of the playground retort. All the devastating phrases
that occurred to me hours after a fight came to her lips in the
heat of an argument as easily as her name and address. She had
been known to leave girls weeping on the pavement. In fact,
more than once I had been one of those girls and probably
would be again, but when Iris took the occasional shine to me I
couldn't resist her.

That day, I followed her out to the back of the house and
watched her offer a salt lick to her horse through the fence. She
never got to ride this horse, and it was probably just as well.
The one time her brother saddled it up, the mare lit out at a full
gallop and scraped him off on a low-hanging branch.

"I dare you to touch it," Iris said.

"Does it bite?" I asked, eyeing the mare's big hatchet teeth.

"Not the horse, dummy — the fence."

I glanced down the wires and noticed ceramic conductors strung along at regular intervals. "Is it on?"

Iris got an unnatural glint in her eye. "I don't know. Why don't you find out?"

"No way, José." I tried to sound cool, but my voice quavered and I took a step backward. "I'll still be hanging there when your dad gets home."

Iris gave me a look of unqualified scorn, as if she were seriously pissed that I wouldn't fry myself on her orders.

Then she broke into a grin. "Just kidding. Christ, did you think I'd let you touch that thing? My dad's got it cranked up to two thousand volts."

Just then we heard gravel crunch in the driveway. Iris's face went white. "Oh Jesus! He's home." She hustled me along the back of the house to a shed, shoved me in, and shut the door. I crouched down under the workbench, breathing in gasps of sawdust and motor oil and batting spider webs from my arms. When my eyes adjusted to the darkness, I saw strange figures on the ceiling and walls, and after another moment they came into focus — *Playboy* centerfolds, tacked up as neatly as wallpaper over every surface, yards and yards of lingerie and splayed flesh. I had looked through plenty of such magazines up in the loft at Genevieve's house, but this was too much — an assault on the eyes. Just when I thought I would have to bust out, commando style, and take my licks from Mr. Sledge, Iris cracked open the door.

"Run," she hissed. "He's coming out here any minute." I bolted across the side lawn, slid under the barbed-wire fence, half expecting to be electrocuted, and sprinted across the adjoining pasture, mud and cow shit flicking from my heels. I was so convinced that Mr. Sledge would try to shoot me, I dodged this way and that like a soldier crossing a sniper zone.

Later, Iris told me that her dad had caught a glimpse of me running off through the field. She told him it was April, the neighbor girl, checking on the cows, and when he heard this, her father threw his head back and laughed.

"Christ, that girl puts pep in her chores!"

It was only then that I made the equation: if I wanted to be

Iris, tough and dodgy and quick on my feet, I would have to live in that house. She probably earned her wisecracks the hard way.

But if the Sledge family formed one bracket to my life, the Norris family formed the other. Deedee, the youngest daughter, ruled our class like a frosty princess; year after year she was never dethroned. The Norrises lived on a ranch set against the foothills at one end of the valley. I decided that Deedee's superiority came down to breeding and hardware: she had a private plane, a dishwasher, and a swimming pool, and a mother named Kathleen, who had thick blond hair, wore riding boots, and carried herself with a stunning hauteur.

Where did that leave me? With a family I would trade in only on certain days. They were decent and kind but badly equipped.

"We're as lucky as we can get without being too lucky," my mother said when I reported on my musings.

"What does that mean?" I asked her. I wasn't sure there was such a thing as too lucky.

"Life gets handed to you on a plate, it loses its sweetness," she said. "I grew these peppers." She held one up, a knobby fist of greenness, smallish and malformed, but so fresh I could smell it from across the table. "They don't taste like the ones you buy in the store."

That year, my father got a job at the Ford plant in Fremont, working on the assembly line. Because he was a new hire, he had to start on the night shift, punching rivets from ten in the evening until six in the morning, while the rest of the city slept. At the end of such a week, the three-hour trip to pick me up for our monthly visits was too much, and so I began to take the Greyhound bus to San Francisco to save him the drive.

Mother drove me to the station on her end, a dusty office tucked behind a drugstore in a nearby town, and waited with me until the bus pulled into the parking lot. I took a seat up front near the driver and waved until she was out of sight.

The ride took nearly four hours, and the bus stopped in a string of small towns along the way. Each station was slightly different, but there was a through line of quiet dreariness to those rooms: men waiting with vacant expressions and bags between their feet, women cleaning out their purses, toddlers digging through the sand-filled ashtrays for butts.

At the first stop, I pretended to scan the vending machines, using the glass to keep an eye on the people behind me. Once I was sure no one was approaching, I took a look at the snacks, and it was there that the first heady wind of freedom swept through me. I could buy whatever I liked — chocolate bars or Cokes or those Hostess Sno Balls that looked like electric pink wads of yarn. Whatever I ate would disappear without a trace. I was miles from home and no one would know. I selected an industrial-sized Pixy Stix, which plunked into the tray like a stick of dynamite, tore open the fat paper tube, and tipped my head back — a straight brain shot of sugar.

"Hey, can you spare some change?" A red-eyed man I'd seen slumped in a corner chair suddenly appeared beside me. He was curled in on himself: hunched back, beak nose, one leg shorter than the other so it hung, bent, beside the other in a gesture that appeared almost coy.

I started to say "Sorry," but that first sibilant shot a cloud of lavender Pixy dust into the air between us. In my palm was a handful of coins, slick with sweat. I had swallowed a nickel once, on a bet, to see if it would go through. I never caught sight of it, but it occurred to me that the thing had probably made its way through the septic tank and out the leech lines and was now lodged deep under the lawn back home. I thought, *I'm rich enough to eat money.* I opened my palm and turned over the change.

I was glad to see that the hunched man went, on heel and toe, and plunked my coins into the coffee machine. He selected extra cream and sugar, and stood rubbing his hands as the machine shot a beige stream into a cup.

"Looks like horse piss," he said. "But it's a meal."

Over the coming months those bus trips would train in me a canny watchfulness. Under the mask of a bored stare, I'd scan the crowd for worrisome types. I got in the habit of dividing up my snack money, putting the largest bills deep in my backpack and keeping a few dollars and change in my front pocket. Soon the vending-machine fare lost its charm, and I returned to pretzels and V-8, my mother's long arm extending all the way to Petaluma, where the celery and tomatoes on the label drew me in with their promise of nutritional virtue.

I took my tomato juice over to the pay TV — a black box attached to the arm of a molded plastic chair — and dropped a quarter in the slot. Leslie had won me over to the tawdry world of daytime soaps. The screen bloomed with light, then sharpened into a scene: two lovers hiding in some artificial bushes. For fifteen minutes I watched *All My Children,* chewing pretzels and studying the scheming heiress, the illegitimate son, then a close-up of their two wrangling mouths. When the engine revved, I ran out to claim my seat and watched out the window as the vineyards gave way to a corridor of malls and car dealerships. Thirty miles down the road, when we came to another station, I jumped out, slipped another quarter in the pay TV, and caught up with the action.

When the bus nosed into the concourse in San Francisco, the door flew open with a hiss.

"End of the line," the driver bellowed. I always hated that phrase. It made me feel ejected. I loitered in the back, unwilling to deboard. I wanted to feel that I'd arrived at my destination by choice, and not because the road had ended beneath me. But perhaps it was more than this that made me linger in the bus. Even after I had mastered my tough-girl pose, the San Francisco station was more than I could handle. Everyone looked bleary-eyed, whether from fifteen-hour journeys or cheap booze and a night on the street I couldn't tell. The walls were dingy and smelled of piss. On the one or two occasions when my father got caught in traffic and wasn't there when I arrived, I hovered near the ticket windows. I figured no one would kidnap me in full view of a person in uniform, even though the tellers, dressed in striped shirts embossed with the bus line's skinny dog, looked like they wouldn't offer you water if your clothes were on fire. When my father showed up, I rushed into his arms.

During that school year, my father and Leslie moved to Oakland to be closer to the Fremont plant. When I came to visit for the following summer, they had found a new way to occupy my days: a summer program at Jarvis Gann Elementary School. My father had met with the principal before I arrived and asked her about the activities. Students took classes in the traditional subjects and spent a little extra time outside doing P.E. The school was set against the Oakland foothills, the buildings gray and unforgiving, but it was near our apartment and wouldn't require a lot of driving to and fro. My father inquired about the cultural mix.

"Oh, it's a very peaceful campus," the woman assured him. "The students are motivated and hard working. We don't have any racial tension, if that's what you mean."

I found out, on my first day, that she told the literal truth. There was no racial tension. I was the only white kid on campus. It actually took me a little while to absorb this. Looking out, I didn't see my incongruity. I took my seat in the classroom, and the teacher began her lesson, and it wasn't until I noticed that she refused to call on me that I began to wonder what was wrong.

"Who can tell us about the Magna Carta?" the teacher asked.

I waved my arm like I was drowning. The teacher called on a quiet girl to my left who had her head bent over her book. I looked around to see what set me apart, and suddenly it was plain as day. Then I remembered Yolanda, the only black student back at my elementary school in the valley. She came to class for six months, and in those six months no one befriended her. She often fell asleep at her desk (we somehow were made to understand that she didn't get much sleep at home); when the bell rang she would rub her eyes and wander the playground alone. I didn't dislike Yolanda, but I had never offered her any kindness. Now I caught a glimpse of the strange world in which she had traveled.

I came home at the end of that first day looking anxious.

"How was it?" my father asked.

"It was okay," I said.

"Not great?"

"It was okay." I was worried I'd get scolded for being so color conscious. I figured my father would say it was good for me to see the flip side of oppression. But when I finally confessed —

"I was the only white kid" — my father was surprised and a little pissed.

"No racial tension! Well, no shit." He let out a rueful laugh, remembering his interview with the principal: "She was like, 'We are all so happy here at Yada Yada School.'" He pursed his lips and steepled his fingers across his chest. Then his face relaxed. "Look, I'm real sorry. We'll find another program. I mean, I want you to be in a mixed school, but this doesn't sound good."

And true to his word, he did find a better program. Caliente, it was called: a day camp run by the Oakland Parks Service. There, in a heavy-beamed building on the hillside, I learned Filipino stick dancing, played congas, and made batik prints. The other kids were good-natured — the happy mix my father had hoped for. We ate our lunches out under the eucalyptus trees, then set up our steel drums and played rounds, the Caribbean rhythms floating down over the cityscape below.

Our new apartment was set up high on the hill, with a deck and a view of the Bay Bridge, but the neighborhood was a bit rougher than the one we had left. Grandma Leila came for a visit and was mugged a few blocks from the house, and my father thought I ought to take a class in self-defense. He had been a black belt in karate back in his Boston days, and so at his behest I went to a dojo for the summer. There was one other girl in my class, a good five years older than me, with legs as thick as tree trunks. She was already a green belt. The rest were boys.

At first I was taken by the rituals of the dojo — the posing and bowing — and the forms reminded me of dance: the slow-motion sequence of leans and kicks and weight shifts that required softness in the limbs and fierce concentration. For the half-hour that the sensei would go over them, I was lost in the mirror, trying to follow his swift limbs.

But karate was an art of self-defense, and soon we would have to bring these elegant movements to bear on someone's body. I remember the day I realized this. My dad dropped me off early for class, and I paced around the lobby, gazing at dusty photographs of the studio's graduates in competition: a boy frozen midleap, his *gi* rippling with effort, his flexed heel just grazing another boy's cheek. In another shot: two boys with arms extended like pistons, both of them wincing: one thousandth of a second in a flurry of blows, only their Afros undisturbed.

"You'll get to that soon," the sensei said, interrupting my study. He had come in noiselessly, a middle-aged black man, serious but kind.

"You mean people are going to hit me?"

"It's all about control," he said. Then he laughed. "Or it should be. A match is won on points and not bruises."

My father was deeply invested in my karate career. He took pictures of me in my white outfit, having me kick for the camera, and what he took for combat readiness was really a scowl of irritation. I had a growing list of gripes about the sport. When it came time to pay for the next block of classes, I begged my father not to send me back, literally clinging to his pant leg: "Please, please, don't make me go. I hate it there." My father seemed shocked at my aversion, which I apparently had never mentioned before. I remember his apologetic tone when he called the sensei to tell him I wouldn't be returning. "No, no, you're doing a great job," he said, tugging on his mustache. "I guess this was more my thing than hers."

It was at that Oakland apartment that Leslie and I got it into our heads one day to give my father a facial. I don't know what possessed us. We must have been reading beauty magazines, a shared luxury we discovered early on, both of us entranced by the stories of everyday girls made glamorous by an ingenious haircut, the perfect lipstick and scarf. When my father came home from work, we made him sit in the kitchen on a plastic chair while we prepared hot washcloths and stirred up a paste of oatmeal and honey in a metal bowl. He was unmanned by our suggestion, and sat in the chair with his arms loose at his sides while we laid compresses across his forehead and smoothed tonics across his cheeks.

"This is amazing," he said, when we were finished and his skin was gleaming. We gave him a hand mirror, and he tipped his chin down and examined himself from every angle. "Why don't we do this all the time?"

Leslie and I laughed. She combed his hair back with her fingers and wiped the cream from around his ears, and I remember the expression on his face, a look of transportation and trust on this man with size-twelve feet and grease under his nails. He was basking, his face turned up the way a leaf tracks the sun.

That summer I was flipping through some old political posters I found in a box in my bedroom when I came across one of my favorites: a group of campesinos in fatigues against a rich red ground. They held hoes and rifles; flares of orange lifted behind them — the signs of distant battle. The text was set in narrow lines: "It is better to die on my feet . . . than to go on living on my knees." It seems strange to me now that I thrilled to those sentiments, for they were the kind of sentiments that had separated my father from me years before. The men in that poster, were they to come to life, would most likely have told of children they had left behind in the villages of their country. They would have spoken in the language of sacrifice.

My father and I sometimes talked about our early years together — or rather he talked, telling me stories of our travels together back east. How I leapt into his arms at a rally and babbled into the microphone, unfazed by the sea of heads before me. How I squelched a bully at our Boston play group by threatening to bite him till he bled. But we rarely spoke about his time in prison or the absence that followed. We each had our reasons for leaving the past behind us. He wanted to be a different father now — more grown-up, steadier, more in control. I think I was afraid to cross the river of hurt behind me. Still, the defiance of those words stirred my blood. I sat on my bed studying the men's rugged faces and wished for something worth laying down my life for.

Soon I would have someone on whom I could heap such extravagant emotions. In early spring I came for a weekend visit, and soon after I arrived, Leslie and my father sat me down in the living room.

"We have some very good news," my father said. Leslie was beside him, beaming. I wracked my brain, trying to think what it could be.

"You are going to have a baby sister," my father said.

I looked back and forth between them, speechless. They were holding hands, leaning forward on the couch in anticipation. Tears welled up in my eyes. I tried to say something, but my throat was stuck.

"Aren't you happy?" my father asked, his face starting to fall.

Happy? *Happy* suddenly seemed like a flimsy little word, paper-thin, trivial, unequal to the waves of joy and relief and gratitude that flooded me. I was going to have a *sister*.

"When?" I croaked, my voice returning.

"Five months," Leslie said, smoothing her shirt over her belly. "It's just a little lump yet. You want to feel it?"

I knelt beside her and put my hands over the faint mound of her stomach. Five months. It wasn't so long. I had waited ten years already. Only five months, I thought, and I would never be alone again.

seven

MY SISTER MIA was born in June, but oddly, for all my anticipation, I can't remember the first time I saw her. I do remember the phone call announcing her arrival. I was at my mother's at the time, watering the garden, laying the hose in a trough between rows of peppers and watching the dirt turn black, when my mother called me to the phone. "It's your father," she said, smiling with excitement, which caught me off guard. "Come quick."

I stood in the kitchen, listening to my father's voice, tinny and light with his news. He was at a hospital pay phone. "You have a sister. Her name is Mia and she's beautiful and she can't wait to see you."

I couldn't wait either, but I would soon discover that my sister's arrival, her presence in the family, was both sweeter and more fraught than I could have imagined. She was a good-tempered baby, with cinnamon-orange hair and a drop-dead smile. I loved to hold her, to stare at the tiny moons of her fingernails, even to change her diaper, that feeling of tried-on domesticity it gave me. But sometimes she seemed too beautiful: I could never compete with that translucent skin, that delicate baby scent that made friends and relatives bury their noses in her fat-creased neck. And there was another thing: she fit in her family. I imagined her somehow always traveling with me, following me from house to house. But she stayed put, and in the end I would envy that more than anything else. She wouldn't share that odd feeling — on holidays, on birthdays — that someone was always missed.

Two years later, Jim and my mother would have a daughter, Alice, and two years after that, Leslie and my father would have a second child, Eva, another girl. At ten, I was an only child with four parents; by fourteen I would be one of four kids. For the most part, I loved that filling of the houses, the clamor, the company. We would be too far apart in age to compete for clothes or toys or a family niche. But I would often have the feeling that they had come too late, that I would have to wait years for them to catch up.

When I was in sixth grade, Mother and Jim sold 12000 Spring Street. They were tired of being landlords, tired of living at the main crossroads of the valley, where your front yard was everybody's business. They bought a house along a narrow river canyon outside town. There, my mother had to give up vegetable gardening. There wasn't much sun under the live oaks, and every winter the river swelled to twice its size and washed trees and deer and topsoil away on a thundering stream.

What we gained at the new place was privacy. You could do a nude interpretive dance in the back yard and wouldn't shock anyone but the squirrels. Technically, we did have neighbors, a city-dwelling couple who owned the lot next to ours. They drove their trailer up for a weekend now and then and talked of the grand second home they were planning to build, which made Mother nervous. She needn't have worried. We soon learned what they were made of. When they arrived on a Saturday, they started construction by raking the leaves. While they raked, they screamed at each other, and at their dog, who soon took to cowering in the willows by the river's edge. By Sunday, when the leaves were in a neat pile, they packed up and left for their city jobs. The wind blew, the leaves sifted back over the lot, and in a month or so, when the place looked just as it did before, the neighbors returned and started raking again. After about a year, they stopped coming.

We couldn't grow anything to eat at the new place, but there were flowers on the banked terraces above the river that were older than I was: camellias the size of haystacks, rhododendrons on sagging trellises, a twenty-bush rose garden in dire need of pruning. The house had been rented for years by a couple who wouldn't have known a hose if it reared up and bit them, so the whole yard was starved and in need of assistance — just the way my mother liked it. She threw herself into weeding and mulching, and in the spring the landscaping showed its more delicate goods: a patch of crocuses at the base of an oak, a raspberry vine that filled out and gave fruit.

The house itself was a modest one-bedroom, long and narrow, with open-beam ceilings and rooms stacked end to end like railroad cars. Off its west corner was a guest cottage, complete with bathroom and kitchenette, and I was to sleep there until we could afford to build another bedroom on the house.

"So how do you feel about staying out here?" my mother asked me as we toured the place. The main room was small, with linoleum and fluorescent lights. The owners had left some white wrought-iron furniture in one corner, and my mother dragged it into the center of the room.

"I feel fine," I said, glancing around. "It seems cool." I was already plotting the transgressions I could get away with under my own roof.

As it turned out, I wouldn't do much transgressing, nor would I sleep there very long. The guest house was a good thing come too early. I was eleven — just shy of laying claim to the place, longing for privacy but not quite over my childhood fears of spiders and storms and the dark. And that place had spiders — armies of them. The house had been on the market for a while, and it had clearly been some time since anyone disturbed the spiders' peace. They crawled the walls and floors as if they owned them, and wouldn't be hurried when I approached with a shoe.

When my mother came out to tuck me in at night, I made her go marauding. She went around the room, crushing spiders underfoot, then chased after the ones overhead with a curtain rod. The ceiling was made of old soundproofing tiles, and when she pressed into them, the rod made a faint crunch that I took to be the snapping of spider bones.

"Spiders don't have bones. They have exoskeletons," my mother said. She had the rod in her hand, a few legs and black carcasses dangling off the end. Then she started to laugh. "I guess that's cold comfort. This weekend, we'll really sweep out the eaves." She propped the killing tool in a corner. "I'll go after them with my spray hose."

When she kissed me and left, I sat up in bed and watched her disappear, then counted to six and waited for the light to come on in her and Jim's bedroom — a mere thirty feet off. It was a comfort to see their shadows cast on the wall.

As it turned out, I would make those thirty feet in record time when the first winter storm broke out, sprinting through the rain in my nightgown, thunder cracking overhead. That night I slept on the foldout couch in the living room. And when the rains went on and I showed no signs of returning to the guesthouse, my mother moved my dresser into the living room. I slept on that sofa bed for two years, an oddly cozy arrangement. I liked sleeping in the center of the house, where it seemed nothing could harm me. In the winter I had a fire beside me in the hearth, and I woke each morning to the rasp of the coffee grinder and Jim whistling along to the radio in the kitchen.

The mail truck retired around then, though it had been running reliably since we left Boston eight years earlier. Jim parked it on a far corner of our two-acre lot, under a bay tree, and painted it brick red to match the house. It soon became another shed, the back filled with plywood and two-by-fours, the cab gathering dust and cobwebs. Once, Jim needed to move it — to get a backhoe by when he was grading the bit of land sloping down to the river that he liked to call "the back forty" — and to his amazement, the engine coughed and turned over on the first try.

"Geez, maneez," he said, shaking his head with a smile. "Can you believe that?" The truck rumbled steadily beneath him, and he cocked his head to one side, listening to the idle the way an acupuncturist listens to a pulse. "We should never have moved out of this thing."

This was Jim's perennial cry. He had a philosophical opposition to material goods, and watched the expansion of the house with a mixture of satisfaction and dread. "We've got to cinch in our belts," he'd say when a batch of bills came due, or, "Man oh man, we're going under."

This talk never worried me much, since it seemed to have little bearing on the actual state of our finances. Mother had a steady job with the school district and was forthright about their habit of socking money away for lean times. She conveyed her usual matter-of-fact faith in our future — not a future of luxury, but one of being well fed, with a roof over our heads — even as Jim seemed braced for a sudden downturn in our fortunes. This difference between them came clear in daily ways, not least of which was their manner of walking the supermarket aisles.

Jim pushed the cart at a snail's pace, leaning over to squint at price tags, ticking items off a short list. It seemed that thriftiness was a matter of preparation and pacing. If you didn't rush, you wouldn't overspend. My mother's style struck fear in his heart. She wheeled through the store at a clip, tossing items into the cart, and wrote the check without a second glance.

Still, even with all the stops out, our life had to be called frugal. We ate out perhaps once every two months, never bought anything on credit. Even the house, their one large expenditure, was added to slowly. Rather than borrow against their mortgage to pay for the additions, they saved the money to pay for building materials, and did most of the labor themselves, hiring out only for the jobs they couldn't do — finish carpentry and tilework.

We'd left Spring Street, but I still went to the same school. Instead of walking a mile down the street each morning, I waited out on the road for the school bus, watching my breath mushroom into the cold valley air and mooing at the cows on the far hill. After school, I still spent most of my time with Alison Rider, and with another girl, Maxine, who had moved to town during the fifth grade.

Alison, Maxine, and I were a trio, which did not mean a set of three equally loyal friends, but rather three variables in a constantly shifting equation. When two of us were drawn together, a third was repelled. When I was on the outs I swore I didn't need the other two; they were pathetic, tucked over there with their heads together. And then something would come between them, a little frisson of boredom or ill feeling, and one or the other would bump up against me in line and make a jibe at the other's expense, and I'd forget any of that trouble had ever happened — until it happened again.

Alison and I had known each other for what seemed like most of our natural lives. She and Maxine, though they had met only lately, both lived with their mothers, and shared a certain jaunty self-reliance. I believe I was slightly more mothered than they were — though I don't think their mothers would feel I have the right to say this — but among us this became a liability; it marked me as soft. The two of them were certainly worldly, considering the backwater in which we lived. They listened to Boz Scaggs, knew how to make omelets, and swept the kitchen without anyone asking them to. Maxine, in particular, seemed to know about sex — not just the facts, but the essence of it. It was there in the way she raked her fine blond hair away from her forehead and trailed her fingers through the ends. Somehow, on her, that gesture didn't look vain, it looked almost weary — a languid, unconscious movement that made the boys flock around her, mooning.

At twelve, I was still a child — bony and restless and given to blurting out stupidities. I remember once trying to calculate Maxine's appeal. She couldn't kick or throw a ball; she screamed and turned scarlet at the sight of a mouse. I paused there, having the vague sense that these might be considered her charms. But there was more: she was flat-chested; her hair was too thin to feather or curl; she had gaps between her teeth and was prone to cold sores. Still, the boys treated her with a kind of breathless reverence. She, in turn, didn't give them a second glance. She was promised to a boy she'd met in Jamaica, where she went during the summers to visit her father.

In the classroom, also, I seemed to be falling behind. The teacher kept a homework ledger, and there were always a few checks just after my name, the good intentions of the early school year, but they thinned out after Halloween, grew patchy by Christmas, until finally there stretched a row of empty boxes. I would ask to see this ledger frequently, hoping for a colossal error in my favor, and now and then I copied down the missing assignments, but I was too demoralized by my own laziness to chip away at the missed work.

Slowly, before my own eyes, I was turning into a laggard and an occasional troublemaker. I experienced this as something happening to me. The teacher singled me out for corrective measures, and under her glare I got jumpy and took bigger chances, flipping her off when she wasn't looking, for the amusement of my friends — except then she *was* looking, and she was *not* amused.

I was becoming corrupted in certain ways, but I was still known among my friends for my sexual naiveté, so it was a relief when I got my first French kiss and could stop listening to Maxine's instructions about tongue rolling and flavored lip gloss. It happened on a Greyhound bus, on my way to a weekend visit with my father. I jumped off at the station in Cloverdale to feather my hair with the bathroom hand drier, and when I got back on, there was a young man in my seat.

"Oh, sorry," he said, when I hesitated in the aisle. "I'll move." He started to pull his bag from the overhead rack.

"That's all right. No one has a seat to themselves," I said, suddenly grateful for the packed bus. He was handsome, in a plain-featured way, and his sheepskin jacket made him look bulky and useful.

"Well, all right then," he said, sinking back into his seat. His name, I soon learned, was Tony. He made a living raising ducks.

"So — mallards?" I asked brightly. Any shred of poise I possessed seemed to have deserted me.

"Yep," he said, grinning wider.

Later, Tony mustered some excuse to compare the size of our palms, and when I held my hand up, he laced his fingers into mine. I never wished that ride would go slower, though I can't remember a thing we said for the next fifty miles. When we got to his stop, he said, "Okeydokey," and leaned over to kiss me, dryly at first; then his mouth opened and — miracles! — there was his tongue. I remember the smell of hay on his coat, and how a strange voice in my head said, *So that's what he wants —*

as if he were taking advantage, and my part was one of womanly forbearance. In fact, the advantage was mine. I knocked off that awkward first effort with a boy I'd never lay eyes on again. I rolled my tongue this way and that, sure that reports of my ineptitude would never make it back from the duck farms of Sebastopol.

When I got to the station in San Francisco, my father was waiting for me, hands in his pockets, his coat buttoned against the cold. He looked worried, and clutched me in a welcoming hug slightly longer than usual.

"Are you okay?" I asked him, my thoughts of the duck farmer quickly fading.

"I'm fine," he said, shaking off whatever had him brooding. "I've got a few things on my mind. But, hey! You're here. We've got some great things planned for the weekend."

On the drive home, I watched clouds of worry pass over his face. My father was never much good at hiding his moods. For that matter, neither was I, and perhaps he caught sight of my mirrored concern. Toward nightfall, he gave up pretending.

"Honey, I need to talk to you." He clenched his lips in a way saved for nervous occasions. I followed him to the living room and sat down, but instead of launching in, he went over to the record player and picked out an album. Celia and Johnny. I thought it was strange — putting on music at a time like that. He slipped the LP gingerly from its sleeve, lowered the needle, and turned up the volume before sitting across from me.

"I'm sorry about the music." His voice was pitched low, below the jazzy blare of the horns. "I'm worried that the house might be bugged."

My stomach turned over. I had no reference point for his worries, no idea if they were well founded.

"Don't worry," my father said. "I'm just being extra cautious. The thing is, there is a chance that Leslie and I might need to move to Kentucky. There's some very important work going on there with the coal miners, and they need our help."

I stared at him in disbelief. I could barely have picked out Kentucky on a map.

"What kind of work?"

"Organizing work. The union is going up against some powerful mining companies."

"Can't the people in Kentucky take care of it themselves?" I was conscious of my petulant tone, but I had a feeling he would cut me some slack under the circumstances.

"They are having a really hard time, honey. It's a crucial fight." I could see his frustration in trying to convey the urgency in terms I could understand. In fact, he didn't have to try. He and I had once watched a film about striking coal miners. I don't remember where we saw it, but the images stuck in my head. Men standing in a muddy road, their faces smudged from a day in the mines, then the rat-a-tat of machine-gun fire, and some of them falling.

Beyond him, out the sliding glass doors, I watched the city lights wink on. I wanted to glide out over the buildings, away from our apartment, which now seemed to be locked in a set of cross hairs. More than my father ever did, I believed in a faceless governmental will. His fears were concrete. He feared phone taps; he feared inflated charges and prison, no doubt, having faced them before. My fears were more vague than that, more high-flown and Orwellian, though I hadn't read Orwell yet. I was a pure-blooded conspiracy theorist at twelve, the product of bad nerves and little information.

"Honey, what are you thinking?" my father asked.

"I'm thinking that I don't want to move to Kentucky!" I said, my voice rising above the music.

My father stiffened and raised a finger to his lips.

"Oh my god," I whispered. "I'm sorry."

"It's okay," he said, seeing my panic. "Don't worry about it."

"It's not okay. I said *Kentucky*. They probably heard me." I felt sick. Maybe I had meant to give us away.

When my father saw me rattled, he forgot caution and turned comforting. He took a seat beside me and curled me to his chest. "Look, I'm sorry if I scared you. It's gonna be all right." He murmured and shushed, and later Leslie came home and we ate around the lamp-lit table. My sister banged happily on her highchair, sucking on one of those horrid Vienna finger sausages, and I tried to forget about what we'd said.

The next day my father and I went to the neighborhood courts to play basketball, and my fears seemed to shrink in the sunlight. Still, when we dribbled back to the apartment I stopped on the street and stared at our building, the neat walkway, the number on the door. I tried to see if it looked different from outside, if someone watching from a far window, a telescope, a parked car, might find something to mark us from the rest.

One morning, on a weekend visit to that same apartment, Leslie called me into the bathroom. She was standing in front of the mirror, a comb in hand, bangs hanging over her eyes. "How would you like to cut my hair?" she asked, flashing me a hopeful smile.

Up till then I had used scissors only to cut paper and thread, but I shrugged and said, "Sure." As in most things, my fear of screwing up was outweighed by my hope of discovering some unknown talent. I took the scissors and sliced the air a few times for warm-up.

Leslie brought in a kitchen chair and sat down facing the mirror. "I can do the front by myself," she said. "But I can't reach the back." She ran her fingers through the hair at her nape. "So, to make layers what you do is comb the hair up like this" — she scooped up a section from the side of her head and pulled it toward the ceiling — "and cut it off straight." She demonstrated with her fingers.

I thought I saw how it worked: "The pieces from the bottom have farther to go, so they end up longer?"

"Exactly," she said, looking pleased. More than once she had lit on the fact that we were visual thinkers: if you gave us directions to your house, we would map the path in our heads, a rat's maze seen from above. When Leslie described to me a dress she had seen in the store — "strapless, with a Juliet neckline, a fitted waist, and a gored skirt" — the dress would come together as she spoke, each phrase adding a detail, until it hung there, whole, in my mind.

Still, it was one thing to visualize a task, and yet another to do it. By the time I lifted the scissors to begin, my hands were damp with sweat. I had noticed, in my short life, that people were unduly sensitive about their hair. I remembered the acts of vengeance I had wanted to wreak on a certain hairdresser back home. She'd been asked for a trim and had delivered a pixie. At least she and I had gone to different homes at night.

Leslie must have sensed my jitters. "Don't worry," she said, turning away from the mirror and laying a hand on my arm. "I can't afford to get it cut in a salon. You can't do any worse than I would do myself."

Reassured, I started in back, lifting up a section as she had showed me. How short to make that first cut? For this, people went to beauty school. I took a deep breath and dove in with the blades. The scissors were loose and dull, so I had to make a couple of sawing attacks. I snipped further to make the ends straight, avoiding Leslie's eyes in the mirror, but by then the hair had slipped a little in my fingers. When I let the hank go, it fell into a jagged staircase.

"I don't know," I told her, looking at the damage. "This might not go well." I used the future tense out of delicacy.

"I don't care," Leslie said, a heartfelt dash in her voice. "It's only hair. It'll grow back. I wear a cap at the shipyards anyway."

Her mood was infectious. A haircut wasn't an epic event. Besides, the mention of the pinched family finances had struck a chord in me. I lifted another section and continued, picking up small advantages as I went along: if you pulled the scissors toward you with each snip, the hair was drawn into the blades and cut cleanly. Still, it was an awkward business. I nicked my fingers a few times. When I combed, I put the scissors in my mouth, and when I cut, I held the comb in my teeth, and soon my tongue was matted with hair. When I finished, there seemed to be more hair on the floor than Leslie had on her head. I had given her a choppy shag, the kind of cut little girls give their dolls.

"It looks pretty good," Leslie said, turning this way and that.

I stood back and chewed my lip while she dug into a drawer for a hand mirror. After some jockeying, she got a look at the back. Her eyebrows lifted. She pushed at her hairline with her free hand.

"It looks terrible," I said, the last word nearly a moan.

Leslie laughed. "Oh, well. Next time it'll be better."

"Next time? There isn't going to be a next time!"

"Why? Didn't you like doing it?"

I considered this for a moment and decided I had liked it quite a lot — the concentration it required, the pleasure when a section fell smoothly. "But look at the mess I made."

"It's not so bad, really," Leslie said, scrunching her hair in the mirror. "It just needs time to settle in."

Slowly, Leslie was alerting me to the subtleties of personal grooming. I had been a tomboy most of my life, and hadn't worn a dress since the first day of kindergarten, but in those years the idea of beauty, of improving ones looks in minute ways, was like a faint signal coming in.

It was a signal I must have heard one afternoon, standing in front of the living-room windows at my mother's house, looking out at the river — that familiar green canyon. I was twelve, and it was dusk, and so the view outside was fading and my reflection was beginning to sharpen in the glass. I had always disliked my profile, and now I turned to the side, studying my nose, the length and slight knob, which I found displeasing.

Earlier that year, leafing through a book on Roman history, I came across a photo of a cameo dug up from Pompeii, a young woman's head and throat carved in bas-relief. That face rang a bell. I took the book to the bathroom and held it up to the mirror, turning my face to the side so our profiles were twinned in the glass. I had to admit we weren't pretty (though she might have gone over better in her day). Our noses sloped off at an angle that seemed insufficiently acute and gave us, I thought, a doleful, insistent air.

But how did we know beauty when we saw it? Leslie had told me about Greek theorems for the ideal proportions of a building, the relationship of column height to roof slope. They were based on human proportion. What we liked in a body, a face, was what we liked. It couldn't be explained.

Now I stared into the plate-glass window and tried to imagine a nose that would suit me better — something narrower, I thought, perhaps an upturned nubbin. But when I tried to envision this new nose, I got confused: all the parts had to work in tandem. You couldn't just cut and paste. Then, suddenly, in a flash, it came to me: God made my nose. It must have been the best nose for me.

For whole precious moments I swung in the hammock of faith, and I wonder if what I felt, for those moments of suspended judgment, was as much about God as it was some version of my mother's native optimism. It was a brief stoppage, at least, of the adolescent's endless second-guessing. Just then — alone in a quiet house — it was a relief to think that nothing more could be done, that there was nothing to strive for. To be powerless was to have no regrets.

Then a dreary thought pulled me up short: I had seen a lovely baby in the supermarket just that week — caramel eyes and a mobile face — and then she turned and revealed a port-wine stain from forehead to cheek. Beauty wasn't fair, or parceled out with any logic. I left the window, more bitter than when I began.

My mother got her share of my scouring gaze. On the weekends, she danced around the kitchen, flat-footed, singing songs from Casey Kasem's Top 40 while I sighed and cringed. That age might have been called the End of Mercy. It shames me now to remember how ruthless I was with my mother's pride. She was looking less and less the earthy hippie: she dressed in plaid skirts and flats, wore her hair short and permed. To look at her, no one would have guessed she once lived out of a truck. Still, I began a campaign against her scrubbed face and simple outfits, and out of some supreme restraint, she didn't react to my barbs. Instead, she let them hang out in the air, hoping, perhaps, that I might recognize my tone and relent.

I didn't. At all costs, I wanted her varnished, like my schoolmates' mothers — ranchers' wives who leaned toward peroxide and blue eyeshadow. Early in junior high, I managed to coax my mother into the bathroom for a makeover.

"See, you just need a little bit of color," I said, guiding her to the toilet seat and fingering the hair away from her face. I swirled pink blusher on the apples of her cheeks, then stood back to survey my work: "You look better already!" My mother stared up at me, skeptical, brows lifted, head tilted to the side — the look we wear when we ask someone to be our mirror. I gave her a coat of thick, clotted mascara, my hand braced on her cheekbone, and pronounced her improved.

My mother wore that makeup dutifully for months, though she disliked the effect and the primping added time to her usual morning routine: shower, black coffee, a quick brush through her hair. I'm sure now that she would rather have spent those minutes staring out the window at the river. Instead, she went into our tiny bathroom — damp, with northern exposure — and leaned toward the mirror, an expression of mild bafflement on her face as she worked with the applicators and brushes.

My mother's confusion filled me with a sense of expertise and pride at my influence. I was accustomed to her competence. When she dreamed of a stone pathway leading from the house to the river, it wasn't long until she had selected the slate, found the quarry, and started hauling and setting the thick stones. So I took a certain satisfaction from watching her squint at the foggy mirror, chin tipped down to survey her lashes, the way she glanced up now and then to see if I approved. I even convinced myself that she liked the results, but years later, when I no longer considered her my hostage in the wars of adolescence and when her makeup had grown dusty in a bathroom drawer, I asked my mother something that had been nagging me. "Why did you wear it? That makeup. You never liked it."

She cocked her head and considered me for a moment: "Oh, to make you feel powerful."

During the school year, while I was living with Mother and Jim, my dad and Leslie often moved from one city to another. They never pulled up stakes during the summers, mindful of my need to land somewhere for the two months of my visit, but their courtesy gave these shifts of city an unreal edge. I would leave one apartment, its arrangements fixed in my mind, and, upon arrival months later, discover we had a new address — the same watercolor prints, stereo, and director's chairs arranged neatly in strange rooms. Until I tried it myself, during my college years, I thought moving a household was mainly a feat of imagination, an airy process by which the beloved objects floated across cities, up stairs, and into new positions.

When I arrived for the summer after eighth grade, my father pulled up at an apartment in East San Jose, a two-bedroom place on the top floor of a stucco building. (The plans for moving to Kentucky had been scrapped, never to be mentioned again.)

Since I had been expressing an interest in drama, my father enrolled me in a musical-theater program, housed in a run-down auditorium in the heart of the city. The parts were to be cast by audition, and my father helped me work on a song, the title tune from *The Wiz*, which we had seen on Broadway earlier that summer when we went to visit my Grandma Leila. I aspired to the kind of effortless verve that Lena Horne displayed on the original-cast recording. I played that album over and over, taking note of where she added a trill, where she backed off. I might as well have been studying Van Gogh's brush strokes. My voice wasn't up to the rendition. I had a tendency to look up and raise my brows when I pitched for the high notes, as if they were physically out of reach; I did a growling business in the lower registers, which I tried to pass off as vibrato.

When the audition day neared, I did a run-through for my father in the living room. He sat down in a canvas butterfly chair with a cup of milky coffee and gave me his attention. "Okay, let's pretend this is the real thing. Walk on from the wings."

I got a knot in my stomach, but I launched in anyway, and by the end I was quite charmed with myself. I even affected a little finger snap to jazz it up.

"That's good," my dad said. "Your voice is strong, but I think you're pushing it a little."

"What do you mean, 'pushing it'?"

"It's okay to sound like what you are."

"What's that?" I asked.

"A twelve-year-old with a damn good voice —"

"Thirteen."

"What?"

"I'm thirteen."

"God, is that right? Okay. Thirteen. Now try it again."

The day of the audition, my father drove me to the theater.

"You nervous?" he asked, clapping a hand down on my leg so hard it made me wince.

I was beyond nervous; I felt damned. I looked out the window at kids stepping into strip-mall doughnut shops with their mothers and wondered if there was some way to swap fates. But the car sped on and I remained inside it: hot window glass, Lou Rawls crooning on the radio, my stomach in a burning knot. After a while, the dread took on a life of its own, and I lost track of what had caused it. Were we going to a funeral? To the hospital for some horrible operation? Then I remembered. We were headed for the theater. I was to sing my song.

A young woman was passing out numbers at the theater door, and my father and I waited in the seats while dozens of kids got up, one by one, to sing a scrap from "Somewhere over the Rainbow" (the ingénue hopefuls) or "Gary, Indiana" (little freckled boys with tumorlike knees). My father was sizing them up, but he knew better than to engage me in conversation. I was fixated on counting the number of bars the kids got through before they were dismissed by a voice from the balcony.

When my number was called, I took my place in what seemed like a half acre of worn hardwood, facing rows of jostling kids and the darkened balcony. I declined the services of the accompanist, who started everyone off in a murderous key, and sang a cappella, surprised from the first note at the voice coming out of my chest. Fear made me bellow. I cut the warbles and trills and went straight for the middle of the notes, hoping not to lose my way. When I got a gruff "Thanks" from the rafters, I bolted like a dog cut from its leash and joined my dad in the seats.

"Ooh, cat! You kicked butt," he whispered, slapping me five down low between the armrests.

I sang well enough that day to get called back for one of the leads in *The Music Man,* but the second audition was a minor disaster and I ended up being cast as a dancer, which suited me fine. While I was tap-dancing to "Marion the Librarian," my father and Leslie were working on the assembly line. I had only vague notions of how they passed their days. I had seen the outside of the plant once or twice, a massive building the size of several airplane hangars. Inside, I knew there were belts and conveyors, and that the cars went by at a dizzying pace. My father always spoke with gratitude of the old hands who helped him when he was a new hire, showing him time-saving tricks, picking up the slack until he got up to speed. I heard in his voice how good it was to have a friend in that place. And there were always stories about the foremen, who could make their lives difficult in small but important ways: refusing to release them for bathroom breaks, saying they couldn't find a floater, or bucking to get them transferred to a tougher part of the line.

My father's involvement in union politics made his position delicate. There were plenty of fervent anticommunists on the line. I was conscious that he had to play his hand carefully. He spoke sometimes of his "enemies," and that word took on an ominous ring in the context of massive machinery. Now and then, cars slid off into the pits, their wheels having been locked in protest against line speed-ups or forced overtime. I imagined my father picking his way amid the conveyor belts, pressurized hoses, and bins of parts. It seemed like an easy place to have an accident.

For a long time I imagined Leslie and my father working side by side, but then I learned that she was assigned to a different part of the plant. By my father's report, she learned quickly the very tasks that had given him trouble. He always spoke fondly of this, her skill with a rivet gun. I think those were good years in their lives. He and Leslie seemed very much in love, and they were comrades — doing common work, making equal pay. Together they were able to buy their first house, the old industrial worker's dream, made real now by two salaries instead of one.

That San Jose house didn't have a lot of character, but it had high ceilings and good light, three small bedrooms, and a kitchen, dining, and living room, all without walls. Leslie applied her considerable design talents to maximizing the space.

She had a few pieces of nice furniture, handed down from her mother, and she would stand in the center of the living room with her hands on her hips, trying to decide how to "reconfigure things." This task was approached with a kind of theoretical rigor. Rather than trying to change the way we used the house, she would change the house to fit our habits. If the laundry was piling up beside the tub, she would search for a hamper that fit in the bathroom. The television would be moved from bedroom to living room and back, following the family's viewing trends. She favored geometric prints, abstract art, uncluttered surfaces. I had the feeling, watching her over the years, that there was a perfect arrangement for the furniture, and that one day we would find it. I say we, because I was quickly brought into the game, asked to help her shove the couch around or offer my opinions on wallpaper. I relished the sense of possibility she inspired: with a keen eye and good judgment, we could make the house into a place of function and style.

That mattered a lot to me. Though I was happily surprised that Leslie and my father had managed to rise into the ranks of homeowners and the house was nicer than I could have hoped for, the neighborhood was a bit of a disappointment. On the corner next to us was a run-down timber-frame house set back under a fringe of pines, which might have been a holdover from the days when San Jose was all orchard land. At night, shouts rang from the open windows, the man's voice rising in pitch until he drowned the woman out. I once caught sight of what I thought were pot plants rising out of the back yard, but when I put my eye to a slat in the fence a pit bull roared up, all teeth and spittle, and I kept my distance after that. The houses across the street were neat but faded: white lava rock in place of lawns, plaster-of-Paris lions lifting their paws beside the doorways, the windows covered with scrolled wrought iron.

The neighborhood was on the border between an upscale development and a hodgepodge of modest homes. Driving to our house from the freeway, you could take two routes: one that took you through blocks of matching ranch houses, another through streets marked by graffiti and corner liquor stores.

When I invited a friend home from rehearsal, I was torn as to which was the preferable approach. The first route led to false expectations, but gave our place a certain respectability by association. Taking the second resulted in a pleasant surprise when we finally pulled into our driveway, but I feared that by then our passenger might have jumped to irrevocable conclusions. Which was better: to be seen as a modest clinger to the hem of affluence or as the crowning jewel on a run-down block? These were the questions that occupied my thoughts. Somewhere along the way, I had become a great materialist. Neither of my two families, at that time, was much concerned with image. My mother put her stock in bettering the quality of human relations, and my father into the bettering of human conditions. I had a fixation with status that made up for the both of them.

When I returned home, my mother's failure to take interest in decor began to gall me. Our walls were hung with my sun-curled school drawings, brass Chinese platters, and hardware-store calendars. Our furniture was a mixture of chipped antiques and hand-me-downs. Soon after we had moved in, Mother and Jim had begun various construction projects: turning the garage into a split-level bedroom add-on, popping out a wall to make the kitchen larger. I didn't know it then, but that house would be under construction for the next fifteen years. There seemed always to be a room with exposed joists or plywood flooring and piles of sawdust in the corners.

I considered it my job to hector them about the schedule: "Why do you even bother calling it my bedroom? I'll be grown and gone by the time it's finished."

"Aww, naw, it oughta be done in another year or so," Jim would say with a laugh.

When my mother asked me once why I didn't invite friends over more often, I told her it was because the house made me ashamed.

"Hmm," she replied, her lips drawn whitely together. "Well, what do you propose we do about that?"

I offered to try improving things through a little strategic rearrangement.

My mother always liked a can-do spirit: "That's fine by me. Do whatever you like."

I spent the afternoon pushing furniture around, making a reading nook out of a pine bookshelf, a vinyl beanbag chair, and a black lacquer table that the former tenants had abandoned. I could never figure out what to do with a certain chair my mother had had shipped out from Boston after we got settled in California: a huge cube of mahogany lined with brown leather. (I didn't dare suggest getting rid of it. Once a week my mother rubbed the sides with lemon oil till the wood gleamed.) It overpowered the couch. When I moved it, the thing left a square of flattened carpeting that never quite bounced back, like the jaundiced grass under a wading pool. And the carpet — the carpet was the hopeless premise that underlay it all: wall-to-wall orange and red shag, so bright it made my fingernails hurt.

I pushed, I scooted, I made minute adjustments to the knick-knacks. Then I stood back and surveyed my handiwork. It was no use: the same junk in new configurations.

That work was an homage, of course, to Leslie's aesthetic. Even when she worked in the auto plant, her wool shirts and head-scarves were neat and well coordinated. I remember a kind of mourning in the family for her nails, which would never come clean, even with scrubbing. My father mentioned this to me once in a hushed, rueful tone. I understood that it was one of the sacrifices of their lifestyle.

On their nights off, when they went out together, I used to lie around on the bed, watching her dress. One outfit stands out in my memory: a white silk blouse with long, pointy lapels and wide cuffs, worn over a wraparound skirt printed with green dice. Green dice. I knew this was hard to pull off, but the white dots on the faces made a crisp correspondence with her blouse, and the ankle-strap heels she put on at the end added a note of refinement — a signal that she knew the skirt was campy, but what the hell. I wasn't overreading this. She paid that order of attention to the width of a collar, the shape of a heel.

When her outfit was complete, Leslie dug around in her jewelry box, slipping on a heavy opal ring passed down from her mother. I loved this ring: the bold asymmetrical setting, the stone shot with black and vermilion, the way it slipped around on her finger, a rare thing casually possessed. This ring came to stand for everything Leslie had and couldn't give me: her fine skin, the oriental rugs and family oil portraits tastefully framed, the talent for putting strangers at ease, and a personal restraint I could never muster.

Later, she would make clear to me the cost of such refinement, the weight of things left unsaid. But back then, I only hoped that she might save my father and me from our wildness, our confusion in the world of manners. And she did apply her hand to my father's wardrobe — weaning him over the years from polyester dress shirts and steering him toward linen and gabardine. But I think, looking back, that much as we admired her composure, Leslie was attracted to our brash ways: my father's broad physical presence and wacky humor, the way our emotional life played out on the surface, a string of moods.

eight

I HAVE SAID that I was becoming a troublemaker at school, and my mother, sensing it to be a case of limited horizons, decided I should go to high school in the neighboring town. I would leave an eighth-grade class of thirty — the same thirty students, give or take a few, that I had started with in kindergarten, our clan so starved for new blood that we pounced on newcomers with a vampirish ferocity — and join an incoming freshman class of three hundred, not one of them familiar.

In those first weeks, before I made any friends, I walked the school during lunch like a cop on the beat. To sit alone was to die a small death; walking gave me the illusion of purpose. I made tours of all the bathrooms on campus — checking my hair, washing my hands needlessly — then looped around the shop building, where a few boys lingered on their lunch hour making slingshots and bongs. From there I circled down to the pool, checking my watch now and then as if I were pressed, maintaining a constant pace until the bell called me to class again. On these tours, I made a minute study of the company I might keep.

There was the cowboy contingent, dubbed "goat ropers," who sat along a narrow wall, their tooled boots dangling, the concrete below them stained with chew; and the athletes, marked by their mesh jerseys and bristle cuts. The smokers were required to puff in a sand pit abutting the dumpsters of kitchen trash; their bell-bottoms and Jethro Tull T-shirts seemed to maroon them in the seventies. I felt some affection for the drama freaks, doing dance routines on the lawn in jeans and leotards. And I slowly inched my way into the fringes of the cool crowd — who filled out the college-prep courses and seemed to spend the weekends hosting keggers on BLM land and having sex in their parents' Astrovans. To join them, it seemed I would need some new clothes: pinwale corduroys, pegged at the ankle; heavy wedge-heeled sandals; and sweaters embroidered with snowflakes or roses.

When my mother picked me up at the end of the day, I was exhausted. We said little during the winding ride back to the valley. Sometimes I leaned the seat back and slept. My mother seemed to understand the strain I was under. When we arrived home, she sent me out to the back porch with a bowl of apples, a cutting board, and a knife. Late in the summer, Jim had built a fruit dryer out of plywood, a box fitted with a rack of screens and a hot fan. (He had quit his job at "the Ditch" to set up an architecture business out of the guesthouse, but things were slow at first and he had time for such projects.) Each day after school, I hunched over the knife, slicing apples and pears so thin you could read through them. It was a relief to give up the ruthless shepherding of my image, to devote myself to a simple task and sit still without guilt. All day at school I was painfully aware of how I stood, how I held my arms, what I said to the girl beside me in the lunch line and how it might reflect on me. I knew very well that those first days were crucial — that they would determine my position for years to come. But on our back porch, tucked down in the canyon, I could chew my lip, let my face go slack and my hair slip into my eyes. When the cutting board was mounded with fruit, I filled the screens and slid them onto their waxed runners. While the fan cycled up to a high whine, I would stare out at the live oaks, thinking of how I would remake myself.

I dried jars and jars of fruit that fall, until I made a friend in my drama class and began to spend the evenings curled up with the phone. Michelle was a senior, a languid beauty with sloe eyes and a sweetly wicked air. She lived with her father at a Buddhist monastery at the edge of town. Before the Buddhists bought the property, it had been a mental institution. Along a curving drive at the edge of the compound was a row of large clapboard houses, which must have once been the psychiatrists' quarters. Too lavish for the monks, most of them were let to nonreligious folk.

Michelle invited me over after school one day, and I was quick to accept. It beat slicing pears. We sat out on her wraparound porch, looking out at the leafy grounds, where now and then I caught sight of an orange-robed figure through the trees. "You're an alto, aren't you?" Michelle asked, propping her feet on the porch rail. "Want me to teach you some harmonies?" Somewhere far off, a gong sounded.

She and I would practice our perfect thirds on many porch-lit evenings at that house, testing, no doubt, the monks' vows. That fall, we entered ourselves in the school talent show. We were to sing "Boogie Woogie Bugle Boy" and waited backstage before the event in vintage suits and netted hats.

I leaned against the wall, dizzy with nerves, covering one ear and practicing my part, not the melody but a whole other path through the song, clear if you stayed on it but easy to lose. At the other end of the hall, Clyde Summers, the lead singer for the Coyote Cowboys — four local boys who had mastered enough cover tunes to give themselves a name — was tuning his guitar. He had unusual composure at eighteen and a narrow, gentle face, and I'd admired him from a distance even though he showed no signs of leaving the backwater in which we lived. His dad was a rancher, I think, and he seemed bound to work at a winery, have kids, and play baseball on the weekends with his old high school friends. It was a testament to Clyde's charm that he made the idea of settling in that town seem briefly appealing. Just then he loped toward us, fumbling in his shirt for a pick, and when he saw Michelle he stopped and smiled.

"You ladies look great," he said, putting the pick in his teeth while he buttoned his pocket flap. *Ladies.* I searched his face for wile, but didn't see any. "So I guess we're going to put on a show here," he said, turning to me with a smile. "I'm Clyde." He held out his hand.

I was so twitchy, from stage fright and his attentions, that I tossed my hat into the air. It was an absurd gesture, something

fitting a military graduation. We all stood still while it completed its wild arc and hit the floor.

Clyde picked it up and handed it to me with a look that broke
my heart, the bemused affection you show a girl who's sweet
but young, far too young.

"Break a leg," he said, putting a hand on my shoulder. Then
he went onstage to sing an Eagles tune, "Peaceful Easy Feeling," his voice drifting back to us in the hallway.

It was under that kind of adolescent swoon that I developed
a weakness for country music, for bland harmonies and twangy
guitar. We are at the mercy of things we come to young. The
next day I bought *Hotel California* and played it on Jim's warped
turntable until the needle got dull and the music became married to a batch of fretful afternoons by the river: Mother reading
or asleep, Jim drafting in his office. It was cool there under the
live oaks, tucked in a cleft in the hills, but beyond us were acres
of dry grass, empty and heat stunned. I could picture what little
went on out there — cattle kneeling in dollops of shade, a man
changing his spark plugs in front of the corner store, a Little
League game at the ball field, where boys in dusty uniforms
clung to the backstop. The world seemed emptied of interest.
Flies buzzed against the window screens, Don Henley sang
"Desperado," and I lay down on the red and orange shag rug,
letting out huge involuntary sighs.

When Jim came in for his lunch — salad and bits of cold
steak — he asked why I was hyperventilating. Then he put on
Sticky Fingers and did Mick Jagger imitations in the living
room, one foot up on the hearth, hands perched at the small of
his back, mouthing the words. "Yeah, you got — satin shoes."
This triggered a wave of nostalgia. "You know, the first time I
heard the Rolling Stones I was in a bar in Cambodia . . ." Jim
had seen Hendrix in a tiny club in Manhattan, back when he
was a maverick unknown. Now he closed his eyes as Mick
Taylor went into the extended guitar solo on "Can't You Hear
Me Knocking," and I dragged myself up from the rug, slid
open the screen door, and let that frayed guitar tumble into the
garden.

To this day, my musical taste runs toward the bands my parents weaned me on: Richie Havens, Van Morrison, the Stones. If asked why, I'd confess an almost codgerly conviction: nothing much good has come out since then. Still, it sometimes strikes me as odd that I tune my radio to songs nearly thirty years old, singing and tapping the steering wheel; my parents certainly aren't listening to Benny Goodman.

In 1982, during my sophomore year in high school, Leslie and my father moved again, this time to Los Angeles. Her mother and father lived there, and the GM plant in Van Nuys was hiring. My father got a job working nights on the assembly line, and Leslie decided to leave work in the auto plants and go back to school for a Ph.D. in architecture, following in her father's footsteps.

I made my first visit over Thanksgiving, pleased to have given up Greyhound buses for airplanes. We gathered for dinner at Leslie's mother's apartment — a place that impressed me mightily. It was four floors up in a tall building off Wilshire, with a wall of windows on each side, but what distinguished the place was Carolyn's furnishings: abstract paintings and Chinese screens, Turkish carpets and mahogany breakfronts and leather trunks covered with thick glass. Carolyn borrowed a little from this continent, that century, and managed to make it all come together. There were family pieces mixed with antique-store finds, and almost everything was blue. This color scheme sounds overmuch, but it was not. The place had panache. I mooned around, fingering the knickknacks and trying to figure out how it all went together. Good taste: I was hoping it could be broken down and carried out of the place like contraband.

On a low table in the living room was a salmon ringed with sliced lemons. I sat on the carpet, nibbling at the fish and trying to look as if I belonged. That morning, I had spent an hour in front of Carolyn's bulb-framed vanity mirror, curling my hair in a fashion that would have offended the Pilgrims. Now I held my head carefully, favoring my ringlets, and watched the guests arrive.

Leslie had manned a post at the door, greeting people and

guiding them toward the hors d'oeuvres. "Kate, you look wonderful," I heard her say to an older woman, draped in gray
cashmere, who had just stepped in. In fact, she did look wonderful. *Well groomed* was the phrase that came to mind. The
kind of grandmother who collected sculpture and took boat
trips down the Nile.

"This is Lisa, Carl's daughter," Leslie said, as I stood up to
shake the woman's hand.

"It's a pleasure to meet you, Lisa," the woman said, a soft
rattle of silver coming from her extended wrist. She looked at
me, waiting for a reply, but my mind was elsewhere. I was stuck
on that construction: "Carl's daughter," the lack of a personal
possessive. There were plenty of times when I was glad for that
distinction. I played up the gap when it served me. But just
then, in the midst of that rarefied company, I wanted Leslie to
claim me as her own.

Later that night, when the guests had gone and we were in
the kitchen washing up, Leslie noticed my sulkiness: "Did you
have a nice time tonight?"

I shrugged. I had had a very good time, tipsy on a few sips of
champagne and the pleasant demands of grown-up conversation, but now I was nursing my grudge of the early evening.

"Why couldn't you say 'our daughter'?" I blurted out, ap-
palled to hear my voice crack. I had planned to be peeved.

"What do you mean?" Leslie was at a loss.

"When that woman came in. You said I was Carl's daughter."

Leslie put down her towel. "I'm sorry if that hurt your feelings. But these are old family friends. They've known me —
they know I couldn't have a child your age. To introduce you
that way would have been awkward."

I could see she was stirred by my request. "I'm crazy about
you," she said, leaning her head toward me. "And I'm glad that
we're becoming a family" — but there must have been some
unreasonable bruising in my face, because she didn't reach out
to touch me. She was saying we had our circumstances; we had
come together by chance, and that couldn't be willed away. It
takes a certain rigor to live with these odd unions, to trust their
bonds all the while knowing that they aren't equal to the bonds

of blood. At fifteen, I didn't have that discipline. I couldn't reconcile the two truths in my mind: she was not my mother, and yet she mothered me. Over the years I would dream of her, take up certain of her gestures and phrases, mimic her handwriting — but I never grew careless of her love.

Years after that Thanksgiving, when I was dressing for a graduation ceremony, half frantic in curlers, pantyhose, and one shoe, I wheeled into a room to find Leslie ironing the panels of my skirt. The sight took my breath away. I stood there on the sill, watching her drive a wedge of smoothness over the fabric — the rhythmic slosh and hiss of the steam, her careful attention to the pleats and darts. It set my scalp tingling with a pleasure only distance could make.

The summer after my sophomore year would be my first in L.A., and my mother and I walked around in the weeks before I left feeling sentimental about the four hundred miles that would stretch between us. My mother expressed that sentiment by giving me lots of yard work.

On one of those June mornings, after spending hours digging blackberries out of a bank, we took a break to cut flowers for the house. Each of us composed for her favorite vase — mine carved out of black marble; my mother's a heart-sized globe her great-aunt had made, glazed the color of wine and milk. I knew nothing of this great-aunt, but her handiwork had ended up in our house: a beautiful vase, almost Japanese in its perfection, that symbolized, in my mind, a world filled with elegant trifles, the world my mother had been raised in.

She was walking along the edge of the lawn, clippers tucked in her jeans pocket, talking nearly to herself: "See, over here, how the ground cover is taking hold. If we just spray that down all summer, it'll really go."

I would be gone in a few weeks, and wouldn't be doing the spraying, but half my mother's satisfaction in these projects was in speaking of them out loud. She looked around, her bouquet forgotten, and assessed the state of the flower beds, the skirt of rotten blossoms under the camellias that made her itch to pick up the rake. That would mean I'd be hauling the tarp, for which I felt no itch. I'd rather be a house girl, reading and arranging flowers.

I spotted a last day lily jutting out of the bank and waded toward it, kicking aside the dead daffodil greens. There under one hassock was a forgotten Easter egg, its grainy lavender shell half crushed.

"Hey," I called to my mother. "I found the last egg."

She came over and crouched beside me. "Hiding there all that time."

I could see that it pleased her, this reminder of a lazy Sunday of omelets and chocolate. I knew from long-ago Easters, before I started spending the vacation with my father, that she and Jim got up early to hide the eggs, then sat on the back deck with mugs of coffee while my sister went scavenging. To me the egg looked forlorn, a lost twelfth cousin, left in the weeds for some snake's dinner. I got a little maudlin when it was time to trade families.

My mother showed no such weakness. Instead, she ordered me around with greater vigor, rousting me to clean out the fridge, wash the windows, or wield a shovel in some trench in the yard. All that week she had been working me hard. Finally I asked her why she was playing the taskmaster.

"So you won't miss me," she said, a gleam in her eye.

When I arrived in L.A., my father enrolled me in the summer program at Crossroads, a performing-arts high school in Santa Monica. Elliott Gould's son went there, and the daughters of the man who directed *Caddyshack*. The kids were all seasoned and oddly sensible at fifteen and sixteen. They wore a kind of drab antifashion — Levi's and white T-shirts and Converse high-tops. They smoked, and went to all-night coffee shops. But as far as I could tell none of them did drugs or indulged in any other depravity. Their parents seemed to be having all the fun.

We spent the summer preparing for a performance of a collection of Bertolt Brecht's short plays, set in Germany during the Nazi period, called *The Private Life of the Master Race*. On the first day we sat around cross-legged with our scripts and did cold readings. I remember being shocked by Brecht. This was a far cry from the saccharine tones of musical theater. I had never come across language in the theater that sounded so much like real life — blunt and plain. As each scene began I felt a quickening suspense: I needed to know what would happen next, and yet I had a pleasant inability to imagine how things might end. Then, in strikingly spare language, in dialogue full of hesitation and surprise, the drama would unfold. Perhaps I was wrong — I knew nothing of fascist Germany, or these lives — but the stories had the ring of truth. I had the feeling that if I could render those lines, I might know how it felt to be human under extraordinary circumstances. At fifteen, I had never heard of Brecht, didn't know he was a Marxist. The play sent waves through me because it gave me the script by which to imagine a certain extremity of experience. Reading those scenes, I caught a glimpse of wider feelings, and with that glimpse came a sense I rarely had at that age — that things could be different.

While I spent my days in rehearsals, my father was working nights on the line. He came home at dawn, packed my sisters' lunches, and wrote them a note before falling asleep. The rind of time left between waking and the next shift was devoted to union organizing. For years he got by on five or six hours' sleep, refreshing himself now and then with a catnap.

"Wake me up in twenty minutes," he'd say, lying down on top of the covers, instantly dead to the world. When I called his name, he would wake with a start, make a cup of coffee, and be on his way again. His life required deep reserves.

Sometimes, when the pace let up, he voiced regrets. "Why is it I never listen to music?" I once heard him ask, sitting in front of his speakers. Marvin Gaye was on the turntable, and there was a soft bewilderment in his voice. "I love listening to music."

It exhausted me to watch his exhaustion. I felt his fatigue as a sympathetic twinge in my limbs and wanted it to stop — as much for my sake as for his. Because over time daily short-changes in sleep added up, and when things blew up between us, they blew hard.

But if I fretted about his schedule, he would protest. He and

Leslie loved their work; it fueled as much as it sapped. And there was so much to be done. That was one thing about the world: it was broken in a thousand places. Once you set your mind on righting it, there was no end to what you could give.

Hard as he worked, my father found time to be the family forager, strolling the grocery aisles and trying to remember everyone's favorite cookie and cereal. He liked to have company, and so I often went with him. While he wheeled the cart from aisle to aisle, scanning his list, I served as runner. "Shit, honey, I forgot the Dijon. Could you get me a jar? Aisle six."

In good times, it was a task he enjoyed, but with Leslie in school and the family living on one income, this ritual lost some of its pleasure: he was pinned between his natural largess and his worry over the bank balance. The shelves of expensive snacks, the coolers of cold cuts and cheese seemed to fill him with a vague unease.

When I tired of watching him fret, I veered off toward the toiletries section, located, to my embarrassment, right next to Feminine Hygiene. Even a sidelong glance at that sign made me flinch. There, in the same bold lettering as Dog Food and Canned Goods, was a reference to matters that I could barely acknowledge in private. While my father checked prices on toilet paper, I breezed past the douches and tampons, settling in front of the shrink-wrapped blusher and lipstick and thinking about what I might steal.

It seems the shame of being nabbed by Mr. Shepherd in the first grade hadn't cured me of shoplifting — it just made me more cautious. I didn't consider petty theft a vice worth resisting; I only tried to swear off getting caught. Still, I have a hard time reconstructing what tempted me to palm a vial of Visine that day. Perhaps I was nervous about the cost of the eye drops, though I have no doubt my father would have paid for them if I asked. I have to think that I simply wanted the whites of my eyes whiter, and felt somehow that I should get it for free.

Once I chose the item, I scanned left and right. The aisle was nearly deserted. Halfway down the length of polished linoleum was a middle-aged man, deliberating in front of the condoms. I had passed him earlier, and he had glanced up with a

stricken expression, then turned back to the packages, feigning indifference. The boxes were decorated with bighorn sheep
and couples posed in skimpy underwear. I thought I understood his embarrassment, and politely averted my eyes. Here
we were, two comrades in spirit, flat-footed and self-conscious
in the clinical glare of the toiletries aisle. Still, I waited until his
head was turned to slip the Visine into my pocket. It didn't even
make a bulge. I fingered a few other items so as not to look
hasty, then made a show of checking my watch and wandered
toward the front of the store.

My father was in the checkout line, a look of pained concentration on his face as he watched the prices ring up. "I'll be
waiting outside," I told him.

Los Angeles twilight. The sky was a dusky orange, lit up by
miles of lights, and there was a pleasant crackle in the air. A
little girl clambered onto a toy horse beside the door and fed a
quarter into the slot, maintaining a grave expression as the
machine began its hydraulic gallop.

"Can I see what you have in your pocket?" The voice behind
me was quiet, intimate, and at first I thought the question was
addressed to someone else. Then I turned and found a man
beside me, short, sandy haired, with a small youthful paunch.
My nervous friend from the condom rack lifted up his badge.

"Please give me the eye drops." His voice was firm. I handed
over the goods, and he took me by the arm.

Just then my father appeared, pushing his cart, looking for
me in the spare light from the store windows.

"What's going on here?" he asked, when he saw me in a
stranger's grip.

"Is this your daughter?" the guard asked him

"Yes, and I want you to take your hands off her."

"She has to come with me, sir. She's stolen something from
our store." He held up the Visine. "I have to take her into the
back room for processing."

My father blanched at the mention of a back room. He was
wary of men with rented authority.

"I think there's been a misunderstanding," he said. "I told
her I would pay for that."

"Sorry," the guard said. "No go. I watched her slip it in her pocket." He assumed a posse lawman's stance: feet wide, hands perched at his waist. I saw a pair of handcuffs glint beneath his windbreaker.

When he saw that the guard wouldn't budge, my father left his cart and followed us through a set of swinging doors to a closet-sized room behind the produce section. Inside were two chairs and a battered metal desk. Polaroids of repeat offenders covered the walls. While my father paced in the narrow space, clenching his teeth, the guard penned an account of my crime.

Date, store, aisle. The guard muttered under his breath. "Total value of item?" He lifted up the bottle of eye drops. "Damn bar codes. Let's say two-fifty."

At the mention of the price, my father's eyebrows lowered like awnings. I sat in the extra chair with my arms folded, a gesture that might have looked like defiance but was in fact the mark of controlled panic. I kept imagining the patrol car cutting in between the taxis out front, the scandalized faces of the widows waiting with their sacks of tuna and milk.

But perhaps because my father lingered there, imposing and clearly concerned, the security guard stopped short of the full extent of the law. He took down my name and address, made me swear I would never set foot in the store again, and let me go. When we got into the car, I sagged against the seat and waited for my father to scold. He didn't, though — didn't even pretend to be outraged. Instead he put the keys in the ignition, sighed, and seemed at a loss for words.

"I'm sorry," I croaked, and I *was* sorry, mainly for what I had put him through. I could see that the sudden appearance of badges and handcuffs had roused old feelings in him.

When my father finally spoke, it was not in the language of morals but of unreasonable costs. "The mood is changing in this country," he told me. "They're cracking down on this kind of thing. It's not worth it anymore." Then he drove me home and never mentioned the incident again.

Some might say my father missed his chance, that he should have delivered a lecture on right and wrong. But that talk would have been lost on me. If my father had tried to speak of

profit margins or the businessman's right to a fair buck, I would
have laughed through my teeth. He had spent his life questioning the rights of big capital; he certainly wasn't going to take
their side over a vial of eye drops. As it was, his warning went
deep, because it aligned with everything he had taught me. If
fascism was coming, we might notice first a time of restriction
and amateur guards, and the wise would heed the signs and be
cautious.

The next day I went to rehearsal as usual, still feeling ashamed
of myself. The play was coming along badly. "I just don't feel
any urgency," said Elizabeth, our director, after a wooden run-
through. "I know it sounds like they're making small talk, but
this is big stuff, this is *How much do you love me?*, this is life and
death."

For a moment, here and there, I forgot myself, and the sadness of the lines swung through me. The menace of the state
looming outside, the ripped-up, roots-in-the-air feeling of parting — I thought that I understood a little of these things. But I
was fifteen and had no real grasp of the play.

To give us an inkling of the times, Elizabeth suggested we
stage mock interrogations. Darren, one of the more gifted kids
in the group, was to play an SS officer. I was to sit in a chair and
answer his questions. To make things more theatrical, he would
pose them in gibberish, one of those peculiar drama exercises
that I found quite stirring at the time. We were meant to focus
on the gist and not the particulars, to hear how much emotion
carried through tone. I was lousy at gibberish. I sounded as if
my mouth were full of dental tools.

"Lisa, all right, okay —" Elizabeth interrupted, dragging a
hand through her hair. "Why don't you answer in English?"

Darren turned out to be a gibbering pro. He had a cap of
blond curls and a body coiled like a spring. When he became
the SS man, his whole posture changed. I felt sure I knew precisely what he was saying. A few years ago, I learned that he
died in a freak accident at twenty-one. In London, where he
was studying theater, the gas heater failed while he was sleeping, and he never woke up. When I think of him, I remember

how he paced around that flea-bitten rehearsal room, muttering softly, then letting spittle fly in my face.

"I don't know," I said, in answer to a particularly harsh outburst. "I am Polish." (I must have gotten this from *Sophie's Choice*.)

Elizabeth sighed audibly from her chair.

The night after our first (and last) performance, my father took us all out to Benihana to celebrate. The Japanese-food chain had opened up not long before that, and it was still something of a cult phenomenon: you sat around an open grill while a man with a chef's hat and two cleavers riddled your vegetables into origami, then tossed his knives like a majorette. I was very impressed with the show, and touched that my father had splurged on such a fancy place, but I hadn't checked my actorly self-consciousness at the door. I wanted to make sure everyone knew I was amazed, so I kept my hands braced on the countertop, my eyes glued on the chef, my mouth slightly ajar. At one point Leslie got up to take a snapshot and captured that bit of business for posterity. I look like a sham hypnotist's accomplice. Everyone else was too awed by the flying shrimp to pay me much mind.

The next night I went off to the cast party, held at the home of one of the students. Another boon of the Hollywood life: they all seemed to have absentee parents. It wasn't hard to find a mansion with no one in charge.

My father pulled up front and eyed the Tudor façade and spotlit shrubbery. "Okay, so what time should I pick you up?"

"Well, I don't know when it's going to end. We might go out to Ships for dessert when it's over." I was hedging. Only a handful of these kids seemed to have heard of the word *curfew*. Though none of them had offered, I was hoping I might be invited to sleep over at someone's house.

I could see my father considering this. He was big on what he called "closure," the wrapping up of a long experience with the proper reflection and ceremony. "All right," he said, patting me on the leg. "Call me by eleven and let me know what your plans are."

The cast party was a fairly dull affair. David Bowie on the stereo, clumps of kids here and there. No one seemed to care that the summer was over; they would all advance together into the fall term. I was like a sailor about to be shipped overseas, full of sentiment and extravagant mood. I knew where I was headed: a winter of rainy Saturday nights in a Northern California town, cars circled in the Lucky's parking lot or cruising up and down Second Street hoping for directions to a keg out some dirt road. In social terms, those parties were the best one could hope for: to drink a cup of warm sudsy beer while huddled around a pile of burning tires — the oily black smear visible for miles — perhaps do a bit of necking in the shadows, and then barrel home down a set of switchbacks clinging to the edge of a cliff. We would lose some of our number, needless to say.

Mike, our cast-party host, had commandeered his father's bar, setting out beer and wine and bottles of whiskey. I wasn't much of a drinker, but that night I made up for inexperience, and soon the room whirled and the faces blurred. All worry over where I might land at the evening's end disappeared. I was just glad to be weaving through the crowd, picking up snatches of heady conversation: "His mother is a costume designer. She once worked with Edith Head. No wonder he got a callback for that soap."

At one point two sisters, Rita and Sharon, noticed my bleary condition and insisted I come home with them. I had been to their house before, an architect's showpiece in Benedict Canyon, where their father, a movie director, made brief appearances. Their mother had moved out long before and was rarely mentioned. I stumbled through the vast rooms, all white and gray and chrome, through the open kitchen with the wall-high recessed fridge and marble countertops. Their bedroom, at the top of a flight of narrow stairs, seemed to belong to another house — a comforting space furnished with wicker and throw rugs and floral bedspreads. I went directly to the toilet and retched, then feel asleep on the rug.

I woke late, my tongue stuck to the roof of my mouth, and tried to remember where I was. Then it all came back to me —

the party, the puking, how I never phoned home. I dialed my father on Rita's Mickey Mouse phone, holding the black ears up to my face.

"Dad, it's me." It wasn't difficult to sound hangdog.

There was no reply.

"I'm really sorry I forgot to call."

"Where are you?"

"At Rita and Sharon's."

"Come home." He sounded livid.

"How should I get there?"

"I don't care. Just come home."

I walked two miles down Benedict Canyon Road, past the circular driveways and stucco walls, stopping now and then to dry-heave into the bushes. Rita and Sharon's life had always seemed a bit lonely to me, but just then I was ready to trade places with them. So what if their father lived for his Japanese mistress and rarely came home? Farther down the road, I saw a maid emptying trash beside a whitewashed villa and wished I could trade places with her. I often had these escape fantasies in unpleasant times. I would do anything not to face my complicity.

I was so busy feeling sorry for myself that I never considered what had brought my father to his rage. There is something about the fifteen-year-old mind — a kind of skin or veil or walling off from feelings not your own. I couldn't get my mind around a father's worry, as the night wore on without word. Or what it felt like to go to sleep with your child at large in the city.

When I got home, he raged and I sulked. "How could you do this do us?" he asked me. I had no answer, and sat in the living room with folded arms. Finally he retreated to his bedroom and slammed the door, and I went through the house in a fit of pique, gathering up every photograph and object that signaled my presence. Once I had dumped them in a pile in my room, I found myself at a loss. I didn't have the nerve to burn them. In fact, I was partial to the one school photo in which I didn't look puffy faced and flat-chested, as I did in real life. What I wanted was to take myself back from him, to gather myself up and exit that house — that embroilment.

In early September, when I arrived back at my mother's

house, my father wrote me a letter about the summer. It began
with news about his work in the union — "I am enclosing a
leaflet we put out to the membership. I wrote it — it's pretty
radical for a union leaflet, especially one with the approval of
the President (of the union — not the U.S.)" — and told sweet
stories about my sisters. Then he turned to a sore subject.

"I feel very badly about the summer. I think it's really important that you correctly understand the experience — because
the tension and unhappiness for all of us will be worth it if it
translates into a positive learning experience.

"In thinking about it, the situation was so potentially positive, and we set such reasonable limits on your behavior — and
yet you pushed those limits, didn't respect our authority, and
manipulated so many situations from such a narrow, short-
term, and self-destructive perspective."

The letter went on in this vein. "Next summer, let's leave
more time and space to take stock and have greater self-control.
OK? It should help."

Then he picked up an old thread: "Lisa, I don't know if you
ever read the *Biography of Paul Robeson* I sent you. Please make
time to read it. I think you'll really get a lot out of it."

When I read that letter I felt a mixture of guilt and fury that I
couldn't sort out. I wasn't sure what kind of guidance Paul
Robeson's story might offer to wayward youth, but I made a
note to give him a miss.

There was a full month left until school started, and so I applied
for a job at the pear-packing sheds. The land around town was
thick with orchards, and in autumn the harvest created a glut of
temporary work. Jim gave me a lift to a cluster of sheet-metal
buildings at the edge of town. The main shed was enormous, a
clanging vault of vats and conveyor belts that trapped the late-
summer heat. Just inside the main door was the manager's
office, and I waited on a bench until I was called in to file an
application. The manager, a fortyish woman with a gray streak
at the front of her head, told me the sorting lines were full, but
that I should come each afternoon a half-hour before the swing
shift and wait.

After three days of waiting on the bench with a few other

high school girls, I was hired on as a sorter. Juana, a Mexican woman in her twenties, gave me a pair of yellow plastic gloves and an apron and took me up to the sorting belts, row after row of wide conveyors set on scaffolding above the shop floor. On either side of the belts were rows of sorters, rolling the pears over and checking them for flaws.

"You stand here," Juana said, pointing between two chutes, one yellow and one green. "This one is for juice and this one for can." She explained the various flaws, then held up a pear with a brown stippled pattern on its skin and a tiny hole near the stem. "Juice or can?" she asked.

"Probably can," I guessed.

"Right. But don't think too much," she said. "Just look quick and keep rolling."

Most of the time, Juana sat on a raised chair at the end of the belt and watched us work. When one of the high school girls began to daydream, rolling the pears absently under her gloves and dropping random pieces down the chutes, Juana grabbed a plastic bucket and headed down to the lower belts. If I bent sideways I could see her yellow bucket swinging beneath us. She followed the line until she recognized the legs of the lazy sorter, then stuck her bucket under one of the chutes, catching what tumbled down. Then she returned to the upper level, stopping on the way to chat with Marta, the forewoman from the next line over, who often passed by on the catwalks on her way to have a smoke in the parking lot. Marta dipped into the bucket, pulling out a perfect produce pear, and the two of them laughed.

Juana walked down the aisle to the girl and tapped her on the shoulder. Over the clang and whir, I could just make out her voice, explaining the sorting rules. Juana was never rude. She shamed us with her exaggerated patience, as if we were troublesome children, slow to learn.

I kept my hands moving, asked for a bathroom break only once a night, and tried to sort as if Juana were under me, checking my chutes. Still, the work was grim. I was assigned to a position facing the main door, through which I could see a row of pear trees and a rectangle of sky. When I started work at six it was a chiding blue, the color of summer evenings at home, when the heat broke and the crickets started up and the blue herons flapped up the canyon. Slowly it deepened to rose, then crimson, then black. That slat of dark made me tired. To the left of the door, I could just make out the manager through the window of the payroll office, her gray-streaked head bent over the books. I often envied her, sealed off from the racket of machinery, adding up figures on the ten-key with long, polished nails, feeding stray paper clips into a magnetic dispenser. But above her office was the worst view of all: a large clock, whose works seemed to be gummed with glue.

The belt chugged past, the pears changed in their minute features, but the shapes were the same, round bottoms, narrow stems — an endless, tumbling yellow bolt. Without the sky and the clock, one hour was indistinguishable from the next. That was the most haunting thing about work on the line: whole nights stretched out unbroken, nothing to distinguish them but the skein of thought played out while the machines shook around us. Above that racket, while our hands flew and our lips stayed still, we were all thinking — the sorters, the packers, Juana and Marta, and the gray-haired woman in the office. I imagined it sometimes as a tangle rising toward the ceiling: stories of mood and memory — some of them dull, some of them elegant, I'm sure, all of them bearing the fascinating hitches and knots of the personal. And all of them lost when the clock hands swung together at midnight and we filed out to our cars. I can no more recall a single daydream from those shifts than I could pick out one of the thousands of pears that tumbled past me. Thoughts take root in events; they get snagged in the debris of action. Work on the line was certainly action, but it was small action, repeated with little variance, until it felt like no action at all.

Two weeks into the job at the sheds, I called my father to tell him about my routine on the line, my boredom and sore feet.

"That's why they call it alienated labor," he said with a laugh. I could tell it pleased him that I shared his familiars — the shift work, the foremen, the rashes and odd pains.

"Yeah, well, I call it 'How I Learned to Hate a Pear.'"

Leslie picked up the phone. "You know, some kids work summers at the GM plant while they're in college." She said it lightly, but I could hear the pride in her voice. I thought of all their compatriots on the line, working overtime to get their kids into college, out of blue-collar jobs. Leslie and my father wanted this for me too — they never expected that I would go to work in a factory — but the line work didn't carry a stigma for them. They had chosen it. And I could tell they thought it was good for me to see how the other half lived. Or more than that: to get a glimmer of how *they* had passed the workweek, for the last seven years of their lives.

My season's wages at the pear sheds, added to the sum of my savings account — every birthday check I'd received since kindergarten, plus some stock my great-grandmother had taken out in her neighborhood bank when I was born, which when cashed out was worth one-tenth what she had invested — gave me enough to buy a lemon yellow 1976 Honda Civic. The car was six years old, and *lemon* would prove descriptive of more than the paint job, but when I first bought the thing, it purred and I was ecstatic. I still had only a learner's permit, so Jim picked me up from school in my car and let me practice on the drive home. The Civic was a stick shift, and for a month or so I would pitch and buck through the high school parking lot, trying to ease it out of first gear while my high school friends howled on the curb.

"Easy now, slow and easy," Jim said over and over, miming the action of the pedals with his hands. On those afternoons, I got the true measure of his patience. He never raised his voice or braced himself on the dash. By the end of the month I could hold the car on a steep grade without touching the brake, balancing the clutch and gas at the precise point of engagement. He had me rotate the tires, so I could change a flat in a pinch, and made me a tire-changing kit, with a piece of denim to lay out on the ground so I wouldn't soil my clothes and a length of pipe to give me extra leverage on the tire iron. He slid the pipe over one arm of the iron and bore down to tighten the nuts. "They call this a cheater. And you never know, it might come in handy for self-defense."

Jim made sure I was prepared for roadside emergencies; my mother wanted to prepare me for more momentous things. She said to me once, "When you get ready to have sex, I don't want you to end up in the back seat of some car. You and your boyfriend can come to us and tell us you're ready to make love, and we'll make sure you get some birth control and some privacy."

This offer made me feel terribly old. "Well thanks, Mom," I said. I had to be a little wry, to save my dignity. "If I get any offers, you'll be the first to know."

I couldn't wait to pass this bit of news on to my friend Michelle. "Can you imagine?" I stood before her in mock sobriety, pretending to be my lust-stricken date. "Sir, Ma'am" — a respectful pause — "your daughter and I would like to make love." I tried to imagine Jim's face should this announcement ever be made. Stupefaction. A deep flush. "I bet that man would go straight for his granddaddy's shotgun." (Years later, I discovered that I wasn't far off the mark. Jim pulled up short when my mother explained her love-at-home offer; it was too much of a stretch for a Baptist boy. My mother said it was one of the few pitched battles they ever had over how to raise me.)

At the time, I told myself that my mother wasn't serious. She was granting me a license she knew I wouldn't take; it was a symbolic invitation, her way of saying: *The flesh is good. You have my blessing.* Some years before, when I hadn't yet reached puberty and sex wasn't such a fraught subject, I had asked her what it was like. She thought for a moment, then went to the bookshelf and pulled down a battered copy of *Ulysses*, cracked the book open to the last page, and bade me read.

". . . he asked me would I yes to say yes my mountain flower and first I put my arms around him yes and drew him down to me so he could feel my breasts all perfume yes and his heart was going like mad and yes I said yes I will Yes."

That didn't much illuminate things. But looking back, in light of this literary offering, I have to think my mother's invitation was sincere. She wasn't by nature indirect. She didn't make false offers or speak in code. I think she believed that I would come to her, date at my side, to announce my interest in sexual congress. And *that* idea strikes me as heartbreakingly naive —

that she didn't see the thicket between us, behind which I had
to make my private way.

Against my mother's earnest wishes, I drove my car to a run-
down neighborhood on the edge of town, where Billy — a boy
from my high school, somehow emancipated at the ripe age of
eighteen — rented an apartment. It was swampy land, near the
river, the houses set back from the road and fronted by snarls of
weeds. There were deep puddles in Billy's driveway that never
drained, even in summer. His place, a claptrap house built out
of plasterboard and plywood, had only the barest furnishings:
an old plaid couch and a TV, a neon Hamm's sign on one wall.
Billy worked at a nearby ranch. On any given day, his fridge
might contain a half-eaten package of franks, a few vials of
cattle vaccine, and a six-pack of Oly. When I came over, he'd
offer me a beer and we'd small-talk our way into the bedroom,
taken up almost entirely by his waterbed, a king-size ocean
with vinyl sides.

There is no word that does justice to the sustained conjoining
of mouths that went on there. It was more than kissing, less
than sex. As the night wore on, shirts and jeans were peeled
off, but it seems sweet, in hindsight, that we felt constrained
by those last layers of cotton underwear. At one point, I remember him saying, "Your skin is so soft," with a kind of twangy
complaint in his voice that I found amusing. I wasn't soft; it
was only his hands — chapped from cold and salt and bridle
leather.

At some hour of my own determining it was "time to go,"
and I retrieved my outer clothing and, after some gentle plead-
ing on his part, tiptoed through the living room, past his roommate asleep on the foldout couch with a girl who had allowed
him more mature satisfactions. Out in my car, I turned the ignition and sat idling in the dark, running a finger over my
chapped lips and waiting for the frost to melt from the windshield.

nine

FOR YEARS MY FATHER had been asking me to move in with him. It was difficult to be a holiday dad. He wanted to do the kind of parenting that dailiness allowed. The issue came up every year through elementary school and junior high, and always I put him off. It wasn't easy to say no. I loved him and I could see how much he wanted this chance; I even played sometimes at sharing his wishes: I want to come, but not this year, maybe next. In my heart, the choice was always clear. I was comfortable with my mother. Things were easy between us. I had my friends, and my routine, and I feared change. By the time I was a junior in high school, the topic of swapping households had ceased to come up.

Then Leslie remembered a program from her days at L.A. High. Bright students who had fulfilled most of their college requirements could enroll early at UCLA. You spent the mornings in high school, finishing up the last units of English and P.E., and in the afternoons took a class or two at the university. Leslie seemed under the illusion, along with my high school counselor, that I was an accomplished student, but my bad habits at the high school were starting to show. One morning at a time, playing hooky down at the doughnut shop, I had made a record for myself, and the record wasn't looking too good. My grades weren't shameful. Plenty of people would have been happy with them, but the gates of the best schools weren't going to swing wide for me, and the financing would be strictly pay-as-you-go.

The best perk of the high school scholars' program was that

you didn't have to apply for undergraduate admission. You were automatically enrolled in the freshman class, and the courses you took during high school counted toward your degree. It was a recruiting program for the kind of students who might otherwise go to Stanford or Harvard. Leslie felt sure I could get in.

Flattered by her encouragement, I filled out an application. It was a small program, and it seemed to have fallen into some obscurity. All applicants who met the minimum standards were called in for an interview. (Some odd formula was applied to your SAT scores; I was lucky the equation favored verbal ability.)

When it came time to fly to L.A. for the appointment, my mother came to my room to help me pack. "How do you feel about the idea of moving?" she asked, trying to keep her voice light.

I shrugged. "I'm throwing myself at the mercy of fate. If I get in, I'll go." Easy to sound carefree: I was sure I wouldn't be accepted. I would be right there, in my same bedroom, in my same house by the river, when September rolled around, so why worry?

The interview was held in the Letters and Sciences Division in Murphy Hall. While I waited in the outer office, students came in to check class schedules and talk to the counselors. There was a friendly mood in the office. A woman came out and offered me a cup of tea, and I took it. "You can bring it back with you," she said, smiling and starting down the hall.

I thought she was the receptionist, but when I followed her into a small office filled with books and dried-out spider plants, she pulled up two chairs and shut the door. "I'm Janice. I run the high school scholars' program," she said, holding out her hand. I gave her mine, still warm from the teacup, grateful that I hadn't had time to get sweaty palms.

Janice sat back in her chair and propped a foot on one knee. "So, tell me a little about your interests," she began. She had a pleasant, open face, the face of someone who was used to being told the truth.

I didn't have the good sense to disguise myself. I told her I liked English quite a lot and Spanish less so. I didn't care much for math.

"I can see that," she said, glancing at my transcript.

I racked my brain. My interests. "I like to dance," I told her.

Janice glanced up from my grades. "As in disco?"

"No — well, yes, that too," I told her, feeling things weren't going well. "But I was thinking more of soft-shoe."

Janice's face lit up. "No kidding? I just started tap lessons last month." The foot came down off her knee and she leaned toward me. "How long have you been at it?"

"Oh, off and on since junior high. I've been in some musicals, so I get practice there."

"Can you do a time step?" she asked. "I have a problem with time steps."

"Sure," I said, suddenly flush. "Doubles, triples."

"It's that first part that throws me off."

I stood up and did a single in front of my chair. "It helps to mark the beat out loud."

Janice got up beside me, tucking the hair behind her ears. "Okay. Shuffle, hop — this is where I get stuck, on the weight change."

We went through a few time steps together, the tile floor clicking brightly under our heels. "This floor is perfect," I told her. "You could practice in here on your lunch hour."

Janice laughed a little, and then seemed to remember the purpose of our visit and returned to her chair. "So," she said, picking up my transcript. She didn't seem to be reading it, but rather musing as she stared at my uninspiring grades. "Goodness, I'm still out of breath," she said conspiratorially, putting a hand on her chest. She slipped a finger under a gold chain at her throat and slid it back and forth, then spread the transcripts out on the edge of her desk, as if they might improve with rearrangement.

"You don't have the GPA," she said, looking at me squarely. "But I think you'd be a good addition to the program. I'm going to admit you, on the condition that you bring your average up by the end of the year."

"That, wow, that would be fabulous." I stuck my hand out and she shook it. "I'm sure I could do that."

"Great," Janice said, opening the door. "I'll look forward to seeing you in the fall."

Buoyed by Janice's gamble, I cut back on trips to the doughnut shop and finished the year with the minimum grades required of me. I was moving to L.A., and though I had scarcely shown any volition for the change, once it was decided, I began to look forward to it. Most of my school friends were a year or two older and would be leaving for college in the fall. I was bored with my routine at the high school. I shrugged and let myself drift, borne along by chance.

Since I was going to spend the coming year with my father, I stayed with my mother that summer and got a job at a carpet store in town. On the weekends, I went to a small swath of lawn beside the lake and met up with Chrissy Taylor, my friend of the hour, who had recently fallen out with her sixty-year-old parents over returning home late from her junior prom. We claimed a patch of grass above the beach and the roped-off rectangle of algae-tinged water, greased ourselves with coconut oil, and lay back to discuss the few available guys who were not either former boyfriends or distant relations.

On one such weekend, we met two men who looked promising. Chrissy spotted them playing Frisbee on the lawn and managed to start up a conversation. Jack, the taller one, was a thick-featured fellow with an unfounded pride in his looks. (I later learned he had spent nearly a thousand dollars at the Barbizon Modeling School in San Francisco, learning runway turns and buying vanity shots for his "portfolio." The handlers took his cash and neglected to tell him that he had wide-set eyes and the blunt nose of a boxer and would never be paid to stand in front of the camera.) Still, Chrissy liked a show horse, as she was a bit of one herself. She was lithe, with white-blond hair, a little-girl voice, and a weakness for sloe gin. The package turned men to putty.

She and Jack quickly paired off, which left me with Clay. "We would take you out on our boat," he said, leaning back on the lawn, a smile breaking over his face, "except we don't have a boat." He had a chipped front tooth that I found oddly winning.

Later, the two of them swam out past the wading area and Chrissy and I went in after them, laughing and gasping at the cold, knowing in a wordless way that we would meet them at the buoys. It was near the end of summer. We were about to start our senior year. The ranks of eligible boys were thinning before us as we moved toward graduation. Out in the deep water, our new acquaintances reached the edge of the swimming area and sat on the ropes, and we breast-stroked toward them, pushing the world of sexual possibility before us in soft waves.

I was tired when I reached the boundary and pulled myself over one of the slick floats. Out there, fifty yards from the shore, it was easy to feel insignificant, a tiny fleck bobbing on the surface, the water a hundred feet thick below, turning darker and colder until it reached the lake floor. That lake was once a valley, and a few hundred people lived there before the county bought them out and dammed the river at one end. Underneath us, in the murky depths, were bridges and chimneys, foundations and old vineyards, the grape stocks still rooted in perfect rows. I had walked through it once, during a drought year, and though my mother assured me they'd been given sufficient warning, I couldn't shake the feeling that all the inhabitants had drowned.

Chrissy and Jack were laughing a few buoys farther down. As I watched them, Clay pushed off from the rope, took a breath and dove under, the water closing behind him. I could just make out his arms, flashing like trout, and above them a line of bubbles headed my way. He surfaced close by and shook the water from his hair. "Don't sink us," he said, floating toward me and tugging on the rope.

A ski boat zipped by, and we rose on its wake, then over smaller ribbons of chop. I thought of that line from *In the Night Kitchen*, "I'm in the milk and the milk's in me."

"What?" Clay asked.

"Nothing." I guess I had been smiling.

"What?" he said, laughing and pulling his way toward me on the rope hand over hand.

I figured this was probably better than anything that would come after, bobbing on a thin rope, over a sunken town, with the crumpled hills black and green all around. We both stared at the shoreline, the guard shack, the toddlers scooping in the shallows, pretending the view was what held us there.

Later, in the parking lot, Clay told me to stop by a bar in town, where he would be working that night. "I get off around eleven. Swing by and we'll go take a hot tub."

I loved his ease with this proposition, even though I was sixteen and had no hope of getting into a bar. It was a far cry from the high school boys who stammered and fumbled and kicked the cement planters in the quad before blurting out their invitations. I couldn't stand the terror in their voices, a terror not of me, or of the prospect of my rejecting them, but of the duty of taking initiative. There was often a note of relief in their voices when they came to the last word, as if they couldn't believe they had given voice to a request, and the answer was nearly immaterial.

Clay may have been like them at sixteen, in fact he almost surely was, but he had passed through that now into some zone of sexual comfort. I looked him over. He was handsome, in a rough sort of way, an affable country boy with a broad back and slim legs. I figured I'd never see him again.

Late that night, I drove around town with Chrissy and a few other girls, trying to find someone to buy us beer. "That guy looks good," Chrissy said, pointing to a middle-aged man in front of a supermarket. He was pacing stiffly, hands stuffed in his windbreaker.

"No way," I told her. "You are not qualified to give advice in this matter." Earlier that year she had asked an undercover cop to buy her a bottle of gin. He said "Sure," took her money, and slapped the cuffs on her. There were probably two undercover cops in the whole town, and she managed to pick one of them.

"Fine," she said, laughing her baby-doll laugh. "You choose."

I remembered my own bad eye for security guards. "I've got a better idea. Why don't you take me by that bar?"

"You're not serious."

"Sure, why not?" I figured I might as well get into trouble through the front door.

Chrissy dropped me off on a side street and I walked toward the glow of neon, my heart thumping in my chest. I peered in first through a window. It was a sports bar, pennants hanging from the ceiling, a long pine counter bristling with taps. I took a deep breath and went in.

Clay stood up from below the bar, a pair of dripping beers in each hand. "Hey!" he said, setting the bottles down. "I didn't think you'd show up." He looked different with his hair dry: it was curly and cut close to his head, almost blond. He beckoned me to the counter and wiped it down with a towel. "What can I get you?" he asked.

His boss was at the other end of the bar, talking on the telephone. I recognized him as a swim coach from the high school. I never swam on the team, so he probably couldn't peg my age, but out of caution I twirled until my back was toward him.

"Nothing for me. I'm fine," I told Clay, a rasp in my throat.

"Come on," he said. "It's on the house."

I stared at him, weighing my options. Maybe he did think I was older than I looked, but sooner or later he'd find out. I put my hands on the counter and leaned toward him. "I'm not twenty-one," I whispered. "I shouldn't even be in here."

Clay let me hang there for a minute as he glanced around the bar, his face unreadable. Beside us were two men intent on a game of dice. Farther down, the boss wrapped the phone cord over his knuckles like a boxer preparing for a fight. Clay took it all in, then bent close to my ear and replied in a stage whisper, "This is a bar and *grill*. People bring their kids in here."

Clay and I spent the rest of the summer together, and I finally discovered what had made Molly Bloom so breathless. For the most part, the two of us had nothing in common. His father was a trucker, his mother a housewife. Clay had never been south of Stockton. During the day, he worked for a tree company, trimming oaks away from power lines. On the weekends, he played basketball on a city team or talked his crazy cousin into taking his ski boat out on the lake. This was an all-day affair. They'd

pack a case of beer and while away the afternoon carving perfect rooster tails across the water.

From Clay I would learn bits of local wisdom, such as, Never
piss by the side of the road during dope-harvest time. That was
when the growers took amphetamines around the clock and
sat in the trees with shotguns, guarding their patches. He had
known a man who once stepped off a back road to take a leak
and had both his kneecaps blown off.

Jack, his friend from the lake, was sometimes in the business
of raiding other people's patches. He'd wait for a moonless
night, put on camouflage gear, and rip some hapless grower's
crop out by the roots. Clay regarded this with a certain con-
tempt — it took months of digging and watering to raise a crop
and only twenty minutes to pick it clean — but he had a grudging admiration for Jack's commando style.

"You know I only steal from assholes," Jack said in his own
defense. "Mayton and Hummer, they're both total assholes."
Besides, any day now his modeling career would take off and
he'd have cash to burn.

I didn't like Clay's friends, couldn't talk to him about books
or politics or music. But the man was unfailingly kind. And he
never played the cat-and-mouse games I'd put up with from
high school boys. Years later, when we had gone our separate
ways, he would still drop by to visit Mother and Jim now and
then, bearing a bottle of wine.

At the end of the summer I packed up my car, and Mother
drove with me down to Los Angeles. I was glad she came
along, because my clutch cable snapped in the middle of the
Central Valley, and every weirdo and meth addict cruising Interstate 5 pulled over to offer us help. That was the beginning of
a bad run for the Honda, but we made it to my father's house
late that night. My mother went to sleep in a hotel, and the next
morning she flew home.

I started school at Fairfax the following week and quickly
saw that there would be no slipping out for midmorning
doughnuts. The campus was ringed by a chainlink fence,
topped with barbed wire leaning in toward the school, in case
there was any confusion about who was being curtailed.

Guards patrolled the halls with walkie-talkies, and there was always someone manning the front door, which let onto Melrose Avenue with its garish lure of tattoo shops, clothes stores, and juice joints.

During my first week at school, I ducked into the first-floor bathroom on a break between classes and found a girl sitting in the sink, head down on her knees.

I stopped in front of her. "Are you all right?"

"Yeah," she said, not looking up. She was birdlike, dressed in black, her hair spilling over her shoulders.

"Are you sure?"

She lifted her head. Her eyes were wild and bleary, but she fixed on me and a childlike candor broke over her face. "I smoked a sherman," she said.

"A sherman?"

"You know, Mary Jane and angel dust."

I remember thinking, *At ten in the morning?* as if the only thing shocking were the hour. Early or late, this concoction wasn't treating her well. She gave me a terrified look. "I feel sick," she said. Then, in the same breath, "I better go to class." Still, she made no move to climb out of the sink.

"I don't think that's a good idea. Why don't you wait here awhile?"

We both knew this was no use. Out in the hall, the bell rang, and soon a female guard would come check the bathroom for laggards. But I didn't think she would last very long perched on her desk in the classroom.

"Look, I have to go," I told her, patting her on her back. "Try drinking some water."

Later someone would point out that it was a bad idea to try to mother someone on PCP, and it was then that I realized what a country girl I had become — friendly to strangers, dressed in pastels. I considered myself a misfit among my rural schoolmates, but over the years I had grown more like them than I'd known.

Most of the year I lived in that house with Leslie and my father is a blur. Certain days I spent when I was seven and eight are preserved more clearly than any in those months. I remember that I missed my mother, missed Clay, felt too old for high school, too young around the students in my college courses — a kind of halfling. My room was white and set at the east end of the house, so that the sun lit the side of my head in the morning, and then over the course of an hour swung around to the little southern balcony, which was too weak to stand on. Now and then I cracked the balcony door and smoked, leaning out over the black railing and the bougainvillea and lemons in the yard. I never worried that anyone would notice the butts I stubbed out in the curlicues of wrought iron. Leslie, my father — the balcony seemed too far from their attention. I suppose I was lonely. I remember crying myself to sleep one night over an infant with cancer I'd seen on the evening news — serious, theatrical weeping. At one point my arms shot into the air in a gesture of query and rebuke, a widow's gesture, fist-shaking at the heavens. I was all of seventeen.

It seems to be another girl who came home from school and ate three bowls of shredded wheat, one after another, chewing with the dutiful, bored appetite of a horse, and then turned on the radio and danced in the bathroom to work it off. When my sister recalls that year, she remembers those cereal bowls, stacked on my dresser and beside my bed, the dried plaque of milk that wouldn't scrub off.

Years later, when we talked about that time, my father was regretful: "We wanted you to come for so long, but then that year was really bad for us. I was doing the night shift at GM and working on the Rainbow Coalition during the day, and then my back went out. I was lifting this part, and I just felt something pop." A shudder went through him, as much at the memory of that immediate pain — his disk had torn — as at the months that would follow. "I needed somebody to tie my shoes, to bring me a glass of water. We were living on my disability check."

So that was the crux of it: we were depressed and had no money. From a distance, it seems simple. Back then, it felt thick as a swamp.

For months after his back injury, my father couldn't sit down. He could either lie or stand, and he couldn't stand for very long. He went to a physical therapist, who prescribed an inversion bed: a canvas cot on a fulcrum. It came with a pair of heavy plastic boots with metal hooks curling off the heels. He buckled them on, fit the hooks over a bar on the end of the cot, and leaned backward. It was adjusted for his height, so that when he laid his arms at his sides the cot hovered parallel to the floor, and when he raised them over his head the cot tipped backward to a slant and he hung by his ankles. Draped there, blood running to his head, my father said the guy who invented it was a genius. For ten minutes at a stretch, his vertebrae unstacked and the injured disk was relieved of a terrible pressure. Still, it made him nervous — all that cantilevering in the midst of pain — and he liked me to stay within shouting distance.

Not long ago, Hana, my only school friend from that time, called me up. We had lost touch in the decade intervening, and yet she remembered everything — the birthdays of every member of my family, my grandparents' names, the time I argued with a Texan in the elevator of her parents' condo over a racist remark. "My mother still remembers seeing you walk down Fairfax with your carburetor. Remember the Lemon? That thing was broken more than it ran. I guess you couldn't afford a tow."

"It couldn't have been the carburetor," I said dully.

"Whatever. Some part. She still talks about that. Or how she used to pay you to drive me to school."

I was curious to hear these stories, but Hana's clarity underscored my stupor. I thought, This is what it's like to be old. You reach back into the past and there are huge holes, as if someone had pawed through a fragile web.

Hana went on, antic with memories: how we spent our Saturday afternoons at the Farmer's Market looking for movie stars (our only luck: Dom DeLuise buying provolone with his mother) or smoked pot out of a tin can in her bathroom, blowing it out the tenth-floor window while her mother crocheted in the next room. On Friday nights, we put on frosted lipstick and short jeans skirts and waited in line for an hour in front of the Hard Rock Café, inching forward on the sidewalk in our high heels; eavesdropping on conversations forward and behind; staring in the windows at the square-jawed waiters, the platters of fries and Caesar salads, the happy tossing heads; reading too much into the glances of men passing by in their cars. On most nights, when we reached the door, we were carded and turned away.

Finally, I had to ask her: "Did I look like I was sleepwalking?"

Hana laughed this off. "Oh my god, remember that thing your father used for his back? He was in it that time and we snuck out for ice cream and when we came back twenty minutes later we could see him in the window, still hanging from his feet."

She laughed, but a wave of sorrow swept through me. I had left him there, frightened and in pain. Somehow, I missed his frailty. Or rather, his frailty had overwhelmed me.

One afternoon in the middle of that winter, I gave my father a ride to the chiropractor. It was February and I hadn't seen rain since I left my mother's house in September. Down Wilshire Boulevard the light had a thick, grainy cast. My father stared out the window, muttering to himself, deep in some private argument.

I took a corner and suddenly he came to. "Please, could you go a little slower?"

"How slow?" I coasted to a crawl. I was an incubus behind the wheel. Before we set out he had asked me to baby-sit for my sisters that weekend. He felt that I owed him at least one night a weekend; they couldn't afford to hire a sitter.

"Leslie and I are having a really hard time right now," my father said. "We need this time." When he saw that I was hardened to his woes, he went on the offensive: "You know, you haven't been doing that much around here. The kitchen is a mess; you're basically doing your own thing, going to school, going to UCLA. I think this is pretty reasonable what we're asking of you."

That conversation was still ringing in my ears as we drove. We were both stiff. That much I remember. Hurt made us brittle.

I was waiting to make a left turn, halfway into the intersection, a stream of cars coming toward us. One thing I'd learned about L.A., you could be sure the stream would continue right through the yellow, until you were stranded in the way of the cross traffic. My father's face, his stern pout, caught the corner of my eye, and then I saw a break in the cars and I gunned it across two lanes. It was an act of vehicular insolence. My father let out a hoarse yelp and braced himself on the dashboard.

"Jesus Christ!" he shouted. "I told you to slow down."

I didn't say anything.

"Lisa, I don't ask that much from you," my father said.

"Yeah, right," I hissed. I couldn't look at him.

He turned toward me then, raising up his hand, and the two of us froze, the magnitude of our positions rippling before us. He looked to me furious and amazed — amazed that we had come to this. I was filled with a mixture of terror and exaltation. He was a fearsome sight, reared up like that with blood in his eyes, but part of me willed him to step over the line. I thought if he struck me he would become irredeemable, and then guilt would lift off me like coils of wet rope, and I would float up, free, into the clear air of the wronged. It wouldn't have happened like that, of course. And as it was, my father put his hand down, suddenly weary. When I pulled up at the curb he stepped out gingerly, walking as if the sidewalk were made of paper; one false step and he'd punch through.

We didn't speak to each other for weeks after that — weeks of passing each other in doorways, hunching over our plates at dinner. Then one of us broke, and we put ourselves into a state of rough repair and went on.

When my father and I quarreled, I saw two choices before me: fury or sadness. It always paid to take the second path. I used to tell myself there was something honorable in this — to say, in the middle of the fray, you hurt me. But somewhere along the way, I got stuck in that pose. Fury was his turf. He would rage until the veins stood up in his neck, and I would cry and slam the door to my room. I wept then until I lost track of what had set me weeping.

Once in a while, when we were on better terms, my father heard my sobs and made a tentative knock on the door. "Come in," I said. That knock held the chance of solace. I can still see the way my father leaned into my room, his head tipped forward in inquiry, one hand on the door frame as if for balance. He held back for a moment, the way you do on the lip of an icy stream, postponing the change in temperature, and in that moment I could see the fatigue in his face, the puffiness, the signs of pain and immobility. Still, he was always heartsick at my sorrow, and so he waded in, lowering himself beside my bed, his bad knee clicking. "What's wrong?" he asked, smoothing my hair.

It seemed then that I couldn't begin to explain. I was awkward and had the wrong clothes and no money and blotchy skin. Adolescent sorrows cut deep, but their telling sounds plaintive and thin. I tried to begin — and quickly stopped. I could see my father's eyes glaze over. His head was brimming with worries, and mine made him overwhelmed, because he couldn't imagine how to fix them. I knew he felt he had failed me.

"I'm sorry, honey," he said. "I know it's a hard time. I'd sit with you but I've got to talk to Leslie. We haven't seen each other for a couple of days, and I promised to meet her at ten."

Leslie and I had our own troubles that year. The admiration I had felt for her when I was a schoolgirl had slowly given way to envy in my teens. And Leslie's private nature, which I had broken through with my childish enthusiasms, was a bad match for a teenager's sulkiness and inward moods. I had also had the chance to observe her up close with my sisters — the way her love for them was of a different order.

Not long after I moved in, Leslie and I were at the beach watching my sisters dabble in the sand, and I said that I couldn't wait to have children, that I was overtaken sometimes with cravings for them, even though I knew the time for having them was still a long way off. She looked surprised. "I didn't have any real maternal instincts until Mia was born," she told me in a wondering tone. Wondering, because now she is the fiercest of mothers — always thinking of her daughters, making allowances for their moods, watching the slow evolution of their characters with careful attention. I sat in my beach chair trying to keep a smooth face. I was seventeen, old enough to pass for an adult, but lacking an adult's perspective. I didn't hear her confidence as a fellow woman. I heard it as the rejected child, and I sat there doing the math in my head: all the years that had passed — from our meeting in Mexico until my first sister was born — without her seeing how I needed her. Of course Leslie had made all sorts of thoughtful interventions in my life, but what pained me was her confession that they didn't come from motherly feeling. I jumped up from my beach chair, leaving her staring, and waded off into the surf.

Living at close range only fueled my jealousy, and that feeling took root in a predictable way: Leslie and I fought over her closet, or rather over its contents. I was not to go in there, not to look through her things, but when she was out I went toward it with a kind of fatal headlong attentiveness. The pleasure of these expeditions was partly sensual: I was a sucker for fabric, texture, color, and found it there in the rows of silk shirts, the stacks of sweaters, bunches of belts hanging from hooks. I remember a wide swath of brown leather that crumpled in the hand like cashmere and hooked with a brass latch, gold belts, tailored black belts with silver buckles, belts of woven rope.

Then there were the shoes: a whole wall of them, slipped into hanging shoe racks. Sandals, brogans, boots. Five species of black pumps, each with a different heel or toe. In a generous mood, Leslie would explain their various virtues. These were retro, perfect with a vintage suit. Those were stiletto dancing heels. These had a square heel and could go from office to dinner.

I kept track of additions to her wardrobe with a caustic eye. Even at times when my father claimed we were flat broke, that he had no money to buy me clothes, new boxes appeared in her bedroom. I dug around for the receipts, helpless to stop myself, and howled when I saw the totals. Didn't he know how much she spent? He didn't, of course. Not because she hid it from him but because he was too absorbed in other things, and because she took care of so much — the bills, my sisters' doctor appointments, all the loose threads of family life — that he probably wouldn't have begrudged her these things.

Once I brought a particularly large purchase to his attention, and for a moment he went for the bait: "Really? Are you sure it was that much?" Then he saw where this would lead him and beat a hasty retreat. "Listen, this is between Leslie and me. You shouldn't be going into her stuff."

And of course he was right. It troubles me now to see how little I thought of her privacy. The pain I felt at not having the right things, not wearing the fashion of the hour, was acute, but I doubt that it justified my trespassing. What seems a shame, in retrospect, was that Leslie and I were never able to speak about any of this. But perhaps there was more to our difficulties than my inarticulateness and her native reserve. Perhaps we couldn't speak because the struggle was, as my father might have said, "structural." I envied her for stealing my father away, and she envied me for having come first, as no child should, and because he kept a special place for me — the lost child who stayed lost because it was her only trump.

All this to explain how I pilfered her scarves and sweaters. She would search my drawers to find the missing items, and I had the gall to be furious at *her* for finding me out in such a way. So instead of conversation, we had this passing of clothing down the hall, and muffled outrage on both sides.

One Saturday, I was sorting through old newspapers in the living room, looking for a topic for my class on current events. Leslie saved the papers in order to clip articles of political import, but the task kept looming before her, and the papers piled up in the entryway, by the fire, under the breakfast table. Just glancing at them made me feel defeated, as if it were *my* task and their rising bulk were a chide against lost time. The papers kept coming, and there was no time to sort out the gossip from the relevant news. Every now and then I dug up the oldest issues and spirited them out to the trash. Or I would ask Leslie, when we were cleaning the house for company, if I could throw them out, and she would sigh and say yes, glad once in a while to clear the decks.

That afternoon, deep in the *Los Angeles Times* stack, I uncovered a pamphlet that caught my eye. On the front was a round-faced man with hollow eyes — El Salvadoran, the caption said.

He had been kidnapped and locked in a trunk for two years. I opened the pamphlet. Inside were more stories, stories so gruesome they made me have doubts. But of course such things happened. People did unspeakable things to one another, and how horrible to tell of it and not be believed. I was suddenly baffled in the hazy sunlight. My life seemed trivial, weightless as air.

I put the flier down and lay on the rug, no sound outside but the wind and the rubber tree, tapping the window. Then a scrap of song came into my head, a Leadbelly tune my father used to sing. "Let the midnight special/shine her light on me." It was a prison song, written when the bluesman was doing time for murder. I had never quite heard how mournful it was, since the melody was so rough and strong. When I was a girl and my father sang it, I always imagined the same scene: a view from a barred window, looking out on a set of tracks and the verge of a dark wood. When he got to the chorus, an engine came slowly round the bend, carving light over the trees.

"What does it mean?" I remember asking my father once. I must have been eight.

"What does what mean?"

"The song."

Most times, my father loved to talk, loved to lean back into the past and call up details: his apartment overlooking Harvard Square, where he threw open his windows and played his stereo loud; the way he and I once laughed so hard in front of the La Brea Tar Pits, over some riff that has since sunk into the muck of memory, that we both fell down on the pavement, shocking the passersby. But his time in prison was a blot. Whatever had happened to him there, it still had the power to chill.

"It's about hope, I guess," he said at last. "Hoping that the train would come and carry you away." I watched a shudder pass through him.

That memory made me sick with regret, as much for the time he had lost behind bars as for the tenderness we had lost between us. Back then, at eight, I could still go to him and put my arms around his neck, as if it were weight he needed, weight to hold him here.

ten

I ARRIVED AT UCLA in the midst of a Greek-system revival; sorority and fraternity membership was up in 1984, after a big decline in the seventies, and the Young Republicans' table on Bruin Walk attracted a constant eddy of men in Top-Siders and polo shirts. There was a small protest movement on campus, an island of counterculture amid the sea of lettered sweatshirts. In a quad near the center of campus, some students had set up an encampment to protest apartheid — a cluster of tents and teepees called "Tent City." I knew of people who lived there for an entire school year, showering at the gym, reading on the lawn under the overarching trees, and blocking the doors to the conference rooms when the U.C. regents met at the campus. Until the regents agreed to divest the university of its South African stocks, the protesters vowed to remain perched in the middle of the lawn that fronted the administration building, bringing a bit of the shantytowns home.

I walked past Tent City nearly every day and never stopped to talk to the people who lived there. If someone had asked me what I thought of their cause, I would have said that I thought they were right, and that I wished them well. But I was attached to my creature comforts and more worried about my grade point average than the school's investment portfolio. Though I wouldn't have admitted this then, I think I skirted that cluster of tents because the whole thing seemed depressingly small-time. If I had caught a whiff of victory, I would have been quick to join the cause.

As it was, an eerie somnolence hung over the campus. The more I looked around at the ranks of groomed and tanned students, the more I wanted to do something wild. But then, my wildness was purely a matter of style. I moved from stone-washed stretch jeans and torn *Flashdance* T-shirts to long skirts and ethnic jewelry, which slowly gave way to tie-dye and Birkenstocks and worn batik dresses with bells on the hems.

It was just as well I favored thrift-store clothes. My money was tight, a cobbled-together mix of family help and financial aid. Two weeks into the fall quarter, I took a job with the university catering company, run out of the cafeteria in my dorm. The good news: it paid $5.50 an hour, a handsome wage in my estimation, and the events were held in conference rooms across campus; I would be saved from wearing a hair net in front of my fellow students. The bad news: female servers were required to wear black frocks with aprons and frilled collars, outfits that seemed to have been bought off a studio back lot, the leftover costumes from a chorus of maids. After I did some abject begging, Ron, the manager, agreed to let me wear the men's version — black slacks, a tuxedo shirt, and bow tie — but he insisted I finish this with a scalloped apron, so the patrons, immersed in cocktail chatter, knew whether "sir" or "miss" would best hail an hors d'oeuvre.

Perhaps because I wore pants and wasn't afraid to jockey the vans around in the cramped parking lot, Ron gave me a shift that looked grim at first to a late sleeper. I was to report at 5:30, three mornings a week, for coffee service at some far-flung site.

"The Norton Simon Conference Center. Where's that?" I asked him.

"Malibu," Ron said. He was a circumspect man, wiry and small, with pocked skin and scuffed shoes worn off at an angle. He seemed to love food service. More than once I would marvel at the way he swung around a corner with a heavy tray balanced on each palm or slipped together the blade and housing of a giant meat slicer — swift and mindful and efficient. "Simon donated a spare mansion to the university," he said, handing me a penciled map. "It's down PCH."

The next morning I rose in the dark and took the elevator

down to the empty cafeteria. Ron had already laid out the pastries — waxy Danishes spiraled on a tin tray — the percolators, and wheel-sized filters filled with ground coffee. I loaded it all into the back of the truck and rolled down the metal door, then pulled out onto Sunset Boulevard with the map in my teeth.

It was only then that I recognized my good fortune. The sun was crowning above the Bel-Air hills, and I was half amazed to be awake at dawn, in a shirt and tie no less, silverware rattling brightly behind me, the steering wheel shimmying in my hands as I took the turns. I had been a licensed driver for three years, but I was still at times startled to find myself behind the wheel — as if someone should have caught my bluff. I followed the road until the hills opened up and then forked onto San Vicente — a wide boulevard split by a ribbon of grass and coral trees — and down a steep incline to Pacific Coast Highway, threading along the sea.

That rattling truck was my passage to freedom. I had left my roommate sleeping in her bed, shrugged off my worry over a looming Spanish exam and reams of back-reading, the whole insular life of the campus. Driving along the hem of the continent, I recovered my perspective — the papers, the grades, someday none of it would matter — and that bulky van, which threatened to drop some essential part at high speed, comforted me with its swaying, a reminder of our old mail-truck days.

I cut across traffic and into the driveway of the conference center, a narrow slot in a long stucco wall. Inside was a Mediterranean-style villa, with wings and porticoes and nooks of tended greenery. I found the conference area, laid out the pastries in a tiled alcove, set the coffee to brew, and made sure plenty of cups and napkins were on hand. Then I took my book and went down a pathway to the beach. The sand was bright white, only a short spill to the sea. Here and there a few Adirondack chairs sat empty. I longed to sit out there, facing the water, but my uniform gave me pause. I might have been taken for a renegade housekeeper, and surely the locals already groused about uppity help. Instead, I banked up a chair out of sand near the house and unhooked my bow tie. I was reading the letters of Zelda Fitzgerald — I can't remember why — and while the coffee brewed and women in tracksuits walked their poodles by the shore, I skimmed through her manic prose.

I worked that shift three times a week, and once in a while, after checking the coffee level in the urns, I would wander through the main house, two stories and thousands of square feet of disinhabited space. Mr. Simon had left behind a marvel of minimalism: stucco walls lit by the sea, wood floors and paper lanterns, here and there a Japanese tansu chest, a polished sideboard without a visible hinge, a pair of couches upholstered in wheat and cream. There were no pens in the drawers, no photographs or mementos on the shelves. It was all gorgeous and impersonal, and I walked the rooms pretending they were mine, imagining the flowers I would place just there, over the mantelpiece, the teacups and books that would collect on the low tables. I lived then in a dorm room the size of Norton Simon's pantry, and I had been lucky to get it, but dreaming like that left me bitter and dry. I drove home grumpy, my shirt stale with sweat, and spent the last hour of my shift sorting silverware and rinsing coffee dregs from the urns.

But, oh, how I loved my little pantry of a room when the alarm clock rang at five in the morning. Leaving my bed was like being evicted from a womb. One morning, blurry eyed and hungry, I backed the van up to the loading dock so hard I cracked one of the taillights. When the coffeepots were wedged in and the cans of creamer counted, I slipped a cheese Danish from the tray and headed back for the silverware. I was just finishing the last bite of pastry when I wheeled around a corner, nearly colliding with Ron. There was glaze at the corners of my mouth and crumbs in the pleats of my tuxedo shirt.

Ron's face furrowed like a pug's. "What are you thinking, huh? Those are precounted." He hurried back to the kitchen, took another Danish out of the box, and carried it out to the truck on a scrap of wax paper. He reminded me of a surgeon — the same white coat and brisk gestures, the pastry limp and pale as a severed ear.

When the Danish was rightfully positioned on the tray, he

turned to face me. "When the order calls for one hundred, we send out one hundred. Never ninety-nine." His eyes burned. "This is an easy job, but it takes self-control."

I saw my mansion dissolving before me, the cost of a lousy Danish. But when I was demoted to afternoon luncheons on campus, I was surprised to find it was the van that I missed. Those drives down PCH, surveying the sea from the vantage of its high seat. The needled dials on the dash panel, the black caulking on the windows, the hollow ring of my shoe in the foot well. It was all deeply familiar, and yet I gained some novel satisfaction from being the one behind the wheel.

In the fall of my freshman year, I got a letter from my mother. She had never been much of a correspondent, so the sight of her upright cursive gave me cheer. "Maybe you should sit down before reading this," it began. That opening, and my penchant for calamity, left me wholly unprepared for her news.

"Your mother is going to have a baby! Arriving in June. We already know it's a boy — to be named James Branscomb the Fourth. Big Jim, as we'll now have to call him, is deliciously happy."

I was surprised at first. My mother was thirty-nine. My sister, her second child, was then six. But the more I thought about it, the more it seemed like a fine idea. A brother. That would be novel. I got out my *Norton Anthology of Poetry* and copied out a passage from Wordsworth — "Our birth is but a sleep and a forgetting" — and mailed it to my unborn brother, who already had a name worthy of a shipping magnate.

My mother called me a few days later. "So, do you think I'm crazy?" she asked.

"Not at all," I told her. Easy for me to say, from four hundred miles off. I would be more maiden aunt than sister, showing up for holidays and doing rare diaper duty.

"Well, thanks for the card," my mother said. "Big Jim thought it was for him at first, and it made his face light up."

That spring, when I went home for Easter break, I flew to San Francisco and took a shuttle bus north from the airport. Leaning at the window as we wound up Highway 101, I saw those coastal mountains as if for the first time. The slopes were a vivid rain-fed green, set off by the darker green of the oaks. Farther north, the road hugged the river, which strained through gravel bars and rocky narrows, the ridges on either side thick with pines. We'd come around a curve and the bus window would frame a swatch of river, hill, and sky that had the suffused palette of an old oil painting. I had driven that road a hundred times, with my father, my mother, on the Greyhound buses. I knew every bridge and winery and roadside curio shop. But it took two years of living amid strip malls to see the quiet lushness that had been spread out before me all my life.

When I arrived home, my mother was in her sixth month, wearing elasticized pants and eating Rolaids by the handful. Other than that, she didn't seem much changed. She tugged on a cardigan and spent the mornings raking the flower beds, pausing now and then to flex her back.

On the Sunday before I left, she and I made Easter eggs, popping the ends of a dozen shells with an opened paper clip and blowing the insides into a bowl. Now that I lived near enough to my father for monthly dinners, I had Easter again with my mother: the paper-light eggs we wrapped with fern fronds, the baskets of fresh grass — all those specifics whose loss had caused me consternation at eight years old.

My mother filled a few bowls with water and tore open the packets of dye. While she stirred, I studied the fullness in her face, the way her belly kept her pushed back from the table. The first time I'd seen her pregnant, I was twelve and hadn't taken much notice. Now I could half imagine myself in her state. I wanted to ask if she ever felt like she was trapped on a runaway train. Instead, I voiced it a blander way: "What about labor, are you nervous about it?" Labor being the terminus that lent that speeding train its threat.

My mother picked an egg out of the carton and shook her head: "It's not that bad. You can either clench up and say, *I don't like this, I don't like the way this feels*" — she whispered the phrases through her teeth — "or you can just concentrate on making the whole thing open. It's not magic, you know, it's a muscle."

I must have looked unconvinced. I was fairly sure I'd be one of those clenching types.

"I remember there was this woman in the labor room when I was in with your sister. Boy was that a scene. She was howling. The whole family gathered round like a Greek chorus." I could hear my mother's impatience with this spectacle. "It gets hard to listen to." She must have seen how I blanched. "Maybe you should come watch the birth," she said, one eyebrow raised.

"I don't know," I told her. "I think I'd be too nervous."

"Well, if you want to be there, you're welcome," she said, bending the wire dipping tool and scrolling the eggs in their baths.

The next morning my mother dropped me off at the municipal airport, where I waited for the shuttle bus. Tiny planes droned in and landed. Two men left the main office and stared over the airstrip as they each fingered in a lipful of chew.

"Take a look at the goddamn hippie," one of them muttered as he passed out to the parking lot. His truck, vaulted like a toy above its oversize wheels, had a bumper sticker on the back window: If You Don't Like Hank Williams Jr., You Can Eat Shit.

I flashed them the peace sign, but after they drove off, I looked myself over with a stranger's eye. I was wearing a long Indian print dress with black work boots. My extra clothes were jammed into a stuff sack, and draped over one shoulder was my mother's old army bag, to which I had affixed an enamel pin of Chairman Mao. I don't know when I had become a caricature of a Woodstock refugee. It had happened gradually. I picked up one item and then another when it caught my eye — the turquoise jewelry, the thermal underwear, the ankh — and when I wasn't out in the sticks, I thought I looked pretty good.

Not long after that visit, my mother had a vivid dream about Franny London, her leather-working friend from the woods near Santa Cruz, whom she hadn't seen much since our mail-truck days. In the dream, Franny had an undiscovered tumor, and my mother woke in a cold sweat, full of fear for her friend. This was an odd thing coming from my mother, who didn't toss salt or knock wood or put much faith in omens. But the dream struck her as a warning, and she wrote Franny a card and made an effort to track down her whereabouts. After a while, the dream's urgency faded and the letter was tucked in a drawer.

I found the envelope in a box of old mementos a few years ago and was stopped short by its hopeful address: "Please deliver to Franny London, who used to sell Light Force Spirulina in Santa Cruz." My mother had faith that a reasonable request, plainly phrased, would be honored out of some basic rightness in the universe. She imagined that note passed on by one helpful soul and another, until it reached the hands of her missing friend.

But inside the card were darker thoughts: "Are you out there, Franny? I just had an intensely vivid dream about you. I hope you are in real life 100% well." Somewhere along the way, my mother had begun to worry about bad outcomes. At the bottom of the letter, she added a postscript that made me smile. "You wouldn't believe it," my mother wrote. "Lisa is nineteen and a sixties hippie lady come back to life."

Back at UCLA, still outfitted in my retro garb, I once passed a man in fatigues in the narrow breezeway behind Pauley Pavilion.

"Chairman Mao," he said, giving me a piercing look. He had a grizzled beard and chapped skin, and for a moment I thought he was unhinged. Then I remembered the pin on my bag.

"Oh, yeah," I said, glancing down at the red and gold button. "A relic of my youth."

The man looked surprised — I could see him trying to calculate my age — and then a memory clouded his face. "I haven't seen one of those in a long time," he said.

Some tone in his voice made me wince — familiarity, laced with bitterness and regret. Wearing Mao's bust on an army bag suddenly seemed like a stunning presumption. I wore that pin because it conjured the spill of fuchsia in the back yard of our Berkeley house, afternoons nibbling cinnamon toast at Edy's Ice Cream or lying in the window seat while my father pelted his conga drums. I had plucked Mao from a drawer in my father's house out of nostalgia and as a nose-thumbing at the right-wing squares on campus. But I could see from this man's pained glance that it meant more than that. When he turned the corner, I unhooked the pin and tucked it into my bag.

My friends and I almost never talked of social issues — a funny thing, considering that I spent a good deal of my life in a household in which politics was the primary subject. I mentioned this once to my friend Wendy, whom I'd met the first day in the dorms, and she shrugged: "There's nothing to say."

I pressed on, but gently: "It seems odd, though. We aren't bloodless people."

"Well, it's just totally depressing," she said, lifting her hand and then letting it drop. "I read about this Iran-Contra thing, I can barely understand all the doublespeak. And soon it will all be swept under the rug." She was sitting forward now, an edge in her voice.

We went on, in a rambling way, because once you pulled a thread, whole swatches of history unraveled — and suddenly we came to a conclusion that exhausted us both: it would take a global effort to clean up the mess. Still, as my friend spoke, I felt a flush of gratitude toward her, for her lucidity and her weariness. She confirmed something I suspected: we didn't know where to start.

Some might say that the hubris of youth is to believe in one's own absolute power, and that growing up is about the waning of grandiose dreams and an increase in concrete abilities. I seem to have missed that early phase. I never imagined I could affect the national scene. What I felt, at nineteen — I am embarrassed to admit — was discouraged. Our president was a senile ex-actor, we were up to our ears in debt, and I was convinced that before long I would be snuffed out by a stray ICBM.

I thought more than I should have about those missiles. Who could dream up a better recipe for dread? They stood ready in their silos. There was no blood, no battle. No one was dying, and maybe no one would — or maybe all of us would die at once.

Leslie was working with a group on nuclear disarmament at the time, and since I had latched on to this specific terror and lost sleep over it, I went with her to occasional meetings and spent a weekend canvassing for SANE/FREEZE in Brentwood. This was thought to be friendly territory: white liberals, movie-industry people with bushels of money who'd be a soft touch for donations.

I walked with my clipboard and literature, and rang the first doorbell.

"Hi, I'm with SANE/FREEZE. Are you in favor of cutting defense spending?"

"No, and I'm on the phone right now."

"Hi, I'm with SANE/FREEZE. Are you worried about nuclear proliferation?"

"What?"

"Hi, I'm going door to door to gather support for a freeze on nuclear weapons."

"Not here, you're not. I'm ready to blow the Russkies to kingdom come."

Every now and then I'd find a person willing to haggle over the issues (on which I was embarrassingly ill informed); here and there I'd get a signature; and at two or three houses that weekend, a pacifist forked over a check for fifteen dollars. I began to read the houses from the outside. A bird feeder was a good sign. No point knocking at a house with a bald eagle on the mailbox. Wood shingle seemed to be better than clapboard. But after one weekend, I gave up. I never had much heart for fighting the tide. Instead I went to the library and found a map that showed the few likely safe regions in the country — places far from hard targets and out of the range of prevailing winds — and plotted when I might move there.

Much as I felt out of sync with the mood at my new school, I was in love with the campus and amazed by the small privileges of student life. At the edge of Bruin Walk was a women's gymnasium, a brick building with a small yellowed locker room where you flashed your I.D. and a woman doled out clean towels from behind a wire cage. The locker room gave onto a small brick courtyard that housed a vintage lap pool. Outside the walls, students streamed by with their books, but the pool was sheltered, a throwback to the days when a woman might like to take a dip in privacy. Nearby was the new rec center, named for John Wooden, whose famous pyramid of success was engraved on a plaque near the door: an ascending pile of abstract virtues that apparently brought home the NCAA pennant ten years running: faith, patience, honesty, poise. The talk might have rung old-fashioned, but the building was not: a pile of glass and steel with racquetball courts, a two-story gymnastics arena, and aerobics offered on the half-hour. The house the boom years built.

I began to take yoga twice a week in one of the lofty second-floor studios. The class was taught by a long-legged Englishman named Christopher Reed. He didn't look like my idea of a yogi — thin and stringy and lithe. In fact, he resembled a doughy Alexander Gudonov. Christopher was a proud man, with a low melodic voice, and he didn't go in for mumbo jumbo. He never once mentioned his third eye or asked us to imagine we were floating on a puffy white cloud. Instead he described the poses in a precise and plain fashion, walking around the room to straighten an elbow here, turn a foot out there. After an hour, the sap of worry over school leached out of me, and by the end of the class, when we were in Corpse pose — splayed out on our backs — I was limp from toe to jowl. It was then that I thought of my father, flipped heels over head in the department store, not giving a fuck-all what anybody thought, because he was human and it felt good to twist this way and that. And how I hid in the clothes rack, ready to disown him. It seemed that I always measured his life as it bore on me.

I was grappling in those days with ideas of separateness and cohesion. Sometimes it seemed that the things that drove my life — my desire to be a good student, daughter, friend; to distinguish myself in the world; to take comfort in clubs and schools and academic allegiances — were made of smoke. We were big-brained animals, smart enough to want life to have purpose and form, so we made up ways to pass our days here — hoops to jump through, invisible rules. I could mind them and be convinced I had distinguished myself among men, or I could tear my clothes and rave in the street: in the end it didn't seem to matter. I was a speck in the vastness, in the risings and migrations and extinctions, a bottle on the waves. I loved that thought. It made me feel free.

I spent a lot of time, at twenty-one, peering into the unbridgeable gaps between people, looking at what got lost, even between those bent on communion, rather than what got through. I think I hated to be alone, but hated worse the idea that no one could comfort me. Better to mask a need than ask for solace and have it go unmet. Clarity was a sham, a false god. If no one really understood the movings of another heart, then why bother trying to be lucid?

These days, I pay more attention to what strains through, despite the limits. What we can say, one to another, even if we can't say everything. But even back then, secretly, I longed to be wrong. And when I first came across some writings about Taoism, it was the calm refutation of our separateness that washed over me like a tonic. I thought I had been sharp-eyed to have noted man's solitary fate, but now I was convinced this view was a delusion, a false stopping place. We weren't linked by some flimsy web of social relations, but we weren't distinct either. We were joined on the essential struts of linked matter.

Of course, the Buddhist doctrine of nonattachment seemed to appeal most to those who didn't have much, or who suffered more than they were glad, so that giving up the cycles of happiness and sorrow was in fact a winning proposition. I suppose it said something about me in those days that I kindled to the words of Thich Nhat Hanh and Shunryu Suzuki. I owned a few clothes, a futon, some boards and cement bricks, and I often felt quite gloomy. Buddhist practice seemed to offer relief.

After my mother's invitation over Easter to witness my brother's delivery, she and I didn't speak about the subject for a while. I got swept into final exams and the topic was forgotten. But when the quarter drew to a close and I thought about my visit home, I turned again to the idea. I would arrive a week before her due date. If I was there for the event, why not see it firsthand? Maybe she was right; maybe it would dispel some of my morbid fears.

My brother's due date came and went, and my mother's doctor finally agreed to induce labor. It certainly made things orderly. We got up early, dropped my little sister off with a family friend, and drove to the hospital. After my mother's waters were broken, Jim and I kept her company while she walked the halls, trying to get things going. The birthing room was done up to look homey, with chintz wallpaper and a window looking out on a bank of grass and shrubs. Jim stayed at my mother's side, stroking her hand and changing the tape in the tape deck. They were listening to the Brandenburg Concertos, which is cheering stuff, but maybe somebody forgot how long the business was. There was no other tape. As the day wore on and the opening concerto began for the sixth or seventh time, I retreated to a deserted waiting room to read back issues of *Good Housekeeping* and pick at my face in the bathroom mirror. Around nine in the evening Jim burst in the door.

"It's happening!" he said, breathless and already sprinting back down the hall. "This is it!"

I was given a gown and a mask and ushered into the room. The bottom half of the bed had pulled away, and the doctor was there, guiding things along.

True to her word, my mother didn't howl. Her face torqued with each contraction, but between them she was composed.

"Okay, push, Ann," the doctor said, radiating calm. He was from the Philippines and had a silky, coaxing voice. "Lisa, do you want to come closer?" he asked when the contraction had passed, motioning to a space behind his back.

A front-row seat. I felt cold and wobbly in the head, but I moved to the spot. Another contraction came; my mother threw herself into pushing, then stopped when the doctor ordered, and our eyes met. Uncomfortable as I was, I tried for a game grin beneath my mask.

"Oh, good," my mother said, beaming at me. "You're smiling."

Then another contraction, and she flushed and turned inward.

"Boy, that's a big one!" Jim said, looking at the monitor.

"I *know* it's a big one," my mother hissed through her teeth. It was the only brusque word she uttered through the whole thing.

"That's good, Ann," the doctor said, his voice rising. "Here's the head."

And then he was there, my brother, little pulpy man, his face furrowed with puzzlement. The doctor cut the cord and laid him on my mother's chest. Jim leaned over his son, grinning from ear to ear. I had never seen the man so blissed in all my life. "Well, neat-o-rooties," he kept saying, over and over, peering at his tiny namesake. "Man alive!"

My mother slumped back on her pillows in ruddy contentment, smiling at everyone.

"How do you feel?" I asked her.

"Oh, I feel great," she said. "How about you?"

"I'm fine," I said, and I nearly was by then.

My brother was given a warm bath in the room, and I put in a call to the family friend, who brought my sister by. Mother had bought her a new Cabbage Patch doll, meant to quell envy, but my sister didn't seem to have any. "Oh," she said, in a mild voice, when the doll was presented. "Thank you." Then she sat cross-legged on the floor while Jim brought the baby down to eye level, and gave her brother a placid, welcoming smile.

"You know what I'd really love right now?" my mother said, looking down on the scene.

"What?" I asked her. I couldn't imagine.

She closed her eyes and tipped her head back. "A roast-beef sandwich with onions."

As soon as I got back to school, I made a beeline for the medical bookstore. It took me a while to locate a text on obstetrics, and the language was a bit technical, but it offered clear descriptions of the various methods of anesthesia. The pelvic block had a few disadvantages: it could be used only late in the game, by which time I might be beyond repair, and it required a needle as long as a drinking straw. I paged right past the section on I.V. narcotics. I had sampled Demerol at eight when I shattered my elbow in a fall from the monkey bars, and knew I wanted nothing more to do with it. It left me woozy and cotton mouthed and made me confuse my mother with a boy from my third-grade class. I finally settled on an epidural, which carried a small risk of paralysis, but which had made certain women report that they barely knew they had a lower half. I was slightly calmer once I had my anesthetic selected, a good decade or more in advance of the event. My mother's bravery and grit had impressed me, but I didn't think they were qualities that I shared.

My investigations into sex and its outcomes weren't purely by proxy. In the final quarter of my freshman year, I started dating Bob, a residence assistant, a liaison in direct violation of the dormitory bylaws. For a number of months it seemed we were both happy. We pretended to study together (he was enrolled in a master's program), met for trays of casserole in the cafeteria, ran into each other in the elevators and kissed from floor to floor. As an R.A., he had a room to himself, with a sleeping loft and an enormous paper collage covering one wall, which an old girlfriend had made. I spent a lot of time staring at that collage. If you squinted, a jester emerged from the layered triangles and squares, balanced, arms akimbo, on top of a harlequin ball.

"She got too caught up in surfaces," Bob told me once, when he saw me staring. I wasn't quite sure what he meant by this, but there were other hints that his ex-girlfriend was slightly pitiful, and that finally he'd been forced to give her up. I always imagined this woman hunched amid a confetti of colored paper, trimming doggedly and pining for Bob. In time, I'd come to think of her as a kindred spirit.

In the meantime, Bob and I took long drives out to Malibu in his 280Z, listening to Al Jareau and letting the city haze unravel behind us. I had rarely been off campus since I left the catering job, and Bob became my escort to the wider world. I was particularly grateful for this one night, when a prankster pulled the fire alarm at 3 A.M. This happened quite often, and each time we had to wait out on the curb, sometimes for an hour, while the fire department checked each floor for the phantom blaze. But that night Bob and I slipped off to his car, rolled out the back end of the parking lot with the headlights off, and drove down to Ships café, where we sat for hours, still in our pajamas, drinking coffee and crisping English muffins in the tableside toasters.

It all came to an end one afternoon when we were lounging around on the couch in Bob's dorm room, talking of nothing in particular. Suddenly he jumped up and announced that he had to go running. He seemed nervous, and paced around the little room, stretching his quads. "I've got to get a regimen going," he said.

"Well, I guess I'll see you later then," I said, confused by this rush to fitness. He had never mentioned running before.

Bob left in a brand-new running suit, and I don't think we spoke for more than five minutes after that. He began a series of elaborate evasions, acting as if there were nothing worth discussing about the fact that we had gone from lovers to strangers in the span of an uneventful half-hour. Of course, it hadn't happened like that. It must have been brewing for some time. Certainly I had been oblivious to the signs and no doubt had played my part, but the question was, In precisely what manner had I made him disappear?

Hoping for an answer, I knocked on his door one night, when I was too drunk to be ashamed. The long hallway was buffed to a shine. I stared down its length, swaying slightly, waiting for the man in the cheerful I.D. photo taped to the door to appear in the flesh. "Hi, I'm Bob," said a little dialogue bubble rising from his mouth. The hallway smelled of laundry soap and stale beer, and from an open door somewhere issued the hoarse strains of Sade. "Smooth operator," she crooned. "You're a smooth operator." I thought I heard voices murmuring from behind the door, and the peephole darkened, but Bob never answered my knock.

Once I was away from Bob and had time to think, I realized that I knew almost nothing about him. Time has not improved my perspective. I would like to say *Bob was looking for—* But there the sentence ends. I was blindly in love with him, and I hadn't the faintest idea what he wanted from life or why he was living in a dormitory at twenty-three, supervising a floor of late adolescents.

After Bob made his exit, I began to sleep sixteen hours a day, pulling myself up like some sluggish swamp creature just in time to make it to class. At one point I called my mother to tell her the sad tale.

"Well, my goodness," she said. "This must be the first time in your life anyone's ever rejected you." It wasn't true, but she meant it as a compliment.

"Is that how you see me?" I asked her.

"Well, you just seemed from the start to be whole unto yourself. Everything you ever really went for, you got. Even your father — you had power over him. You were the first person he changed his life for."

I was quiet, taking this in.

"What you need to do now is expand your options," my mother said. "Check out the bulletin boards around campus. Take a dance class. Join the spelunkers' club."

What could I say? The last thing I wanted was to go tramping around in a cave with a bunch of headlamped troglodytes. I already felt like I was underground. I didn't hazard this, though. I said sure, I'd make an effort, and mumbled my way off the phone.

My mother would have liked to give me strength. And in odd ways she did. On the path from the dorms to the campus I had to pass a hedge of *Daphne odera*, a shrub with clusters of citrusy flowers that grew around my mother's house. I wanted nothing more than to go back to sleep, but I plucked a sprig and held it to my nose, and that scent was restorative; it led me down the path. As I walked, an old Latin hymn she used to sing drifted into my head. *Dona nobis pacem.* A simple phrase, carried on a changing rivulet of melody. I sang it over and over until I reached the doors of the classroom, unaware of what the Latin meant: grant us peace.

I barely remember studying that quarter. When my midterms arrived with As and Bs, it seemed to be the work of some other girl. In the mornings, after rising from my narrow bed, I would slide the window open and sit with my feet out on the ledge, staring at the banked greenery of the rec center and the shimmering blue rectangle of the pool. From down on the pool deck, the residence hall loomed above the trees like an enormous waffle iron, its windows framed with concrete squares. When I had been in better spirits and spent my afternoons down there sunning on the grass, I used to count up and over from the edge of the building to find my particular box, and I remember thinking of the oddity of this arrangement, the way we were housed like rabbits in a hutch, pacing within feet of each other, walled up with our private worries and wishes. Walking down the hall to the communal shower with my towel cinched modestly around me, I was aware that I lived in a hive of other girls, but once I returned to my room and shut the door, the world dropped away around me. The walls jutting out from the window frames seemed designed to prevent us from catching sight of one another, or perhaps they were meant to prevent drunken rabblers from dropping bottles on each other's heads. Either way, when I sat at the window, feeling virtuous for getting myself a little sunshine and air (it wasn't spelunking, but it was a start), I could see only my allotted square of the view. There might have been another girl, one window over, leaning out beside me with a similar expression, but I would never have known she was there.

When my depression didn't let up, I made my way to the psychology clinic on campus, where I was assigned to a young man named Charlie, who would meet with me once a week for three months as part of his clinical training. I didn't ask to be assigned to a man. There was some question as to whether I would be assigned to anyone at all — I wasn't an emergency case — and then this chance came up. But in hindsight it seems lucky that I went each week into a tiny room with two chairs and a desk and a box of tissues and spoke to that dewy-faced man. He restored my faith in the gender. I thought I was there to tell him the story of Bob and my broken heart, and I did talk of this now and then, but I was surprised — though surely Charlie was not — to find that I filled the bulk of those hours with stories of my father. It was as if I had lost him all over again. Out came stories of his long-ago disappearance, which was preserved in my toddler's mind with the same abruptness, the same lack of explanation. Charlie listened carefully, while pulling on his mustache, a delicate boyish fringe. I had the impression that he was afraid to say much, for fear of misstepping, but his face was the most marvelous tonic — full of curiosity and compassion — and little by little, sitting across from him, I recovered my spirits.

I remember only one thing that Charlie said in those months, and he said it hesitantly, with a brief glance at the tape deck whose reels spun silently on the desk, recording our sessions for his adviser's review.

"You know, I'm feeling angry at your father, listening to your story," he said, placing a hand on his chest as if to make clear the prejudice of this emotion. His admission shook me like a thunderclap. I had talked over those early years plenty of times, and they summoned in me a variety of feelings, but anger wasn't one of them, at least not one I could admit to myself then.

At the end of that session, I bumped into my father on campus. He had been given a fellowship by the Institute of Industrial Relations, and was taking a three-month sabbatical from the line to do research for a book on the labor movement. I left the air-conditioned lobby of the clinic, saw him walking up the path, and my first response was delight. That familiar face, that reliable enveloping hug. He asked how I was doing. There, in the face of the actual man, I couldn't bring myself to speak of resentments. I shrugged and looked down at my feet. I was wearing red Converse high-tops, borrowed from a friend, and a shirt patterned with red paisleys. I realized it had been months since I'd worn anything vivid, or taken care, for that matter, with what I wore. I felt as I were resurfacing from a dream, and in that first flush, my gripes didn't seem worth mentioning.

"I'm doing fine," I told my father, smiling.

"You look good," he said. "I mean you always look good, but you look happy." He seemed honestly glad of this — his face buoyed up — as if knowing I was content lightened something in him. I was grateful I'd held my tongue. We walked together into the campus, talking about my sisters, his relief at being granted time to think and write, until we came to a fork in the path.

"Hey, Converse," my father said, catching sight of my shoes. "You know how I love those."

It seemed that only a few weeks later the quarter was over and I was out on the curb, my clothes stuffed into plastic garbage bags, waiting for my father to pick me up for the summer. I could barely stomach the giddy atmosphere. The walkway was lined with piles of monogrammed luggage. Someone's dad, a man in a pink polo shirt, snapped photos and glad-handed the residence staff. Everyone around me seemed to look on the summer as a respite. They whooped and cheered, waving from car windows as they pulled away. I sat on my trash bags, indulging in bitter thoughts. They would return to neatly manicured homes in the suburbs, where their mothers kept the counters wiped and served fruit plates in the afternoons. They would take jobs lifeguarding at the local swim club, and drink beer in the evenings with their high school friends.

I seemed to be the only one who wanted to remain in the warrenlike coziness of the dormitory. I had found there the first breath of independence, the merest whisper of what it would be like to shape my life. I knew no one from my year at Fairfax High; Hana had since moved to Boston. And, truth told, I dreaded the return to my father's house, where the tensions of the previous year still hung in the air. My father and I had been jousting for so long, we didn't seem to know any other way. We were like exhausted boxers who refuse to call the fight. When the bell rang, we both came out of our corners.

That summer, in the mornings, before I reported to my evening shift at a furniture-rental store, I drove to UCLA and wandered around the campus. Perhaps I wanted to reassure myself that the scholarly life was not an illusion, and that I might still belong there. I slipped into Powell Library and read newspapers in the domed rotunda. Above me, the walls were set with Moorish tiles; below me, the stone floors polished by countless feet. I put down my paper and walked through the stacks, pulling out titles at random. I didn't read much, but I liked knowing it was all there: yellowed maps of Namibia, the complete works of Flaubert.

It was on one of these nostalgia visits that I ran into Mike, whom I had met in a history class during spring semester. He was attractive, in a generic, hulky kind of way. He wore Bermuda shorts and thongs and seemed glad to see me, which caught me off guard. Amid the ranks of sun-kissed sorority girls, I was certainly no prize. When Mike invited me to a party at his fraternity that weekend, I agreed to go.

That Friday, at eight, I changed in the bathroom at Easy Rents and locked up the store. I had spent hours that morning fretting over my outfit, and it is a measure of my self-consciousness that I can still remember exactly what I wore: a long straight skirt with a black hieroglyphic print, a mango-colored tank top, and silver earrings. I drove down Wilshire Boulevard, parked outside the fraternity house, and had a momentary crisis of confidence. I imagined myself braving a solo entrance only to find Mike tucked in some corner, nuzzling with his early pick of the evening. The vision nearly made me turn over the engine and head home, but in the end the relative desert of my social life forced me out. I picked my way up a yellowed stairway flanked with men and headed straight for the keg.

I was in line, plastic cup in hand, when I spotted my old boyfriend Bob. He hadn't caught sight of me yet, and for a moment I considered tossing my cup in a corner and fleeing the scene, but instead I froze. Just then he turned and called my name, walking over with a smile. I don't know what attracted him — perhaps the novelty of my presence at a frat house whose members were known for their thick necks and bad motives.

"Hey, what have you been up to?" he asked, moving as if to give me a hug, then settling for an awkward open-armed gesture. He seemed drunk.

"Not much. Working." I was embarrassed to mention my job. "How about you?"

"I'm getting my real estate license. Doing an internship at Coldwell Banker." He bent his head forward and gave me a sly smile.

"What happened to the master's program?" I asked, stalling for time. I was trying to figure out how I could cut him off — a small blow for the misery he'd caused me — when I felt a warm hand on my shoulder. It was Mike, looking surprisingly sober among his sodden brethren. He barely even glanced at Bob, who underwent a sudden adjustment of scale. I had never noticed how insubstantial he was.

"I'm so glad you made it," Mike said. "Can I get you a beer?" Bob saw the lay of the land and mumbled a quick goodbye.

"Old friend?" Mike asked, after Bob had disappeared into the crowd.

"Barely know him," I said. It struck me then that this was the truth.

"We've got a few of those oldsters hanging around," Mike said as he filled my cup. "College is over and they keep coming back for the free beer."

Mike's payment for my rescue was made in the usual coin of the realm. We rode his motorcycle to his apartment in Benedict Canyon — he was an upperclassman, and moneyed; the fraternity was purely a social affiliation — and had dull, drunken sex. In the morning, he gave me a lift to my car and saw me off with a flannel-mouthed kiss.

Monday through Friday at the furniture-rental store, I overlapped for an hour with Laurie, the woman who worked the day shift. Laurie was blond, heavyset, with a Bo-Peep face and a slightly wounded air. She sat behind the teak desk, and I took a seat in the customers' chair, and gradually we got to know one other. Looking back, it seems to me that she took on the role of confessor or shrink, with the desk between us as bulwark. A practicing Buddhist, Laurie occasionally coaxed me into chanting with her when business was slow, and when I came in one day looking gloomy, she managed to tease out my worry: I was late for my period, and feared that my evening with Mike was the cause.

When a week had passed with no results, I found a free clinic in the yellow pages and drove out to Santa Monica for a pregnancy test. I sat in the waiting room with women eight months along, with teenage girls thumbing through fashion magazines, beside a pale young woman who clutched at her boyfriend's hand. If only my mother could have seen me then: not much wiser, for all her frankness, than the girls whose mothers told them babies came from storks.

The test was simple. I filled out some forms, turned in a urine sample, then waited to be called into the examining room. "It's positive," the nurse practitioner told me, in that marvelously flat voice health care workers use to deliver ambiguous news. "Have you decided what you want to do?"

I shook my head.

"Well, if you decide you want to terminate the pregnancy, you need to make an appointment for a follow-up exam."

Terminate, exam: I pushed away the words the way you kick off a heavy blanket on a stifling night. "Thanks, I'll think about it." I grabbed my purse, paid the receptionist, and hurried out to the parking lot.

Once in the car, with my seat belt fastened and the keys in the ignition, I realized I had nowhere to go. There wasn't a soul I wanted to tell — not my dad or Leslie, not my mother, not any of my distant college friends, certainly not the father, whose last name, to my embarrassment, I suddenly couldn't remember. I started the car and merged into the traffic on the Santa Monica Freeway.

I was only blocks from the Pacific, at the tab end of an interstate that unfurled all the way to Jacksonville, Florida, and for a moment I considered taking that road, past the downtown high-rises that jagged up from the freeway like a deadly EKG, past the palm flats of San Bernardino, into the desert, through Phoenix, Tucson, El Paso . . .

Just the thought of that drive made me weep. All those lonely towns and truck-stop motels. I would never make it. I wasn't the running type. Besides, my trouble was my own, and it would come with me. Instead, I knew that I would get off at La Brea Avenue and drive to my father's house and go through my sister's room to my cubicle against the wall, trying to put on a cheerful face. Eva was only four, but she had a radar for sorrow, and thinking of her made me pull myself together. I found a tissue in the glove box and wiped my eyes and nose, and then out the side window I caught sight of a motorcycle cop, keeping a steady pace beside me. I had no idea how long he'd been there. He didn't turn on his siren, but looked my way and tipped his helmet toward the shoulder.

I pulled over and watched in the rear-view mirror as he strolled toward me. I must have been speeding. Or perhaps my registration had expired. I felt a flicker of panic at the sight of his tooled belt and holster. When he came alongside my open window, he bent over and flipped up his windscreen.

"Miss, are you all right?"

I stared at him, baffled.

"You know, at times like this, it's best to pull over and take a breather."

Nothing fans my self-pity like the kindness of strangers. I leaned into my hands and sobbed.

"You wait here till you feel better," the policeman said, putting a gloved hand on my window frame. "Then be careful pulling out into traffic."

All that week I went to work as usual, and when I wasn't sleeping or helping a customer, I chanted with Laurie. I didn't call the clinic. I didn't even keep track of how many days had passed. I told myself I would never go back to that place.

If you had asked me to define my character in those days, I would have said I was distractible, lazy, prone to fads of the spirit. But with fear at my back, I began to chant with an unwavering discipline. I chanted in my car, driving down Wilshire Boulevard to the showroom. I chanted in my bed at night, soundlessly, so I wouldn't keep my sister awake. Keeping my mind clear was like trying to balance on a wet log. I slipped off and found myself listening to the traffic outside or trying to remember if I'd put gas in the car. Then I'd steady myself for the task and begin again.

In my mind, I traced an image of my reproductive tract, half remembered from my high school biology text, a narrow stag's head with curving antlers. Somewhere in there was an egg, and now I hoped it would go the way of countless other eggs with bad beginnings. I hoped that it wouldn't catch hold. But how to

find a way to fix on something that was no more than a complicated infolding of my own flesh? I wanted to find a way to exert
my will that bore the commencing life no ill feeling. I had set
this thing in motion, and now I wanted it to stop. But it seemed
callow — even dangerous — to make it alien or wish it harm.
The chanting, those nonsense syllables, offered a way to focus
my thoughts, a path of sound on which to make this moral
stepping, and as I went on I began to feel a kind of unfamiliar
hope — hope that I had the power to change the course of
things. After all, wasn't faith the agent by which people lifted
cars, walked for days in the snow, or turned to someone who
had wrecked them in some often revisited hour and said, "You
are forgiven"? I walked around in the summer heat feeling
alive to every shift and mutter in my blood.

When I came to work one Monday, Laurie had brought me a
present, a small cardboard shrine with a scroll mounted inside.
"It's already been blessed," she said, her eyes shining with
reverence. That shrine must have been the starter model: a
stippled brown box with an open front. It looked like the package for a blender or a baseball mitt. But the scroll mounted
inside caught my eye. At the top and bottom were strips of
Japanese paper — delicate leaf patterns highlighted with foil —
and the columns of brush strokes were lovely, if inscrutable.

"These characters represent all the possible states of human
existence," Laurie said, running her pink nail down one column.

"Really?" I couldn't quite stomach her solemn tone, and it
must have shown in my face.

Laurie gave me a level stare. "Things are going to get better
for you," she said.

Despite my flippancy, I took the shrine home and mounted it
on the back of the bookcase that walled off my bed. I didn't
believe it was the strongbox of my soul, but I had a tiny super-
stitious fear of throwing it out.

When I told Laurie that I'd hung the shrine in my room, she
asked if she could meet my father: "I'd like explain to him a
little about this stuff, so he won't think you're associating with
a nut."

"I don't think he cares one way or another," I told her, but Laurie insisted it was for the best. She came by on a Sunday evening and settled herself on the couch while I went to get my father from his study. He was at his desk, a welter of books and papers around him.

I rapped on the door frame. "Dad? There's someone here who'd like to meet you. The woman I work with."

He paused in his train of thought. "Sure, honey. I'll be right out."

Laurie stood up when he came into the room.

"Dad, this is Laurie. We work together at Easy Rents."

She offered her hand.

"Nice to meet you," my father said, looking vaguely confused by the formal mood.

Laurie sat down. She had both hands in her lap, and she was fidgeting. I'd never seen her like this. "I wanted to talk to you because Lisa has been getting interested in this group I'm involved with — I'm sure you probably saw the shrine she brought home — and I just wanted to let you know a little about it."

My father smiled. "Well, you're welcome to tell me about it," he said, "but whatever Lisa wants to do is okay with me." He looked amused by Laurie's earnest appeal to his authority.

"I don't know if you're familiar with Buddhism," Laurie ventured. She had rehearsed her spiel and wouldn't be stopped. When she was finished, she smiled expectantly, ready to answer questions.

"Well, like I said, I have complete faith in Lisa's judgment," my father said.

"Because a lot of families feel nervous — you know, with the chanting."

"It's not a problem with this family." He and I exchanged a small smile. "We've seen it all."

All that week the sun was scorching. The lawns looked like cut paper, heat shimmered up from the avenues, and I had to put a towel over the black vinyl seat of my car. I felt slightly sick — from the weather or the flu, I couldn't tell. One night, when the midday heat didn't lift, I slept on the couch in the living room, where a faint breeze came in through the western windows. After lying awake for hours, chanting softly under my breath, I slipped into a dream with an odd awareness of the change, as you might slip sideways though the curtain of a waterfall, surprised to find you can breathe on the other side. I was asleep, but I knew I was dreaming, and the knowledge filled me with a sudden exultancy: if this was a dream, I could do anything. Quickly, eager to do something impossible, I vaulted up toward the living-room ceiling. Once there, I felt a little sheepish, but it was pleasant to be weightless, and so I dipped out of an open window, out over the chain of headlights pulling down Olympic Boulevard, and floated west toward the sea. From my vantage point in the air, I could make out each street corner, exactly as it looked when I drove past it in daylight: there was that scrap of pink chiffon snagged in the fence at La Cienega and Wilshire; over there the store on Pico where checks could be cashed with a purchase of meat. I was floating above the Los Angeles basin, a great bowl of steel and light, and yet at that same moment I knew I was asleep in sweat-dampened pajamas, on the second floor of our tile-roofed apartment, under the boat-shaped leaves of a rubber tree. That doubleness was like another dimension; the world widened out on all sides. I skimmed out toward Pacific Palisades, executing rolls and barrel turns, and all the while I could hear the faucet drip in the kitchen at home, the refrigerator click on and whir. Up ahead was the ocean, and I moved out over it, unafraid. When I reached Catalina Island, I circled the lighted dome of the casino, flew over bison sleeping upright on the hills. Coming back, skimming low over the waves, I saw that the water wasn't dark, as it looked from the shore. It was illuminated by the city lights, miles of extra wattage spilling over the sea, a broad gold band that broke to pieces on the chop.

I woke the next morning to an unmistakable cramping. In an odd way, I was grateful for the pain, for the corrective it seemed to apply. I had been granted a reprieve — I wouldn't have to go back to the clinic, wouldn't have to pay the consequences of my bad judgment — but I felt that I should suffer for my carelessness. I went into the kitchen to make tea, and my father came in.

"Are you all right?" he asked. "You look pale."

"I'm fine," I told him, lightheaded to say the words and believe them. "Everything's fine."

I drove to the showroom and sat down across from Laurie in the cushioned customers' chair. I didn't have to say anything. The relief was all over my face. Laurie beamed. "I knew it would work," she said.

I could see she was happy, but the certainty in her face made me stiffen. "That what would work?"

She faltered for a moment. "The chanting."

My friend was convinced those syllables did the trick, the magic syllables and the box and the scroll. I wanted to believe it was my own doing. But even that wouldn't hold up under scrutiny. Nothing could be proved by a sample of one. It might well have been luck. It might have been chance.

"We don't know that for sure, do we?"

"No, of course not," Laurie said, glancing down at her nails. She deferred out of politeness, out of gentleness, but I could see in her tipped-down face that she still believed.

eleven

I WENT BACK to school in the fall with three thousand dollars in the bank, a feeling of pleasant self-containment, and the vow not to fritter any more of my time away with men. Then, midway through the school year, I fell in love. I didn't know then it would be more than a passing fling.

I got to know Mauricio through an American-history section. I sat up front, monopolizing the classroom discussion and mooning over the T.A., a sharp-featured young graduate student with an infectious passion for his subject. On our first day in class, Mark asked us to write our names, majors, and any other salient facts on a three-by-five card. Then he went around the classroom asking what we'd like to be called, and marking down any unusual nicknames or pronunciations. Somehow, despite his dedication, he got the idea that Mauricio wanted to be called Bruce, and Mau (pronounced like my old familiar, Chairman Mao) never disabused him of the error.

I never took note of Bruce's presence — he sat in the back and rarely spoke — but he took note of mine. He claims he found me insufferable, my endless comments, my transparent crush on the teacher, but that couldn't have been the whole story; he can still remember certain outfits I wore to class.

We were in his dorm room when this slipped out. I had been led there by Wendy, who knew Mau from the campus coffee shop. It was late on a Friday night, and I was bored. Mau didn't make much of an impression. He was listening to Jethro Tull, and some high school friend of his was there, sniffing amyl nitrate from a tiny amber jar, then flopping backward on the bed. He kept offering it to Mau, who kept declining, which seemed prudent.

Then Mau told me that we shared a class.

"Really? I don't remember seeing you." This was odd. There were only thirty students in the section.

As proof, he slipped into an imitation of our T.A. at the blackboard. "So, what are the basic tenets of federalism? Class? Anyone do the reading? Lisa?"

"It's my fault I do the reading?"

"No, of course not," Mau said. "Just as long as you admit you're motivated by lust."

I fessed up. "All right, so I have a crush on him, a Jewish guy with a mustache and nice muscles. And he gives those inspired lectures on the Bill of Rights."

Mau, I soon learned, was Jewish, too. A Jew from Mexico, no less, with freckles and blue eyes. He had left Mexico City at twelve and spent his adolescence in Orange County, trying to transform himself into a surf rat.

I sensed a fellow misfit. "That must have been a bizarre transition."

"Yeah. I never wanted to invite anyone over for dinner. I thought our house was too ethnic. My mom served chilies with everything."

Later, I would discover that we shared other connections — divorced parents, step- and half siblings to spare — and nearly shared a birthday. It seems Mau and I were born one day apart, in 1966, our mothers — one in Newark, one in Mexico City — overlapping in labor for a brief time.

Mau owned a truck, and for our first date we drove east, under a lid of singed air, to a library and botanical preserve in Pasadena. We had known each other two weeks, and this was our first official date: to go look at exotic plants.

We paid our entrance fee and walked a little through the landscape of succulents and cacti. Mau was absorbed in the plants, in studying them. He had a lack of self-regard and a wonderment at outward things that reminded me of my mother.

"I can never remember the difference between euphorbs and

cacti," he said, squatting down in front of one of the beds. He often began his sentences with a qualification, a doubt. "In one, the spines are considered leaves — hardened leaves coming off the trunk — and in the other, the spines are really modified stems and the leaves are so tiny you can't see them."

We moved from the desert to the flowers and manicured herbs of an English garden and sat on a bench. It was scorching there against the Pasadena hills. My mouth felt mothy and dry, and I asked Mau if he minded waiting for a few minutes in the shade. We had been walking very slowly, almost drifting along the path, but even this began to feel like too much progress. He put his hand on my knee — a steadying gesture — and for a moment I couldn't remember who he was. Friend? Brother? It was akin to that moment of waking in a strange room when you turn and turn, trying to latch on to some clue to your whereabouts, so that you can couple up to the world again and go on. Whoever he was, he had good manners. His eyebrows came down a little, and he cocked his head to the side: "I think I see a water fountain up ahead. Why don't we walk a little?"

What I liked about Mau, early on, was his rationality and calm. And that he was humble and doubted himself. Much of this would cause us trouble later. One day I would throw a shoe at him to try to raise his ire, and at times his shyness became a trial. At parties, he'd often go missing without a word, and one night I found him in a closet, sipping a beer on a pile of dirty clothes, happier there than in company. But just then he seemed to be my perfect complement. Gentle, with an oddball humor, attentive and self-contained.

We strolled on into Japan: through groves of bamboo and over orderly rivers. Inside a high wall we found a rock garden, a bed of blue-gray stones combed into undulating waves, which a plaque told us was meant to inspire tranquillity. A handful of visitors milled about, staring at the rocks with expectant expressions, then grew restless and passed out through a door on the far wall. Mau squatted down beside the rock waves and, after studying them for a moment, reached his hand over the barrier.

"Can't you read? The sign says no touching!" The voice was

high-pitched, but the body that delivered it, which was advancing upon us, was enormous — a pear-shaped man in a security uniform.

Mau stood up, apologetic but calm. The rocks seemed to have worked their effect on him. "There was a break in the pattern," he said. "I was going to smooth it out."

I went directly into my unctuous mode, my ass-kissing authority mode, which I hated in myself and was helpless to resist. "Sorry about that," I said, trying to arrange my face like that of a reasonable person. "He didn't mean to disturb."

I walked with the guard toward the exit to show him we meant no further harm, and Mau trailed behind, looking backward at the rocks as if at some unfinished business.

"This must be a tough job," I said to the guard, going into overkill. Then it struck me: it probably was tough. The boredom, the low pay, the daily enforcement of rules that you didn't devise and that people chafed at and blamed you for. This kind of thought came to me from my father. He often asked people about their jobs: supermarket checkers, car-wash boys. And the stories they told him were always slightly unexpected, a glimpse of work from the inside. At the end of the day, if the register didn't balance, you were docked for the difference, or, look at this, the wheel glaze made your hands break out in a rash.

"Well, it's the best work I can get," the security guard said. "I've got some abnormalities." He made a sweeping motion over his gut, and I thought I caught a glimpse of webbing between his fingers. In my heat-struck state, the guard was beginning to look like a cartoon — that enormous waist and tiny head — with a cartoon's putty-colored flesh. Mau pulled alongside us at the mention of abnormalities and began examining the man with interest.

"My mother, she had three arms," the guard told us, glancing back toward the rock garden to see if anyone was within earshot. "I was a rough sort, and she'd wash the dishes with two hands and slap me with the extra."

We stood before him, rapt.

"She didn't even have to turn around," the guard went on,

warming to his subject. "It came off her back, sort of." He gestured toward his shoulder blades.

I tried to think of something to say. "Well, we're sorry if we caused any trouble."

At the reference to the rocks, the guard seemed to remember his duties. His chest swelled and his head reared back: "The sign was right there, plain as day: don't touch the rocks. But he had to stick his paw in." He kept a wary eye on Mau as we walked away.

Later, we left the gardens, and Mau bought a pineapple at the supermarket — it seemed just the thing — and sliced it on his tailgate with a bowie knife. I felt as if I had known him for ages. Years later, it was the guard we would remember when we recalled that day, his webby hands, his haunches tapering to tiny feet. A vast man, deerlike and sad, stationed at the doorway to the Garden of Tranquillity.

Every month or so during the school year, I got together with my father for dinner. He would drive out to Westwood and we'd meet at Mario's, a small Italian restaurant with empty Chianti bottles strung from the ceiling and candles in red glass orbs. A meal at Mario's was always reliably middling: salad in checkered wooden bowls, pasta with meat sauce. The waiters served with bored efficiency and then left us alone.

My father loved that place. He loved all good things that stayed the same. When he moved to a new neighborhood, he would find a dry cleaner he liked — one who did decent work and settled without a fuss when a shirt got ruined — and an honest mechanic, and then repay them with unflagging loyalty. For twenty years he had been ready to upend the status quo, but in his private life he preferred ritual and regularity.

One Sunday night, I walked down the hill from my apartment and met him at the restaurant door. My father gave me a hug and paid his perennial compliment: "How do you stay so thin?" Once upon a time, I would have given him a few ill-informed dietary pointers. Now I just shrugged and pulled away.

The maitre d' remembered my father's face, if not his name, and gave us a quiet booth. My father sank into the vinyl and sighed: "God, honey. I'm so tired."

We were all of ten minutes together and already peevishness had settled over me like an old coat. He was just a man, trying to make his way like anybody else, but I took his exhaustion personally. I suppose I wanted to see him on an even keel, wanted him to model a life of moderation and balance. Even then I knew it wasn't fair: you have children, and suddenly your life is no longer for itself.

"What have you been up to?" I asked him.

"Well, I'm almost finished with the book, and there's still a lot going on with the campaign. We're still in the middle of a very important struggle . . ." He trailed off.

The campaign had been his lifework for the past few years: a fight to keep GM Van Nuys open, the last auto plant in California. I had followed the main turns in the battle and had gone to a few rallies, but it was typical that I couldn't say now what events he spoke of that day or why they were important. I had my ear tuned to only one thing: his boasting, which filled me with scorn. "I'm playing a very pivotal role in this fight," he was saying. "And it's a fight that is going to have national significance." I didn't let him get away with much. If he crowed over a triumph, I heard only the crowing and missed the chance to savor what he'd won. I was prideful to a fault, but tried to assume a public modesty. What I didn't see: that his boasts covered the pains of questioning and self-doubt.

I spent those dinners in bitter quiet, withholding my full attention to signal displeasure, but never daring to flush the topic into the open. My father wasn't insensible to this. He saw my cinched-up face and talked past it, afraid to face things head-on. I may sound harsh in the recounting, but I suffered from my own pose. I was ashamed to love him. Once I saw his faults, it seemed foolish. I held him at a distance in order to ex-amine him, but then I couldn't examine him. It was like looking at the sun. He stumbled ahead, raw, full of expectations, trying to check his desires. "Is it all right if we talk about my work for a while?" he'd ask, and I'd feel sheepish that he needed permis-sion. Then he'd talk too long, a breathless detouring monologue that wore out my patience.

"You know I ran into a friend from college the other day — god, has it been twenty years? He was pretty progressive back then, had pretty good politics, but now he's totally dropped out. Just trying to make money. I mean, we made so many real gains in the sixties — in civil rights, putting some kind of check on the worst excesses of imperialism — but there's so much to be done, it's really frightening."

(Indeed it must have been grim to watch all his old comrades defecting. I noticed, around then, a grudging admiration when I told people of his generation — my professors, my friends' parents — what my father did: "He's still an activist. A labor organizer." When they heard this, I watched them go through some kind of momentary reckoning.)

While my father went on talking, I watched a piece of carbon cycle in the hot candle wax. It occurred to me that he and I were like magnets turned to the wrong ends — drawn together, and when we came closer, driven apart.

"So what do you think?" he asked.

"About what?"

"About what I was telling you."

This was a crucial moment, one we'd come to a hundred times. He'd said his piece and now he wanted me to "engage." As it was, I couldn't even offer a few comments to appease him, the kind of exchange I would have granted to a stranger. While he talked, my mind had wandered, and now I hadn't a clue what he had said.

When my father saw that nothing was coming, he changed his tack. "God, there was something I was going to ask you," he said. He cocked his head to the side, chasing a stray thought. "Oh, yeah." He put his hands on the table. "How are you?"

We stared at each other for a beat, then burst out laughing.

Only when it was time to go did I truly soften toward him. My father and I said goodbye on the sidewalk, and I watched him walk away. At the end of the block he paused, hands stuffed in his pockets, unsure as to where he had parked. That confusion, so familiar, struck me like a blow. I thought, Someday he'll be dead. It was half dread, half furious wish. I stood there in the middle of the streams of passersby, trying to imagine it, gingerly, the way you'd thumb the edge of a bruise. I wanted to know what I would lose. All I could come up with were a few simple things: some songs my father had taught me; the way he laughed with his whole body, convulsed.

I didn't often indulge in fears of his dying. It was my mother I lost over and over, the way as a child I used to throw my favorite ring down in the grass for the strange pleasure of seeing it lost among the blades. My father seemed immune to death. He was rarely sick and came from a line of Methuselahs, his grandmother still alive then at ninety-three, still alive now at one hundred four. He insisted he would live to be ninety, and I believed him. But guilt made me see the mortal man, the one I loved more than I could show. I started to run down the street to tell him this, but then the crowd converged around him and he was gone.

I had bad luck in the enrollment lottery the next quarter and had to stand in line for hours to try to pick up an extra class. The line snaked through Ackerman Ballroom, a vast hall where hundreds of students napped or read or slumped against the walls, waiting to hear their numbers called so they could scan the lists of open courses. What was left was usually the dregs: the history of Mesopotamia; a seminar on *Beowulf*; Advanced Logic. The only class I could find that day was a philosophy course on the mind/body question.

I was a little breathless on the first day, as the professor sketched out the topic. Are the mind and body separate? Is there such a thing as a soul? Those questions made me feel muddled and ill-used, yet filled me with a quickening faith in myself. I think I even harbored some hope of contributing to the great philosophical debate on the subject, but I cloaked this hope in the garb of self-exploration. I marked off a section of my three-ring binder. There, in those pages, I would make an inquiry into the state of my being, and in the bargain I'd try to land an A in Philosophy 107.

To aid in this important work, I sometimes got stoned with my friend Alex before class. Alex was my roommate. Her father was the Rodney Dangerfield of Hong Kong. He started out as a dishwasher in China and now made ten movies a year and lived in a villa in Kowloon. Her mother was English and a dead

ringer for Nanny in *Nanny and the Professor.* Alex looked like a
very beautiful boy, with spiky hair and slim hips. She wore
motorcycle boots and a Hello Kitty backpack and rode a skate-
board across campus. At Christmas break she went home via
the south of France and Phuket. The world seemed very small
to her and, hence, dull. Pot seemed to ease her ennui.

Our class met in a Moorish-style building in South Campus
— traditionally science territory, where I rarely set foot. Alex
and I met in the courtyard and sat in one of the sandstone
arches passing a pipe back and forth. She was meticulous with
her equipment: a metal pipe with a cleaning tool that she used
religiously between bowls, and a small box of wooden matches,
to which she had affixed a strip of grip tape as a striking surface. When the deed was done, we went in and took seats at the
top of the steeply raked auditorium. I never thought it strange
that we were to learn the intricacies of one of life's great questions at a ratio of two hundred students to one teacher; nor did
it occur to me that I was failing my end of the bargain by
arriving stoned. I was just grateful not to have to make eye
contact with the professor, and to be able to slip out unobtru-
sively if the lecture got dull.

Professor Howe was fat and stooped, with a monk's fringe of
white hair. He paced back and forth across the dais, one hand
tucked at the small of his back, the other holding a tiny microphone, designed to clip to a lapel, which he pressed to his lips,
so his sibilants rasped over the PA system.

I expected, when I signed up for the class, that we would be
taught some basic ground rules for philosophical writing, and
then be asked to expound on the mind/body question. My first
assumption was quickly disproved: Professor Howe cared not
a whit what we thought about the matter. Surely the man knew
well what kind of work would be turned in — late, of course —
if he opened the door to our native philosophical charms: un-
supported theories laid out in butchered prose, pages and
pages of meandering without the spoor of an original idea. I
was sitting up in the nosebleed section, a little toasted, a little
exhilarated at the chance to let my mind run, when Professor
Howe whipped out the syllabus and cut me off at the knees. We
would spend the entire ten weeks studying Descartes's *Medita-*

tions. It was a very subtle and complicated piece of work, Professor Howe explained. He had spent his whole life studying its proofs, but in ten weeks, if we paid meticulous attention, we might trace our pens over the great man's argument and perhaps get it straight.

Late in the quarter, when I had resigned myself to the structure of the class, I watched Professor Howe go through a fit of inspiration. His lecture style was generally dull and droll, but one day he came into class with a sheaf of papers in his hand and his hair worked up into a silver laurel around his ears.

"I have come across something interesting. It is probably nothing, but I think —" He fumbled through his notes, leaned over the lectern, and lowered his voice to a whisper. "I think I may have discovered a flaw in Descartes's argument."

Professor Howe launched into the details of his discovery, but he never once looked up into the seats. He was lost within himself, the microphone held so closely he was practically chewing on it, and he might as well have put the thing down, as he had all but forgotten his audience. It was a private performance. He was running his idea through a system of checks, and we were the silent witnesses, present but unnecessary. There was a faint ripple of interest in the class. A few people folded their newspapers and sat up straighter, watching Professor Howe pace and gesticulate below. Anyone could see from the man's restless energy that something grave was at stake. I had the feeling that I was privy to a great event, the significance of which was lost on me. I craned to get a look at the teaching assistants, who sat in the front row. They were all at full alert; some of them were taking frantic notes.

From what I understood, his discovery was deceptively simple. Descartes, it seemed, had committed a fallacy of substitution. That is, he had "proved" an idea in one context, and then — considering it a firm block that could hold the weight of further suppositions — he had shifted it slightly, so it was used in a different way on the next go. "Descartes has pulled a feat of legerdemain," Professor Howe muttered. "A very clever one, mind you, hard to pin down, but nonetheless a fallacy . . . It's right here."

I found it hard to believe that in the 340 years since Descartes had penned his theory, no one had noticed this error. But Professor Howe was obviously well versed in the debates held in learned circles, and he was quite lathered up over his breakthrough.

At last, he wore himself out. "Well, maybe it's something or maybe it will come to nothing at all," he said, looking at his feet. After a moment of silence, he glanced up into the seats, and seemed surprised to find all two hundred of us sitting there.

"That's it," he said. His shoulders went slack and he looked over at his teaching assistants with a blank, wondering look, as if to say, "Have I done it, or am I out of my mind?"

The next week, Professor Howe came to class a changed man. His clothes were neat, his hair was combed, and he looked like he'd been popped with a pin. All the wild-eyed vitality had left him. He clipped the microphone to his lapel for the first time and put both hands on the lectern to steady himself. "Last week . . . it was all a mistake," he said, clearing his throat. "Now let's turn to the third part of Descartes's theorem 'Of God, That He Exists.'"

That was the end of my high-flown hopes of defining the mind/body connection. If this man had thrown himself against the ramparts and failed, I didn't see much point in my trying. But it occurs to me now that the whole thing might have been a charade — a great performance to stir the curious few into wakefulness. Perhaps Professor Howe staged his discovery to dramatize how much was still at stake in the dried pages of a three-century-old thesis.

But what of my own opinions on this weighty subject? Did I believe in a soul at all? I think I did. It didn't have anything to do with God; I just couldn't believe we boiled down to a bit of electrified neurochemicals. There was something more than that to being human. The sum was more than its parts. We could change the shape of our bodies, after all, we could smooth or ruffle our pulse, and perhaps — as I had tried that previous summer — we could alter other, deeper workings. It seemed a shame, and somehow vain and improbable, that nothing important to being went on outside our skulls. A bit of us had to travel out — I might have said it like that. I sometimes imagined each of us with a kind of nimbus of self or will lifting from our bodies, until it became indistinguishable from the air.

Between classes, fifteen hours a week, I worked as a clerk at the anatomy-department office, typing up invoices for white mice, monkey food, and human legs. And there I did a bit of research into the mind/body question.

One door over, Benny, the mortician, received the cadavers that had been donated to science. Benny was a dapper man with a belly as round as a medicine ball and a graceful walk. He was responsible for draining the corpses, pumping them full of formaldehyde, and, sometimes, cutting them into parts. Very few people donate their bodies to science, and those who do are often chopped up in order to get the most use out of them: heads to the eye surgeons, legs to the orthopedists, and so on. Benny often wore a blood-spattered smock, its active pattern of russet drops making my stomach turn when I passed him in the hall. Underneath the white coat, he wore expensive suits, and when there was downtime — there seemed to be lots of downtime, between deliveries or while the bodies drained — he played poker in the office with his assistant, a doleful Italian man who rarely spoke. I was in awe of these men, their droll, efficient handling of triplicate forms and death. On Benny's desk was a paperweight — a cross section of a human arm encased in Lucite — which I studied with mild horror whenever I came in for his signature. It bothered me that the bone was off center — a white round near one edge, with the marrow showing. I knew so little of what went on beneath my skin.

Now and then a body arrived when Benny was out of the office, and I would guide the delivery man and the covered gurney down the hall and let him into the morgue. There was an anteroom with steel tables and sinks, a wall of windows that let onto the anatomy labs where the medical students did their dissections, and at the back of the room a massive door that led to a walk-in freezer. I felt a nervy fascination when I entered that room. I examined the scrubbed tables, the tubing and pumps against one wall. Everything looked tidy and sterile, yet I had the feeling that if I stayed long enough in that place, some mystery of life would be revealed. But before I could reach any conclusions, the smell of formaldehyde would overwhelm me and I'd hurry out, yanking the door shut behind me.

Of course, it had to happen sooner or later. A body came; Benny was out; I took the key from my desk and let the delivery man in. Normally they walked out with me, but this man was in a rush, fumbling with his clipboard and pen, and after I signed he left me in the eerie quiet. Usually the tables were empty, but that day there was a body on a table near the freezer door. I could make out the jut of feet and a head beneath the plastic sheet. I walked toward it and paused, then passed on, drawn toward the giant door of the cold storage.

I pulled on the silver handle, half expecting it to be locked, and the sealing popped. A stinking waft of cold air hit my face. There in front of me, hanging from giant hooks in their ears, were thirty or so naked bodies. They dangled limply, toes pointed toward the floor, their skin pale as bread dough. On carts against the wall were a few others, limbs sprawled this way and that, their genitals exposed. I had the urge to cover them. And because there was no sheet, no privacy, I shut the door.

I took a few heaving breaths with my back against the stainless steel, then walked closer to the lone body and lifted the sheet. I wanted to see everything. I knew I wouldn't go back there again. Underneath was a woman — an old woman, I was relieved to see. She was unmarked, except for a shunt coming out of her neck. The faint whirring sound that I had heard without noting was a pump on the side of the table draining her blood.

Perhaps it was something about the surroundings — the chemical smell and machine hum — but I felt nothing of the frisson, the faint charge in the air around a living person. Whatever animated her had gone. I felt it in my chest and fingers — an absence of feeling — and I thought, *This is just a husk.* What hopefulness, though, that I imagined her intact somewhere, as if the integrity of the self couldn't be dismantled, but only evicted from its housing. And perhaps she was intact in a way, held for a while in the minds of those who'd known her, loved her. With a pang I saw that her fingernails, curled against the steel pan of the table, still bore a fresh coat of polish.

I dropped the sheet, feeling guilty. The dead are so helpless. But I knew one thing about this woman, or the woman she had been: she had willed her body to science. She had signed papers that described how her corpse would be embalmed and then slowly defleshed by anatomy students. She had offered up her unique case — the tendons gnarled by use, the organs swollen or misshapen — a body quite apart from the clean diagrams of the textbook. I thought a woman like that might have forgiven my curious stare.

I spent the rest of the afternoon typing up invoices as I normally did — 100 white mice, 2 human heads — except the words no longer seemed rhetorical. Those were individual heads, the detritus of individual lives. I took comfort from the thought that whatever mattered of those lives had long since slipped free.

When I showed signs of interest in the life of the mind, Leslie began treating me like a fellow scholar. She was in the middle of her architecture Ph.D., and her thesis took her into realms of theory where few people were inclined to follow. It must have been a lonely thing, to work so hard at something you couldn't usefully discuss outside a small group of colleagues. I knew she longed for more people with whom to worry the kinks out loud, but she had become accustomed to the idea that most of the jokes weren't worth explaining. Once in a while, I'd ask her to decode some term I'd heard batted from the lectern, and gratitude would break across her face. After that, she began to tell me a little about her work.

"It's about — well, you'll understand this — it's about the pedagogy of design." She talked then of Hegel, Gramsci, and Derrida, and in fact I didn't understand most of it. Still, I was grateful that she considered me worthy of real conversation, and I tried to pay attention and keep my head clear.

I remember Leslie once talking about a theater of ideas — a mental theater, in which the seating chart reflected the relationship of different schools of thought. We were sitting in the breakfast room, a narrow room with a bay window, and she spread her hands out across the sunlit panes as if she could see that theater before her. The oldest ideas had orchestra seats, and as things got more complicated you moved toward the mezzanine and wings, until finally, at the far-flung reaches of the balcony, there were the poststructuralists, postmodernists, and their ilk. Her mental organization left me in awe. In the theater of my mind, there were whole rows of empty seats, important members were unaccounted for, and at times — when I got in a panic — there was a headlong stampede for the doors.

But it was a relief to see things becoming easier between us. Once I moved out of the house, the bad business about the closet and borrowed clothes faded into the background, and meantime my sisters were getting old enough to do some trespassing of their own. "I guess I'm doomed to have my closet raided for another fifteen years," Leslie said, and we managed to laugh about it.

Now and then she and I would run into each other on campus, and Leslie, who had always looked young for her age, looked younger when I saw her on those brick-lined paths. She was buoyed up by the chance to steep herself in research, theory, academic intrigue. She was still a Marxist. I understood that much. But now that she had left off working on the line, I couldn't imagine how she stayed at it all those years.

I spent most of my free time on campus at Kerckoff Hall, a Gothic building overlooking the center of campus. My friend Wendy managed a coffee bar housed in the east wing, so I was treated to endless cups of free espresso. I drank mochas and lattes, cappuccinos and straight shots with lemon peel. Then I went upstairs to sit under a leaded-glass window and try to read, my heart yammering in my chest.

One afternoon, I was in Kerkoff's second-floor bathroom, which gave out onto the roof of a side wing, when on a whim I hoisted myself to the windowsill and out to the gravel-lined rooftop. There wasn't much to see, just ventilator shafts and the tops of nearby buildings, but I felt a small surge of triumph, and when I saw a nook cut into the main tower, which rose up another two stories, I decided to sit there for a while. I was filled then, as I often was in those days, with a sense of pregnant confusion, as if I were on the brink of discovering something that would change my life. This promise was ever receding before me, and the pursuit led me out of windows and onto cigarette-strewn rooftops, where I lost the trail and got muddled.

This feeling may have had something to do with caffeine. In addition to the four or five espressos Wendy slipped me over the counter, she and I took five No-Doz a day — two with breakfast, one with lunch, and two with dinner, as if they were vitamins. We figured that in order to compete among students of the highest caliber, it was of primary importance to be alert.

So I must have been fresh off a double espresso and my lunchtime supplement when I sat on that rooftop, confusing an exploration of the campus architecture with getting an education. By chance I looked up and saw that the nook in which I sat was in fact the bottom of a narrow stone chute. Along one wall, receding up into the darkness, was a metal ladder. I took hold of the cold rungs, and began to ascend into the dark. The sunlight shrank to a distant square below me, and my eyes slowly adjusted to the dark, until I bumped my head on what seemed to be a trap door. For a moment I imagined myself popping up in the chancellor's office in the middle of a meeting or, more likely, into some steamy boiler room filled with bare wiring and rats. Then I pushed up on the door. A crack of sunlight. I had reached another roof, this one small, perhaps thirty feet square, and bounded on all sides by high parapets. It was the top of the tower, a sort of useless open-air room, but jutting into this space was a structure housing the final leg of the building's stairway, a clapboard wedge with a glass-windowed door. Someone had braced a plank against its roof, and when I climbed up there I could see over the parapets: a 360-degree view of the campus, the city, the hazy Bel-Air hills.

I took my mother up there once, when she came to visit the campus. Jim waited in the courtyard with Alice and my baby brother in a stroller. When I showed her how to step on the sink, my mother hesitated for a moment, then shrugged and clambered up, laughing as she slipped sideways through the narrow window.

Together we climbed through the dark chute and up the plank, and when we reached the top she turned in a full circle, hands on her hips. Then she broke into an incredulous grin. Now that I lived far away, nothing pleased her more than my confidences.

The two of us leaned over the wall and watched students moving in streams across the courtyard, eddying at the path-side tables. It was late May. The lavender crowns of the jacaran-das seemed to float above the flagstones, their trunks obscured from above.

By her misty-eyed quiet, I knew my mother was full of her days at Cornell. She was nostalgic for stonework and ivy, for musty libraries and carillon bells. To her, those were the tex-tures and sounds of a young mind cut from its leash. And I saw then how much of my pleasure in college life had been pre-pared by her descriptions. Her stories shaped the air of certain places, so I walked under the columned portico of Royce Hall with her delight slipping around me like an invisible current.

"Look at that sloped lawn," she said, nodding toward the smooth waterfall of green at the edge of the courtyard. "There was a lawn like that in front of Grandma Wood's house in Great Neck. It was so steep, the gardener tied a rope to the mower and pushed it off the hill."

Suddenly my mother spotted her husband among the fore-shortened bodies below: "Hey, there's Jim!" I could hear in her voice that pleasant shock of coming to his familiar shape and not knowing it for an instant, so that to recognize him was to be plunged back into his dearness.

I stared at my mother — leaning over a gargoyled parapet, three flights up and miles from her country home — and was swept by a similar sense of wonderment. That she didn't ask where I was taking her. That she was willing to hoist up her skirt and follow me.

In the years since I had left home, I had made a fiction of her: sensible earth mother, raising her kids without fuss or decorum, shoveling manure to make her plot thick with greenery. In the sculpture garden at the north end of campus was a statue by Gaston Lachaise, a towering ur-female with enormous hips and breasts, and I once bought a postcard of the piece at the campus art gallery and wrote my mother a note on the back: "This woman makes me think of you." No doubt she was less than flattered. When I mentioned the statue a few months later she looked blank.

What I failed to say was that the resemblance wasn't so much physical as symbolic. My love of that sculpture had everything to do with how I saw my mother: figure of bounty and unabashed strength, feet planted wide, hands on her hips. It was my mother of the Spring Street garden blown up to mythic size. What I had seen in Lachaise's *Standing Woman*, and what I wanted to see in my mother, were the shapes of motherly nurturance.

All that year I wrote her ardent letters, one of which turned up not long ago in a box of family photos: "It is a very quiet night, I can hear the city crickets. I have been looking around my house and thinking of the transience of all this — I will move from this place, these people will pass out of my life — and it all seems so simple, so logical, the evolution of each of our lives, and doesn't make me feel sad as it sometimes does.

"I love you so terribly much, because you are Ann, and I think the fact that you are my mother must be some cosmic coincidence, because not all daughters love their mothers like this. We are kindred spirits, I would know you if I found you anywhere, but instead, we are living at the same time, linked by blood, one sprung out from the other. Tonight this seems a small miracle, and if you think about it maybe it will seem such to you also."

My mother may have heard these cries of kinship, but she didn't respond. For weeks after I sent that particular letter, I checked the mailbox for a reply. When none came, I called her, the talk on my end wooden as I waited for mention of my note.

Finally, I had to ask. "Did you get my letter?"

"Your letter?" A long pause. She was skimming back through the days. "Oh, yes, that was very nice."

I didn't have the sense to let it go at that. "Well, did you . . . I mean, what did you think I was trying to say?"

"Hmm, let's see . . ." I heard the clattering of plates in the background. I could just see her at the sink, the windows blackened before her, the phone tucked into her shoulder. "I think it said that you liked me quite a lot."

I may have believed that I wrote out of pure emotion, but of course it was more tangled than that. I wrote for effect; I wanted to stir something in her, some reciprocal passion. What pained me most was the feeling that I had failed to find words to rouse her.

But, of course, it was a failure not of language but of subject. My mother preferred to talk of the world: "So it's a good day here. We went to Conway's and loaded up a whole truckload of manure. He's getting out of the dairy business, so we're determined to get his last barnful."

Then she told me that the birds around the house had become interested in their reflections. She noticed it, she said, because on hot spring days she left the car windows open and their droppings had slid into the interior. Soon the pattern became clear: a spreckling of white and black along the door and on the gravel below the rear-view mirrors. Then one day she caught sight of them, perched on the passenger door, peering at themselves.

"Who knows what's going to happen next?" she said. "I mean, at some point we made the leap from patterned behavior to learned behavior, and the birds might just do it too. It might happen right here in our driveway — bird consciousness." She let out a wry laugh.

I drove up to my mother's house the summer after my junior year and spent a week working with her in the garden. One afternoon we crouched together weeding around the swimming hole. It was easy work. The plants came out of the sand with a toothy rip, and we didn't need a rake or tarp. We threw the pigweed and hemlock into the river and let the current take them down, no doubt destined for some distant neighbor's bank.

While we worked, my brother sat naked in the shallows, scooping mud into a watering can, and the sight made my mother reel back to our days at the communal house in Manomet.

"You were that small then," she said, pointing to him, "and, boy, you had moxie. You had barely learned to walk, and you could kick your legs up waist high, like this." She demonstrated for me then, hands on her hips, making like a majorette across the sand. "I was like, 'Hot damn! Look at those motor reflexes.'"

That memory had surfaced many times over the years, and by now I was tired of the little girl in the story — that wild thing who ate butter sticks and shat in the sugar bowl — tired of the way my mother's voice turned breathy over her charms. She swept into the tale as if for the first time, and I stared down at the sand, turned up in dark mounds where the weeds had come free, feeling bored and churlish. I was twenty. Would I always be the sullen child? All winter I had missed her, and now she was here, telling me a story that had only to do with love, and I could barely meet her gaze. I forced myself to look up — at the sunbursts around her eyes, at her hair fleeced with gray. That story was more hers than mine. She was twenty-four years old then, on a grassy bluff above the sea, watching her daughter march naked across the lawn. After her lonely months in a Lower East Side apartment, she suddenly had a surfeit of company. It struck me: that story was like a much-loved tune, an anthem for happiness. She liked the sound of herself singing it.

I waded out into the current and floated on my back. At the water's edge, my brother harassed the water with a stick. Higher up on the beach, Alice sat in a lawn chair reading. Something thick, I couldn't quite make out the title.

I asked her, "What are you reading?"

She closed the book and looked at the cover: "*Hawaii.*"

James Michener. Pulpy as it might have been, it was adult pulp and she was only seven.

"It's not very good," she said, "but Dahlia and I are having a contest to see who can read the book with the most pages."

Later that night, after we had rinsed the sand from our feet and eaten dinner, I tucked my brother in, lying beside him on the short bed that had once been mine, my heels pressed against the footboard. One wall of his room had windows from floor to ceiling, which looked out onto a slate patio and the lacy branches of a dogwood tree. My mother had laid the patio herself, and she liked the activity so much — the pleasure of fitting the slabs together like a jigsaw puzzle — that the slate soon spread, taking over the lawn and part of the flower beds, running up the retaining wall that extended off my brother's room. Hung on this wall was an enormous mask that Mau's parents had brought back from Mexico, which passed through him to my mother. It was cut from weathered wood, a rough-hewn jackal's face, the brow and chin curving forward, a brute nose jutting from the center. The evening clouds shifted, and a beam of moonlight fell against the wall.

"Look at the light on the mask," I said to little Jim.

"Yes," he said, in a sleepy, offhand way. "It's dancing light."

We were quiet for a while, then he piped up again: "Last night I dreamed there was a raccoon."

"Was it a good dream?" I asked.

"It was trying to get in."

"Maybe that's because of the raccoon that was on the porch the other night. You saw the real raccoon and then you dreamed about one." What hollow comfort — to try to knit fast the worlds of sleep and wakefulness. I tried again. "Dreams are strange, aren't they?"

"Yes," he said, tucking one hand behind his head. "Dreams tell you what's in your heart coming now."

My dreams in those days were of what I could become. At UCLA once, in the student health clinic for a flu shot, I noticed a Goethe quote taped to the wall: "Whatever you can do, or dream you can, begin it. Boldness has genius, power and magic in it." I was about to pass out from the injection — the needle slid in and my palms turned wet — but I happened to see those words, and they provoked in me a momentary swell of courage. I took deep gulps of air and didn't faint, full of momentary resolve to learn fencing, go to Spain, make the dean's list. Soon this courage dissolved, but those lines stayed with me: an enticement and a goad. I knew fear held me back. *From what?* someone might have asked me. If I sifted through possible answers I might have said, *Fear kept me from happiness.* I had bought my mother's line: action lived apart from feeling. It had its own engine.

I drove back to Los Angeles at the end of that summer, down Interstate 5 in my old Honda with all the windows rolled down. That highway was straight as a ruler. You needed only one finger on the wheel, one toe on the gas to make progress. The heat hemmed me in — my hair flew up in strings around my face, my lips were chapped — but after a few hours a pleasant stillness set in, and my mind would run. I drove down the dry belly of the state, past Coalinga, through the methane-reeking hills near Los Banos, where the cows stood in pens of bare dirt, past Chowchilla, a town that would forever recall a busload of kids buried by kidnappers and miraculously freed after a week in the dark.

I didn't like to pull over. Those towns made me lonely. I'd stare at the girl behind the checkout counter, her thick mascara and chewed nails, and imagine myself stranded like that, miles from nowhere, ringing up drinks and gum for luckier people, people in motion, speeding away toward better things. It was best not to stop. I packed food and water and pissed in a juice jar while driving, capped it, and threw it under the seat. I even read part of a novel on one trip, holding the book in the dip of the steering wheel and glancing up every sentence or two. None of this seemed strange to me. If a cop had stopped me and pointed out that I had an open book in my lap and a jar of urine at my feet, I'd have been nearly as astonished as he was. When I came as close to forgetting myself as was possible at that age, I slipped back to the lawlessness of my youth.

My car was like a private universe, and as such I thought it should reflect me. I hung bells from the rear-view mirror, burned incense in the ashtray, and deliberated long and hard about a bumper sticker. What did I want to say to the thousands of strangers who would tail me on the freeway? For years I could think of nothing I felt comfortable trumpeting. There were plenty of causes I believed in, but no single one I favored over the others, and I worried about plastering over my whole trunk and back window. "You've got to pick your shots," my father used to say about organizing work.

I can't remember him ever putting a political sticker on his car. His back bumper was smooth chrome, broken only by an AAA logo. You couldn't pick him out of a line of traffic as someone whose life was devoted to — I want to say social change (but that says everything and nothing), fighting monopoly capitalism (not sure that's right), rebuilding the left (rings vaguely rhapsodic). Difficult to sum up my father's work in a phrase, but easy to say he didn't wear his commitment on his sleeve. Now and then he wore political T-shirts, but only about causes to which he had already devoted countless hours, so that the T-shirt was a matter of gruff pride, the badge of the home team.

"Isn't it terrific?" he said about one, plucking at the hem to pull the silkscreen straight: a crowd marching with signs, the photo trimmed around their heads, so their placards carried the message against the white space: Keep GM Van Nuys Open. "Leslie designed it. She's got an amazing eye."

Perhaps my father's blank bumper was also a matter of caution. Once, years before, as he drove me home from one of my visits to San Jose, he noticed a patrol car following him over several miles. He cut his speed and pulled into the slow lane, but the squad car stayed glued to our tail. After a while the sun went down, and behind us a pair of square headlights flipped on.

"What does this guy want? I'm not speeding." My father checked the speedometer again.

"None of your taillights are out?" I asked.

"I don't think so. And if that's the problem, he would have pulled me over by now."

We were quiet for a mile or so, both of us willing the cop to tire of this cat-and-mouse game. It did feel as if he were waiting for us to make a mistake.

After half an hour in the cop's high beams, I started grasping at straws. "Do you have any bumper stickers on your car?" I asked my father. "You know, something . . ."

My father gave me a quick glance. "No, but that's a good point, honey." I didn't see him breathe easy until the cop swung around us and sped away.

Four years after I bought my car, I finally came across a bumper sticker I thought I could live with: Think Good Thoughts. The phrase was printed in serif capitals, the type small against the white background, and I was taken with its modest, uplifting tone. Now it strikes me as a ridiculously tiny suggestion, pared away from all action, the smallest unit of good-deedery imaginable. But the dusty back window of my Civic bore that appeal for years, until I cut someone off — on Telegraph Avenue in Berkeley, no less, bastion of the lefty bumper sticker — and the offended driver leaned out his window in disgust. "Think good driving!" he yelled.

I was out the next day with a straight-edged razor blade, scraping that thing off.

Sometimes, when I was driving, a phrase would pop into my head, and I'd fumble in the glove box for a pen. "A peppering of crows over the hills." I wrote slowly, with a white-knuckled grip. After years of unsatisfactory grades in penmanship I tried, even in private jottings, to be legible. What I really needed, I was convinced, was a mini cassette recorder. I had the idea that it would make composition effortless (an idea that should have worried me). You'd press Record, open your lips, and great runnels of prose would spill forth. I coaxed my mother into buying me one such little gadget and returned home from Christmas break with a fist-sized Panasonic.

How my friends tolerated me then, I'll never know. At a party, when I had an important thought, I would run to my room and spend a few minutes muttering into the microphone. What was laid down on those tapes? Drunken rambling about the streetlights, a moment-to-moment catalog of my feelings — some of the most self-conscious utterances of a self-conscious age. When I played them years later, it took strength not to wince with shame. My pretensions were so plain, and had been so hidden from me then, that I could listen to them only when I was driving on the open highway. Even there, sealed behind glass with the road noise as cover, I pressed on the accelerator during the most ridiculous patches, as if a witness were tailing me.

Wendy used to beg to listen to those tapes; it was a guaranteed dose of hysterics. After carefully cueing up a tape to avoid the most humiliating swatches, I'd press Play and watch her dissolve on the floor. I figured I owed her this much, since she had to live with me when the document was made. One day, after she'd wiped the tears from her face, she sobered up and put a gentle point on it: "It was like you wanted to record your existence, but you always had this thing in your hand, so your existence was totally contrived."

I remember Wendy telling me one day to write something. I say "telling" me, because it was like that. "Write something," she said, in the tone you'd use to tell a bear to dance. Her boyfriend, Tommy, was over, and Wendy probably hoped the dare and the appeal to my vanity might keep me occupied for a while.

Bearlike, I went for the bait. "About what?"

"I don't care," she said, slumped on the couch.

Tommy was glam, with a crest of chemically treated hair and a face perfected by white pancake. After they made out, he'd look up with the foundation wiped away around his mouth, so an oval of reddened skin showed through. It made him look undone — crazy with appetite.

I sat down at a card table in the living room and faced the typewriter, a gift from my father. It was a Smith Corona, a die-hard machine that made it through four years of term papers pounded out at the eleventh hour. It made a rattling sound when you flipped it on, and I soon came to dread that rattle: it was the sound of beginning to write, an awful, beggared state. But that night, swollen up with my commission, I managed to peck out half a page of moody surrealism. Half a page: that was my limit. After that I stalled out.

Strange to be able to look back and say that's where writing started, while my patron sat by and necked with a willowy glam-rocker. I didn't write stories in high school, nor had I been a childhood diarist. People might have said that I was an imaginative kid, but though I had some of the trappings of this type

— the books, the love of gnomes and underworlds, the private games — I was not particularly creative. I loved to read but rarely wrote anything. I made hand-lettered signs for the hill-side across the river and stuck them into the dirt — The Bad-lands, The Misty Wood — but I never pretended to play in a hexed kingdom. I was dull as a surveyor, pounding my stakes into the mud and moving on. This is something I shared with my mother: the love of naming *how it was*. A very different thing from imagining how it might have been.

It seemed I'd found a happy middle ground in academia: it required writing but not art; it was political but didn't require action. In my senior year, I began to lean toward anthropology and enrolled in a seminar on economic development. The class was led by one Professor Hudson, a rather handsome and la-conic man in his middle fifties, with bushy white eyebrows and Southern drawl.

Our mission in Anthro 127A was to look at development strategies in Third World countries (though first the term *Third World* had to be examined gingerly). But the course quickly broke down to the most basic human questions: Can one per-son help another person in a lasting way? Do we all share the same ideas about what makes up a good life? Is happiness relative?

The discussions were fierce. References to outside sources quickly flew out the window. We all came into the class know-ing what we believed about the world; little of those beliefs would be changed in the process. There was a wide range of students fanned around the long conference table. A Mor-mon economics major who had great faith in the International Monetary Fund and made frequent references to his upcom-ing mission. Manuel, an officer in student government, who wore La Raza T-shirts and had the smooth voice of a radio announcer. "Population control is always pushed on Africans, Indians, Latinos," Manuel said. "What about the Mormons? Haven't we got enough white people already?"

I often found myself seated beside Ferdinand, an intense, stocky young man who had a habit of sucking air through his lips before he spoke, as if he were sipping hot tea. He found the class very upsetting, and often started confrontations with other students. At these points, Professor Hudson would inter-ject and try to direct the conversation toward more neutral ground.

One day, when things rose to their usual boil, Ferdinand slapped the table in frustration, shocking the class into silence. When the hour was over, I saw Professor Hudson take him aside. The older man appeared kindly but firm, one hand tucked into the pocket of his slacks, the other turning over and over in the air between them as if demonstrating the two sides of a problem. Ferdinand looked sullen and squinted at some-thing down the hall.

The next week, Professor Hudson opened the class with a discussion about academic research. "Some of you have great passion for your studies." He didn't look at Ferdinand, but we all understood he was addressing the furor of the previous session. "Passion is essential, but it must not be foregrounded in your work. You must strive to be objective. Objectivity re-quires rigor. If love for your subject serves as fuel for this rigor, that's a good thing. But you must never let your passion be-come the subject."

As he spoke, Professor Hudson placed both forearms down on the conference table in a kinglike gesture and stared at them, as if the key to this objectivity was in his tennis-honed wrists and manicured nails. I didn't think Professor Hudson's caveat was out of line. In the context of the classroom, I was grateful to him for preventing further scenes. But at the same time, some-thing in me reared up against his patrician reserve. I was afraid I couldn't manage his beloved rigor. I told myself I was more interested in what was going on in Ferdinand's loopy head than I was in social stratification in Togo.

I took Ferdinand's part, the madman over the man of reason, but this was a careful hedging of my bets. I was just miserable enough in those days to think I might go mad, and I wanted to reserve some sympathy for the mad in case I ended up among them. Now I can see that I was in no danger of losing my mind; I suffered from garden-variety malaise, but it made me feel sufficiently cut off from myself that I didn't know my own mind or its limits. That dislocation seemed to forebode some greater dislocation, and so I often felt, with a kind of fatalism, that I would not last out my days as a contented woman, that at some point I would "go away." That was the phrase that popped into my head: whether to a mental ward or a monastery I wasn't sure. This inevitable journey away from myself, from dailiness, was a future I looked forward to with a wistful regret, as if it couldn't be helped. Of course, I never became that person. I remained myself, and when I got sufficiently sick of my own morbid nature I tried to improve my outlook in tiny ways.

As often as we could, Mau and I drove his truck into the Santa Barbara mountains, where we'd spend a few days hiking through the dry hills, desperate for water and often lost, and the nights huddled around a fire, talking in a rambling way, checking our blisters and eating Top Ramen. Those trips were good for us. Mau got noticeably more relaxed the farther we got from smog and traffic and meter maids — three facts of city life that drove him into a sputtering rage — and he loved to snap branches over his knee and tinker with the propane stove. The stove came with a tiny needle tool, which seemed brilliant when you were in a clearing of twigs and blunt stones, miles from the nearest safety pin, and the only thing between you and hot dinner was a dust plug the size of a pepper grain. What I came to love was Mau's primal satisfaction when that ring of blue flame leapt reliably up from his match, the way he'd say under his breath, "Best thing I ever bought," as if it had just occurred to him. But on the rides out to the woods, stuck into the cab together, I often got on his nerves. I talked as if we might never see each other again, amped up by the view, and the pleasure of being on the road, and his profile, chopped out of the blue of the far window.

He would catch hold now and then, but for longer periods he was quiet, watching the road, so I started to see my effusiveness as a kind of curse. The more he brooded, the more I aimed to be winning. A bad habit, and an old one, learned on those drives of long ago with my father. I was full of outsize moods, outsize expectations — for feedback and affection, someone to ground me. When I was a girl, I used to think that getting older was in part about getting quieter. That I would become more reticent as I aged. Ten years later, I was still talking. On those rides, I tried to take my cue from Mau, tried to see what pleasures he found in keeping mum.

During my senior year, browsing through the course catalog, I saw a poetry workshop offered through the English department. The class was to be taught by Carolyn Forché. Her name, at the time, meant nothing to me, but the idea of writing poems instead of papers greatly appealed. I typed up some of my scribblings, hitting the carriage return now and then so they had the look of poems, and typed my name on each page. I considered writing a cover letter but didn't know what to say; I hadn't published anything, nor had I studied with anyone of note. I was an absolute beginner, and I disguised my shame at this with a bit of preemptive defiance: the work, I told myself, should speak for itself. (Alas, it would.) On the way to mail my submission, the poems fell onto the floor of my car and accumulated a few muddy footprints. This pained me, but I was too lazy to type them over again. I wiped at the tread marks, slipped the poems in the envelope, and sent them off.

The list of those selected for the workshop was to be posted on the classroom door. You had to show up for the first day of class and discover in front of the other petitioners whether you had been chosen. When I arrived, a group of students was already gathered at the door. A few of them found their names on the list and went in. One woman, who had been craning over their shoulders, took a quick inbreath and walked away down the hall. I read the list twice, in case there had been a mistake, and then followed her.

Out on the granite steps, I paused for a moment in the face of a free hour. I ticked off my options. A cup of coffee at LuVal Commons on an unforgiving metal chair, listening to black-clad film students argue over Fellini. A nap in the sculpture garden. Some much overdue reading on the Jacobins.

I turned around and went back to the classroom.

Most of the students were turned toward each other in their chairs, making small talk and sizing each other up. I slipped past them and took a seat in the back. Ms. Forché stepped in a few minutes later, making such a quiet entrance that no one much noticed at first. She looked pale and more staid than she appeared in her jacket photos, in a long wool skirt and a simple blouse. She looked sensible. While people turned toward her and the chatter died down, she smiled mildly from the front of the classroom.

"Hello. I'm Carolyn Forché. I've been told we've been given a smaller room in another building — I've asked for a round table instead of these chairs — and we'll meet there next week." Drab as she looked, her voice was surprising, low and musical and clear. "To begin, why don't we go around the room and introduce ourselves?"

One by one the students said a few words about what they were up to. Most were graduate students in literature: "I'm doing my thesis on Proust. I've published a few poems here and there." All of them looked terrifically poised, or at least able to breathe and converse naturally in front of a group. At their feet were worn leather satchels bulging with books.

My heart flipped like a dying fish. I had no idea what to say when my turn came. It struck me that coming back had been a terrible idea, and that the only sensible thing would be to grab my backpack and make a run for it.

"And you?" Suddenly Ms. Forché was there, leaning her head around the row of students ahead of me. It was my turn. One or two people turned in their seats.

"Actually I wasn't selected to be part of the class." No one said anything, so I went on. "I very much want to learn how to write better poems; I'm sure the ones I sent in were terrible, but I don't have any idea how to make them better. I was wondering if I might audit the class." A woman near me cast her eyes down in embarrassment.

Too earnest, I thought. Nothing like bald pleas from the uninvited. Ms. Forché advanced down the aisle. "Well, I think poets sometimes cultivate mystery about the form. And it's not useful." She paused for a moment and looked around the room with a keen eye. I could feel that the classroom, the whole atmosphere of the university, was alien to her, that she was looking at us from a remove. She turned toward me. "I'd be happy to have you join us."

Later, when the class had dispersed, I went to the front to have her sign my enrollment form. "Listen, I really appreciate the chance to sit in."

"Why do you want to audit?" she asked. "Do you want to participate or not?"

I was taken aback. "Of course, I would love to enroll. I just didn't think —"

She signed the form and handed it to me. "Enroll then. I'll see you next week."

I'm sure there were many times when my fellow classmates wished they had piped up that first day and objected to my intrusion. The poems that I submitted over the quarter were appalling. They weren't grounded in anything real. Once, I brought in a poem that began with my feeling the pulse in my neck and went on to describe a kind of fish — *bloodfish*, I coined them — that swam through my veins. I had written it at my typewriter at the anatomy department, while Benny sawed off arms and legs across the hall.

When I read the poem out loud in class, a heavy silence fell over the group. I had hope that this was the long inbreath of appreciation. But then a man named Bruce, an accomplished poet, took up my poem, fingering the corners gently as if their sharpness might lend him words. "*Are* there such things as bloodfish?" he finally asked, clearing his throat.

"Well, no," I said, feeling scalded. "I made them up."

Bruce nodded politely. It all made sense to him now.

Years later, I would come across a line from Wallace Stevens that made clear the trouble with my poems. "The imagination," Stevens wrote, "loses vitality when it ceases to adhere to what is real." My real life seemed dull, and I was desperate to make something vivid. To what purpose, I had no idea.

*

Carolyn, as she insisted we call her, didn't seem well, though I couldn't say in what way. Even in the sunshine, her hair gave off little light, and she winced quickly now and then, as if at some internal pain. When I saw her walking across campus with the professor who acted as her patron, an association that he clearly seemed to think reflected well on him, she carried herself with the deliberate gait of someone who has been ill.

I imagined it might have been an illness picked up on one of her far-flung journeys. She had been on a tour of some of the world's war zones — El Salvador, South Africa, Beirut — and she seemed steeped in their desperate moods. Now and then she'd let a story slip out: while in Soweto, her husband, a photojournalist, saw a man tied up by a rival faction, ringed by old tires, and set on fire. This friend had been tortured, that one jailed.

Her poems took up these stories, and it was something she'd taken flack for — writing of material not her own. But what I took away from her poetry was not politics but language, the shapeliness of her phrases.

Still, studying with her, I sometimes felt the weight of the century's barbarism clamoring outside the poems. My story would always be a story of privilege; it was a question of being a lucky person and what to do with it. While I circled around writing poetry, I waged a battle in my head. What was the use of art when the world was full of trouble? I liked poetry, but I didn't think that it made me a better person, or that it made my life hold together on different terms. And art that set out to change people's lives — it would take a genius to conceal that much intention.

In the back of my mind was an inscription my father wrote in a book he gave me when I was nine: "There are two ways to live your life: for yourself or for other people." I doubt he meant it as a chide. He held up a mirror, as any parent does, and what I saw there was his vision of me: wiry, tough, funny, a little brash, a little lazy and prone to forgetfulness, but smart, with a big heart — all in all, a good kid. But when I read that phrase my spirits sank. I knew then that I was selfish, and in the years intervening my judgment hadn't changed. Poetry seemed like a frivolous pursuit.

Imagine my thrill when I came across a stray line from Heidegger: "Poetry is the most rigorous form of thought." It sounds defensive to me now, perhaps because I once used it as defense. I had no idea what that sentence meant or what else Heidegger had to say, but I plucked the phrase out of context and laid it in front of me — a sandbag for my bunker.

It wasn't that my father or Leslie ever came out and said art was superfluous. On the contrary, my father once spoke of his feelings directly. We were at Mario's again, and somehow, over the salads and house wine, the subject came up.

"I don't believe that art has to carry a proletarian message," my father said, choosing his words. "I mean the Soviets got into that for a while — that there was no such thing as art for art's sake — and I think that it's wrong. I do think all art is political, in some sense, either in the way it engages or doesn't engage on political terms. But I don't think that's the only level on which art should be measured."

He certainly never behaved like a censor. He loved entertainment — sappy movies, television. He followed sports, in particular his old New York teams, with a singular passion. But still, the bulk of his energy was devoted to political aims, and I watched my parents far more closely than I listened to them. The work of my father's life, if it could be reduced to words, said that one must apply oneself to human suffering in the most concrete of ways. To avert one's eyes was to be some form of coward. I had the feeling that poetry — things told slant, as Emily Dickinson called it — was a fancy way of averting one's eyes.

Just before my college graduation, my father invited me to a play, whose name I've now forgotten, downtown at the Mark Taper Forum: "It might be sold out, but they always have a few tickets on sale an hour before curtain. I figure we can go down there early, wait in line, then go to dinner before the show."

From the moment he picked me up, I was roiling with old resentments, over his preoccupation, his way of sighing as if the world were on his shoulders. He talked about his work. "I've been through a very rough period. Trying to finish the book and feeling like I need to do everything myself, the promotion, the publicity. I think this could be a very important book. A real tool for studying the labor movement."

I stared out the window as he drove downtown, only half listening. He had made this gesture, and still I was bucking to spoil the evening.

While my father waited in line for tickets, I wandered toward the Dorothy Chandler Pavilion, hands stuffed in my pockets. I was halfway across the courtyard when a stream of water shot out of the pavement, not six inches from my face. For one heart-stopping instant I thought it was a broken water main. Then all around me, out of the slate, more streams rose in counterpoint, water stiff as lengths of rebar, falling apart in the air and pooling at my feet. I had walked halfway into a minimalist fountain: a suite of holes bored in the concrete and a slight concavity to catch the flow. That fountain pissed me off, as did everything else that evening. I backed out of range and sat on a nearby bench, hoping to watch someone else get soaked.

My father came out to find me. "It's going to be a while. The tickets don't go on sale for half an hour. Why don't you keep me company?"

His eagerness set my teeth on edge. "You know what, I can't go see this play."

"Come on, sweetie. I know you'll like it."

"No. I don't care if it's good," I said, suddenly barefaced in front of him. "We need to talk."

"Okay," he said, his voice softening. "I know a restaurant nearby. Why don't we go have dinner?"

We walked the few blocks in silence, neither one of us knowing what to say. When we were seated at a table, and the waiter had brought menus and bread, we managed to look each other in the eye.

"So what's going on?" he asked me.

"I'm pissed at you," I said.

I saw his face working to stay smooth. "About what?"

What was I pissed about? Things so old, so layered, that to speak about them seemed useless. "Everything — that you always get your way, that I can never win an argument. I'm sick of how you're always case-making: that I have to have reasons why I feel the things I feel."

"That's not true, Lisa. Come on. I listen to you. I have tremendous respect for you. I disagree with you sometimes, but I always take you seriously."

He was right. I was overstating things. It only made me feel wilder.

"You mean the world to me," my father went on. "I mean my life boils down to two things — my work and my family — and I think I've done a very good job of balancing the two."

That word — *balance* — struck me like hammer. "Then how come you left?" I don't know how I veered into the heart of things. But there it was. Eighteen years later, and that question was still on my lips.

The waiter came to take our order, his smile dying as he saw my tear-stained face. My father shot him a nervous glance: "We'll need a little more time."

"Are you ashamed of me?" I asked, when the waiter had left. I couldn't stand such propriety from a man who once did yoga in department stores. Now that I had crossed the line, I was feeling reckless, ready to say anything.

"Of course not," he said. "Look, what happened when you were little —" He broke off. What happened then, that whole era, seemed to strain the limits of words. "I felt terrible to leave you, but it was a very important moment in history, and there was so much at stake. I remember taking you to the park and explaining to you about the war — how our country was bombing these innocent people. And you were wonderful. You listened and you asked me if there were fathers and daughters over there like you and me — god, were you three? I remember you being so thoughtful — and I said, yes, there were babies over there and I wanted to help them. And you said you understood. That if I had to go away you understood."

I looked at him, framed against the restaurant's wood paneling, so calm in his recounting. I had my hands out on the tablecloth, and my whole body shook with terror at what I was about to say. "You didn't *have* to go. You *wanted* to go."

He looked defiant. "That's true. I was doing what I thought was right." Then he took a deep breath and sighed. "Look," my father said, "I adored you. I didn't want to go to prison. And as soon as I got out I came back, and I think I was a pretty good father. I tried very hard to make up for the time we missed, driving up to Ann's, putting a lot of energy into our summers together. I don't know what to say. The work I do, I do for you kids. I have three copies of each of my books on the shelf — one for each of you. And I hope someday you'll look at what I've done and be proud of your dad."

"Look at your books?" I couldn't stop shaking. This was the difference in how we measured our lives. "You're my father. What I'll remember is our time together."

He was quiet for a while. "You know I feel very guilty about how much that hurt you, my leaving. I've made a lot of mistakes in my life. I was twenty-four years old when you were born, and I was still trying to figure my life out. I always tried to be conscious of you, but I've been on my own trip, and I don't think that's a bad thing — I don't think the only positive value I can have as a parent is to keep everything safe and stable. We're living in a very dangerous time, families are falling apart under the strain, and I'm trying to do something about that." He stopped and looked at me, searching for some sign that I heard him, that I understood. "I hoped that you could learn something from my struggle."

twelve

AFTER THAT DINNER, things seemed easier between my father and me. Easier for being out in the open. In my final few months of college, I found that I called home more often, that our dinners in Westwood didn't leave me drained. It would be years before the conversation we started that night would be finished, but I felt a weight lift off me just to have begun.

Meanwhile, school was ending and I had choices to make. I was still thinking that I wanted to be an anthropologist. Still thinking, but I had my doubts. It's easy to say, in hindsight, that it all came down to language. I remember going to Powell Library to read dissertations by women who had done ethnographic studies in Malaysia and Bangladesh. It was plodding stuff. So little of the life there came through: no chicken squawk or food smells, no sense of the way people talked. What did come through, here and there, was the loneliness: "This area certainly warrants further study, but in the eleventh month of my stay, I contracted cholera and was forced to conclude my fieldwork." I tried to read on, but my eyes glazed over. Late at night, in a carrel deep in the stacks, a leaky hut in monsoon country sounded like exile.

Still, something in that vision must have compelled me. Late in my senior year, I decided I would travel through Asia. I told myself it was a trip fitting a future anthropologist, but I think it was mostly an impulse to see things bent and strange. I wanted a complete torquing of dailiness — the dress, the clothes, the type of shoes, the plates, the shape of the drinking fountains, how one hailed a bus, the strange fruits, literally. I wanted a wilder life, and a test of my mettle, and in the bargain I thought I might come up with a possible site for a field study.

That spring, I applied to graduate schools in anthropology and also for a traveling fellowship sponsored through the honors department: ten thousand dollars of unrestricted travel money, no final project or thesis required. I knew about that award for a year, and wanted it so badly I could taste it, yet I waited until the day the application was due to type up the essay in the computer lounge. "Through my major in history and secondary focus in anthropology I have become interested in the intersection between historical practice and anthropological methodology. By combining a structural, historical approach to examining social structures, class conflicts, and the comparison of pre-capitalist and capitalist forms of production with an anthropological systems approach which examines the relations between environment, technology and demographic growth, I would like to study the differences between socialist and market economies' efforts at agricultural development."

I may have been bored by other people's turgid prose, but I waxed on myself when I thought the occasion called for it. Those suffocating, generalized phrases rolled from my fingers, but I had a harder time with the particulars. I spotted a woman two terminals down who looked like she might have been from India.

"Excuse me," I asked her, "do you know where in India they harvest the most wheat?"

She laughed. "Uttar Pradesh, I think."

In it went: "I plan to spend two months in India visiting Bengal, where rice is farmed, and Uttar Pradesh, which is primarily a wheat production area."

That cobbled-together document got me into the finals, along with two other students. We were all to be vetted by a panel of professors. I didn't prepare much for that interview. I didn't know how to prepare. I thought they might ask me about my specific travel plans, how I would get from Delhi to Uttar Pradesh and that sort of thing, so I rushed to the library the morning of the interview and photocopied some maps. Many of them were so old they predated partition, but I folded them neatly and brought them to the conference room in the honors department, where four professors faced me from the end of a long table. After a few introductions, a dour older man posed the first question: "What exactly *is* the intersection between historical practice and anthropological methodology?"

The maps wouldn't help me there. I hadn't the faintest idea what to say. I blundered into an answer, losing my train of thought, freezing for whole seconds in search of a word, so that another professor, a kindly woman, took pity and tried to put words in my mouth. The older man, my interlocutor, didn't look at me once for the rest of the hour. He had heard enough.

So of course I lost the fellowship, but decided I would go to India after all; I'd just have to pay my own way. I became more of a scrimper than I already was — living on Top Ramen and peanut butter, buying only thrift-store clothes, working longer hours at the anatomy department — and six months after I graduated I had collected enough to last me half a year in India.

I wanted Mau to travel with me, but he balked at the itinerary. India wasn't his first choice. He was leaning toward South America, where he could speak the language, where he might do more than just gawk. Unlike me, he didn't seem to be frightened of traveling alone; rather, he was frightened that the rigors of the road would put an end to us. Better to put an end to us now, he figured, so he wouldn't end up stranded in Rajasthan, nursing a broken heart, when he could have been a footloose bachelor in Peru. Perhaps we both needed some air. We'd been together three years and were barely out of our teens. It made a lot of sense — our relationship was already showing its strain — but this decision to go on separate journeys strained us further. We held on during the last month before we set off out of laziness and residual affections. And whenever our old oppositions reared their heads — my clinginess and operatic emotion, his impatience and inward moods — we remembered that they'd soon put us on opposite sides of the globe.

The night before my flight, I lay awake in Mau's darkened basement room, poring over the horrible visions I had compiled in preparation for my trip — snapshots of the disasters in store for me. I would be stoned to death in a remote village for showing too much forearm. I would get dysentery and languish in a dank hotel room, unfit to beg for medicine in the local tongue. As for Mau, it seemed likely that this would be our parting of ways. He seemed exceptionally sweet to me in light of this. He had been my friend. In the morning he would take me to the airport and put me on a plane for a distant continent and I might never see him again.

As the night wore on, I spiraled into pure anxiety. Desperate for sleep, I went upstairs to the kitchen and tossed back a water glass of chardonnay, the only sedative I could find. Then I went back to bed, queasy now and no less awake, and stared at the curve of Mau's back until the alarm went off.

Five A.M. He jumped up without complaint and pulled on his clothes.

"I feel sick," I told him, burrowing deeper in the covers.

He brushed this off, but while he searched for his keys, I went to the bathroom and crouched over the toilet, feeling that telltale rush of saliva.

"I can't go," I told him. "There's no way I can get on a plane like this."

Mau handed me a zip-lock bag and a box of saltines and led me to the car.

At the terminal, we spent a desolate fifteen minutes or so in the waiting area. I laid my head on his lap, trying to find the one spot where the room didn't spin, thinking, *These are our last moments, I've got to make the best of them.* But it was no use. Finally, Mau walked me to the gate, gave me a quick hug, and took off.

When I was halfway down the boarding ramp, with passengers sandwiched in front of me and behind, I threw up into my cracker box.

"I'll be boarding late," I told the flight attendant. I walked back up the ramp, against the crowd, and tossed the box of vomit into a trash can. In the bathroom, I took stock under the fluorescent light. My skin was blotchy, my eyes rimmed red. I splashed water over my face, rinsed my mouth, and took a few deep breaths. I looked like hell, but I was feeling better. Suddenly I thought of Alison Rider, my soul twin from junior high, how we leaned into the mirror on those frost-raked winter mornings before school, assessing the goods. "I look like shit warmed over," she'd say. To which I was expected to reply: "How many times?"

As far as I knew, she was still in that tiny valley up north. I'd run into her once at a sports bar in town, not long after I'd moved to L.A. She was the same girl she had been at eight years old, sweet and tough and frail-boned, and glad to see me in a way that broke my heart. I had loved her once through and through, without a sense of how we differed, but that day I saw her from a distance, too thin in her stained parka, dragging a hand through her hair, brushing her chapped knuckles over and over against her nose.

In that stuffy airport bathroom, I couldn't say what seemed worse, staying put, as she had, or leaving everything I knew. Still, hitting rock bottom held an odd solace. "Oh well," I said out loud, my voice pinging against the empty stalls, "it can't get much worse." Then I walked down the gangway and into the plane.

Years later, I told someone the story of that wretched departure, and the first thing she asked was, "Why did you go?" That question stopped me short. Much as I dreaded traveling alone, I never seriously considered scrapping my plans. I thought I was a failure for being afraid of adventure. I thought I had to go, precisely because I wasn't suited to it. If I didn't, my anxiety might spread like a poisonous mold. I would become a shut-in, with the doors triple-bolted, the bathtub plastered with grip decals, every heavy object bolted to the floor. This wasn't the whole answer, though. I went not just to conquer my fear, but because I wanted to go, wanted to see the countryside of Buddha and Krishnamurti and the buildings Jim had projected on our living-room wall when I was a child. If no one would go with me, I would go on my own.

I had read descriptions of Bombay before I arrived — the squalor and heat and strangeness — but none of them prepared me. My flight landed late at night, and I was lucky enough to have been offered a ride from the airport by a family whose daughter was an acquaintance of Jim's. They sent the grandmother out to the airport, along with the baby of the family, five years old, and a driver. Somehow we found each other in the crowd outside the terminal, which was nothing more than a dusty hangar with a lurching baggage carousel and a few officials tallying the arrivals in moldering notebooks.

"We thought we'd never find you!" the grandmother said, leading me to the car. It was an old British sedan from the forties, from before independence no doubt, with curved fenders and weathered seats. We piled in, the driver in the front, Grandmother and baby and I in the back, and the boy soon fell asleep across her lap. While he dozed, she commenced a brisk patting against his cheek, which somehow failed to wake him, all the while telling me stories of a near accident on the drive out, how they'd nearly given up on finding me and returned home, and how the baby — *smack, smack, smack* — was too thin and refused to drink his milk. I could barely listen. I was transfixed by the view outside the window: miles and miles of shantytowns, rivers of sewage by the roadside, bands of children dancing before open fires. I told myself I wouldn't last in that country two weeks.

The Lalvanis were well-off, and their house, set in a genteel section of Bombay, was very comfortable: a formal living room with embroidered pillows and a hanging swing; a long hallway, where breakfast was served, opening onto a leafy courtyard. I was to sleep in the guest room with Grandmother, who was visiting from Hyderabad. I soon saw, when I was shown to the room, set with heavy furniture and a single queen-size bed, that they meant this literally. After I got over a bit of shyness and changed into my pajamas, this arrangement comforted me. It seemed like a week since I'd woken up, nauseous, in Mau's bedroom. I curled up under the bedspread, and Grandmother, leaning against the headboard, kept me awake for a good hour, telling family tales and combing her long gray hair.

I spent the next few days wandering through Bombay. Reading back over my journal, I am struck by the inconstancy of my feelings. I was happy when an old woman pinned a marigold in my hair at the bus stop, and then lonely in the middle of the mad crowd jostling for the bus. The seats were taken by the strongest comers, and the brave bulged out the door, hanging from a rickety bar. I let four buses pass before I had the nerve to fight my way on. Finally I made it home to the Lalvanis', the old house looking patrician above its skirt of refuse, the latticed balconies elegant despite their chipping paint. I went on like this, slipping in and out of moods, feeling bereft at odd moments, then somehow sated, as if going wherever I wanted, in silence if I chose, were satisfaction enough.

On one of my first days in the city, I met a Belgian woman in the marketplace. Her name was Corrine, and I was struck by her easy bearing, her weightless silk shirt and silver bangles.

We walked together through the packed stalls, and finally I asked the question at the top of my mind: "So, how is it, traveling alone?" I was drawn to other people's courage the way you lean toward a fire on a cold night.

Corrine looked at me for a beat. "Well, you're alone. How do you find it?"

I was startled to see she was right. "But you don't seem . . . miserable," I told her. *Alone* had come to mean: alone and liking it. That I had yet to master.

Corrine was headed for Goa, a beach community swamped by hippies. "They have the best banana pancakes," Corrine told me. "And the beaches are wonderful." I agreed to join her there in a few days, and she picked a hotel from the guidebook where we would meet.

A few days later, I went to Victoria Station to catch a train south. At the concourse, families were sprawled out on the floor with their bags, eating curry out of tin dishes. Children ran between the columns, dodging the nightsticks of the railroad policeman. I went to a bookstall in the station to buy gum and scan the reading material: mostly Indian comic books, but near the front a selection of paperbacks, stacked six deep, each volume secured with a rubber band: Joan Collins, Robert Ludlum, William F. Buckley, *Joy of Cooking*. That last title made me pine for my mother, who knew the pie-crust recipe by heart, but still opened to the appropriate flour-dusted page out of ritual while she pinched and stirred.

Twenty-four hours later, I arrived in Goa, took a bus to the beach, and got off at the main intersection. It was Sunday, and I could hear singing from a white building by the road — a church, by all appearances. I walked down the dirt track toward the sea, looking for signs of rented rooms. On either side were rice paddies, neatly squared. The air was faintly salty, and bird cries sifted down from the palms. I passed a small shack where a man sat in the doorway paring a mango, and farther on, a large house, which looked from far off like a military bungalow, the porch fronted by a wide set of stairs. The stairs were flanked by long concrete banisters, which ended in two smoothed seats, shaped like cupped palms. In these seats were two old women, arms folded across their chests, who watched me as I passed.

I hated the faint disgrace of entering a new town, guidebook in hand, travel weary and half lost. From a side path, a couple strolled past in swimsuits and lungis, sandals dangling from their fingers. They looked me over and quickly glanced away. A week before, they had probably arrived with the same awkward packs, but now they were unburdened and nicely browned, and they preferred not to be reminded they were tourists.

I walked on to the end of the road, without catching sight of the hotel Corrine had selected. It seemed that many more shacks had sprung up since her guidebook was published. It wouldn't be easy to find her. I stood at a sandy turnaround, trying to decide if I should turn back or walk along the beach to the few hotels I saw facing the ocean, when a group of boys approached me.

"Good hotel? We are taking you. Right now, madam."

"No thanks, I know which hotel I want."

"Which one?"

"The Laksmi."

They waved their hands in protest: "No, no. Not possible." One of them, a heart-faced boy with glossy hair, spit in the dust to register his distaste. "Five rupees. We take you to excellent place. Top-notch."

"Well, thanks for the tip, but I'm going to the Laksmi. My friend is there."

"Friend? And what is he looking like?"

"She. Tall, blond hair, orange backpack."

The boy's face lit up: "I have seen her!"

"Yes? Which way did she go?"

"Five rupees." He held out his hand.

"Oh, Jesus. I'll find her myself." I started to stride off, though it was hard to look cutting with my huge bag and straw hat. The boy pulled alongside me.

"All right, madam. She is going this way." He pointed south along the dunes. "Not far. Laksmi Hotel." The other boys gathered around us, grave faced, arms draped around each other's shoulders.

I looked at the boy for a long moment. There was no sign of duplicity in his face. "Well, all right, thanks," I said, and headed across the dunes in the direction of his hand.

It was slow going. I sank into the sand with each step, postholed by the weight of all my trinkets and toiletries. The sun was harsh, unfiltered, and the sea, though not far off, didn't offer much of a breeze. After about a half mile, I began to doubt my young guide, and a quarter of a mile farther on, I came to a low-ceilinged shack tucked into the dunes. The place looked deserted.

"Hello? Is this the Laksmi Hotel?"

A woman stuck her head out of the doorway, shielding her eyes from the glare.

"Hotel Laksmi?" I asked again, knowing it was hopeless, but wanting to explain why I had intruded on her sandy yard. The woman shook her head.

I started back. Sand had worked into my shoes and was grinding my heels raw. Rivulets of sweat rolled down my stomach. With each step, I planned the exact phrases with which I would curse the little scoundrels when I got back to the road. I started up the face of a steep dune, lost my footing, and pitched forward, propelled by the weight of my pack.

Facedown in the sand, a little snort escaped me, then more giggles. I imagined those boys, doubled over with glee to see me trudging off in the wrong direction. I caught my breath, rolled onto my side, and got up. I had sand in my hair and between my fingers. My thighs looked like two breaded cutlets.

When I reached the road, the boys promptly appeared, feigning concern, a few of them smirking into their hands. I handed over my five rupees without a word and let them lead me to a room.

I stayed for several weeks in the house of Fatima Fernandez, an Indian Catholic, her faith a relic of the days when the Portuguese ruled Goa. She was a soft-spoken woman, a widow, with three daughters and two sons. Her husband had left her the house and an enormous mud oven in the yard, where the boys baked bread for the town. To make ends meet, Fatima rented out rooms to foreigners for a dollar a night.

The shower was in the kitchen, and so the slap of water and the smell of lather mixed with the curry bubbling in a cast-iron pot on the stove. I wasn't sure how to negotiate this mixing of rooms with sufficient modesty, and finally settled on entering the shower fully dressed, piling my clothes on top of the concrete slab that walled off the shower from the rest of the room, then wrapping myself in a lungi behind the damp curtain and scooting through the kitchen with my shoes clutched to my chest.

There was no indoor toilet, only an outhouse set back in the palms, past a scraggly patch of corn and a bare yard strewn with kitchen scraps. My first visit there was made after sundown. I found the hut by flashlight and unlatched the door. Inside was a raised concrete platform, with a slanting chute cut down to the ground. Propped in one corner was a long stick and a pile of newsprint. There was no bucket or tap. Once I was up on the platform, I cut off the light, but soon I heard a wet snuffling sound echoing through the darkness. I fumbled for the flashlight and cast its slim beam around the hut. Nothing. Then the suckling began again, and I located its source. Directly beneath me, at the base of the chute, was a tiny pig, eating with evident relish. He was soon joined by a brother, who butted him aside and tried to scramble up the sluiceway. All at once I divined the purpose of the stick, but it was another thing to get it from its spot in the corner with my pants around my ankles and a flashlight in my teeth. Once claimed, I used it to keep the piglets at bay, though if I looked down I could still see them waiting, their tiny snouts tipped up in expectation.

I wished I could tell Mau about the pigs. He spent hours watching nature shows and was always charmed by animal resourcefulness. But he was already in Venezuela by then. It would be eight months before I could reach him by phone. I went back to my room and stayed up for hours, listening to Bach's Magnificat in D on my earphones, shining the flashlight down at my feet, which cast great paw shadows against the wall. I was alone on that enormous wedge of subcontinent, and yet solitude wasn't as bad as I'd feared. I pressed the flashlight against my leg, and the beam sank into my flesh. I stared for a long time at that pink halo, shot with arteries like the roots of trees, the only patch of color in the darkness. I was alive, and whether I was lonely or not, my blood kept moving.

The next day I took a walk on one of the rust-colored roads beside the ocean. After a mile or so under the palms, the dirt track veered toward the water, and I came across a battered school bus parked beside a dune. It didn't look like a local bus; the paint job was too drab and there were no statuettes or garlands on the dashboard. When I came closer, I saw a weathered blond woman in the driver's seat, plaiting her hair.

"How's it going?" I asked her, approaching the truck.

"Very good these days," she said. She had a lilting accent I couldn't place.

"Where are you from?" I asked.

"From Denmark."

"You drove?"

"Yes, we came overland."

Now, *there* was a journey. I came closer and peered into the cab. Same high leather seat, same glass rounds over the gauges. "I lived in a mail truck when I was a little girl," I told her.

"Really?" The woman brightened. "It's a fabulous life, eh? The only hard part is finding gas. We had some troubles in Afghanistan. I'm Sylvie, by the way." She extended her hand.

Just then a small boy, fair-haired like his mother, poked his head out from the back.

"This is Jan," the woman told me.

The boy scowled and cinched the curtains around his neck. He looked like he was prepped for the guillotine.

"Jan, will you say hello?" His mother reached out to brush a lock of his hair, but he reared back from her hand.

The woman sighed. "It's hard on him, this road life."

She said *hard* with her tongue pulled to the roof of her mouth, and the long vowel made the word seem softer, tinged with tenderness. She didn't need to explain the boy's sulkiness. But as I stood in the foot well, it was Sylvie I felt myself drawn to. She was living the kind of dream most people never took beyond their armchairs: to fill up the tank and drive into the day, unfettered, everything necessary for living rolling along behind.

I wished her good luck and walked out to the sea, where the breakers rolled over in neat sets, thinking of my mother, the way we used to sit in the sun-warmed cab of the mail truck, eating tuna fish on saltines and singing Woody Guthrie tunes. I was slowly catching up to her happiness.

I had been in India for nearly a month when I realized I'd all but forgotten my plans for anthropological fieldwork. On the long bus rides, swaying on a narrow bench for twelve hours at a stretch, there was nothing to do but think, a long undulating quilt of thought, stitched out over the miles. On one of those journeys, the bus radio blasted a tune from a Hindi musical, and a little boy did a skittering dance in the aisle, shaking his hips and making the passengers laugh. He leapt into his seat, every bit the bored satirist, and stared out the window. Suddenly I thought of my kindergarten friend Scotty Randall, no bigger than this sly sprout, his pinwale cords barely clearing the tops of his cowboy boots, how we wanted to be actors. We were so sure of our vocations at five. I was so sure. What had happened to that? I spent half my life wanting to study music, dance, and then I gave it all up. It seemed that these half-mastered skills were like lost limbs.

The bus stopped at a bend in the road, where a small stream cut down the mountain. There was a tea stall against the hill, and while the women bought chai and bags of peanuts, the men strolled over to the water and pissed in the creek. I don't know why this made me delighted — it wasn't such a good idea for the people who lived downstream — but it did. The animal pleasure of it, adding water to other water and watching it churn away.

There I was, taken by my surroundings, and yet I never once thought of kinship systems or agrarian reform. When I realized this, I felt relief, followed by a sobering dread. Maybe I wasn't meant to be an academic, but I had no alternative plan. If I had the nerve, I would go home and get some silly job and try to write poems. Or maybe I could open a café, or become a clothes designer, or at the very least sew my own clothes — vests and paneled shirts that borrowed some of the jaunty style of the men in dhotis at creekside. I made frenzied sketches in the pages of my notebooks, bought peanuts from a roadside vendor, pressed my face to the window and dreamed.

Darkness fell, and the bus passed down a tunnel of banyan trees — each trunk glowing like a great arched rib in the headlights, so we seemed to be traveling down into the belly of the night. In the road ahead was an ox cart brimming with hay. I could see a man perched on top, curled over in sleep. The cart made me think of Ferdinand the Bull, chewing clover on his way to the fights. It was this kind of thought — a fishhook snagged on some childhood flotsam — that made me feel farthest from home. I turned to the woman on the bench beside me, an old woman with gray hair and seamed cheeks, and wished we could share some bit of useless conversation.

The bus passed the ox cart and cut across a darkened plain. A dry wind blew in the windows, and in the seats ahead of me a few passengers' hair climbed upward — wild tentacles lit by the headlights. The old woman and I moved to tame our stray locks, and in the mirrored gesture we glanced at each other. Her face was settled; it seemed to be the face of someone who had reached some kind of rest. When the bus rounded a turn, momentum carried me toward her until our hips pressed together on the bench. I took comfort from the heat where our bodies joined, the way we swayed together in echo of the road.

Toward morning, we pulled into the station and the bus hissed to a stop. Hyderabad. I thought of that line from *Light in August* when Lena, after tramping across three states, says, "My, my. A body does get around."

I could just imagine her voice: dust-choked as Faulkner's prose, slow as the pace at which he followed her over the roads. It was a phrase that bloomed open after a while. First, an idle exclamation, and then a kind of quiet comment on the piling up of experience. It seemed that a body, pushed around like freight by the implacable will, could take so many turns in the road that the early miles seemed to have been walked by another person.

Hyderabad was a big city, with a large telegraph office, so I put in a collect call to my father. After I filled out a form and waited half an hour, a clerk shouted my name and pointed frantically to a booth against the wall. The phone looked to be forty years old, with a frayed cord and a heavy black handset. I shouted into it: "Hello? Dad?"

"Lisa? Is that you? Hello?"

My father and I talked for a few minutes, his voice so familiar beneath the crackle and static, it didn't matter much what we said. I had caught the family during breakfast. In the background I could hear my sisters, shouting hellos. So normal, all of it. I could imagine the room, where each of them sat.

"Well, you sound like you're doing great, honey," my father said. "You're really amazing. I'm going to put on Leslie and the girls." The phone was passed around and then came back to him.

"Any word from grad schools?" I asked.

For a moment I thought the line had gone dead. "I'm sorry, honey, the news isn't too good. Berkeley said no. So did Cornell. No word yet from Michigan."

"Oh, well. To tell the truth, grad school doesn't sound so good lately."

I figured my change of heart would disappoint him. When I first declared my intention to study anthropology, my father thought it was a great idea. He seemed to like picturing me as a junior Margaret Mead. "You're so smart, you could do just about anything," he said. "But anthropology's cool." Now I braced myself for some protest, but I'd forgotten my father's loyalty, the way he turned as fast as a jib in the wind. "No shit. Who wants to spend ten years doing a Ph.D.? You're doing great out there on your own."

I left the telegraph office elated. Miles away, someone knew me, remembered who I was. I had a life there and I would go back to it. My father understood how I needed that grounding. I found out later those calls cost him a hundred dollars a pop, but he talked as if we were sitting at the breakfast table, passing scrambled eggs and salt, his voice easy and unhurried and full of love.

I went farther south from there — to Madurai, a beautiful inland city — and found myself a room near the train station. After dinner, when the suffocating midday heat had lifted, I walked through the still-warm streets to the temple. Inside, the Brahmins carried a statue of Shiva to the goddess Parvati's bedroom for a cosmic tryst, the palanquin carried by two emaciated men, staggering in time to a squealing clarinet. There were a handful of children hanging at the fringes of the procession, barefoot, dusty, jostling one another.

One of them approached me and pointed to his chest. "Arjuna," he said.

I shook his hand. Arjuna, named for a mythic warrior, came up to my hip and had the shaven head and deep-set eyes of an old man. He stood there, chin tipped down, smiling at me, hands tucked into the pockets of his shorts. He looked to be about my brother's age, maybe four or five.

I strolled around the temple, and Arjuna followed. He seemed to sense that I was charmed by him. When a group of devotees approached, and we stepped aside to let them pass, he leaned gently against my leg, a babyish softening in his face. We had stopped beside a small shrine to Ganesh. Arjuna bent over and brushed his finger in a pile of powder at the elephant's feet, daubing it on his forehead and miming at me to do the same. I gave myself the red dot, though I knew I would regret it when we were out on the street. The boy nodded his approval and led me out of the vestibule, a new directive briskness to his movements.

Out on the street, I searched for my sandals in the pile by the door. A group of boys were gathered out front, and when they saw us they rushed forward. "Come, madam, one rupee, one pen." A thin boy of about ten was at the head of the bunch, and as he recited the litany he plucked at my sleeve. There was no heat to his voice; it seemed more a bit of business that had to be done, and a pen or a rupee might come of it, but if it didn't someone else would come along. Meanwhile, there was a bored inspection going on beneath his banter.

"Madam, what is your good name?"

"Lisa," I said, moving toward the tea stall across the road, where a man was lofting a thick stream of tea from a pitcher above his head and catching it in a waiting glass.

"And your country coin?" the tall boy persisted.

Arjuna huddled beside me, clutching my hand.

"The penny," I said, "which has developed a bad name."

The tall boy gave Arjuna a little kick. "Why this boy? This ruffian?" he asked, pointing at my companion.

Arjuna looked stricken. He was younger than the other boys and didn't yet know how to manage his emotions. They were tough and sly, full of the brassiness that street life required, and you could fault them for it — their tricks and taunting — and allow yourself to pass them by.

"He's my friend," I said. I knew from my playground days that he would pay for this later.

The tall boy smiled and shook his head. "I am your friend. Why not giving me one penny?"

"I don't have any pennies."

A muscle rippled in the boy's cheek. He looked down at Arjuna with a raptor's cold eye. "Why not bring your friend to the festival?" He turned in the direction of the main boulevard, where a crowd was gathering, and strode off at the head of his crowd.

After the gang had gone well ahead, Arjuna and I followed.

The boy was glued to me now. We wove through the thickening crowd, and he looked up from time to time, flashing an artless smile. His belly bulged beneath his frayed dress shirt.

"Where do you live?" I asked him.

He shrugged. Still, my attempt at conversation made him quicken, and when the procession turned a corner and we were alone on a darkened street, he tugged at my sleeve. I bent down to his level — he seemed to want this — and he pulled a fist out of his pocket and opened it in the light from a nearby storefront. On his palm were a watch without a band, a bottle cap, a pretzeled nail. I stared at the stuff, uncertain what he wanted. He moved his hand forward a little.

I picked up the watch, and turned it over. It was a cheap Swiss round-face, lost, no doubt, by some tourist. The glass was smashed, stopping the hands. "It's very nice," I said, putting it down next to the other items.

Arjuna picked up the nail and held it out.

"I can't take it," I said.

He stared at me for a moment, then tucked the stuff away. We walked farther in silence, past the tailors' market, where a few men in dhotis still toiled over their pedal machines. It was nearly ten at night. When we turned the corner onto Dingigul Road, Arjuna took my hand and I noticed a movement in his pocket. He was fingering those bits of junk, turning their surfaces over and over. I thought of my velvet box and the lonely months I spent at Twin Oaks School in Eugene, how I passed those days with a hand in my desk, stroking the weathered nap of that fabric. I knew then why Arjuna had emptied his pocket. He wanted me to see his secret talismans.

By now, the procession had broken up. Soon my hotel would close; the doorman would pull down the corrugated-metal door and go to sleep on a pallet in the hall. Up ahead was a soda stand. I stopped and asked for a lemon drink, gesturing to Arjuna to pick something out.

"Take something, boy. She is offering," the shopkeeper said. Then he spoke to him in Tamil.

"He doesn't want anything," he told me with a shrug.

From Arjuna's darting glances at the soda rack, I could see

this wasn't true. He was thirsty. I couldn't imagine why he would refuse a drink, unless he feared sullying our companionship. That restraint, that giving up of one thing for another, endeared him to me.

"Can you ask him where he lives?"

The shopkeeper posed my question in Tamil, and the boy answered.

"He is living with his uncle. The mother and father are dead."

"Why doesn't he go home?"

When the man questioned him again, Arjuna went still; even the hand in his pocket ceased working. When the boy finally answered, the shopkeeper's shoulders went soft. He had been curt with us at first — peeved, no doubt, at the boy for hanging on to a tourist, or peeved at me for my bleeding-heart attentions, which he knew wouldn't last out the hour. But while Arjuna spoke, the man's brows knit together. He looked straight at the boy for the first time.

"The uncle is beating at the wife and striking at the boy with a stick. He is afraid."

He paused for a moment, then said something in Tamil, something gentle and coaxing, and when Arjuna nodded, the man took down an orange soda from the rack and flipped off the top.

"Thank you," I said, and paid with two rumpled bills. While Arjuna and I sipped at our sodas, the man polished his countertop with a rag. From down the street came the rattle of shops locking up for the night. Squares of yellow light winked shut on the road. I drank very slowly, and the boy, sensing my cue, did the same.

What to do? I could take him to my hotel. The doorman would object, but I could probably soften him with a bit of money. But then what? Sooner or later I would leave Madurai, and he would be back on the street, just as I had found him. This was what my father had tried to teach me. If you didn't judge the world by its systems, if you didn't confront its inequalities at the source, the small sorrows would break your heart.

When our sodas were finished, and the shopkeeper had returned the bottles to their crate, I knelt down next to the boy. "Listen, I have to go to my room now."

For a moment he pleaded. "No," he said, holding on to my hand. He said it in English: "No."

"I'm sorry. I can't take you," I told him, starting to cry. In some odd way, my tears seemed to steel him. Perhaps he knew they meant I'd made up my mind. He let go of my hand and stood there in the street, staring while I fumbled with some bills.

"Please, take this."

He pushed the money back at me, but I tucked it in his pocket, the empty one, the one across from his collection of precious things, and turned away, down the shadowed street toward my hotel.

I traveled alone for the first month in India, and then I ran into Nitzan, an Israeli, in a small town near India's tail. We traveled north together for over a month, glad for tolerable company headed the same way. I was fond of hieing off the beaten track, but Nitzan was fonder. He couldn't miss a single temple or ruin or game park. I always swore I was going to take a day to relax, sit in town drinking chai, and pass the midday heat under a ceiling fan, and in the end I always went along. It was Nitzan who insisted we take a six-hour bus ride into the desert to visit Ranakpur, a temple set deep in the Rajasthani desert, with nothing around it for miles.

When we got off the bus at the compound gate, we were greeted by a toothless old man. "You are arriving to Ranakpur, India's most famous Jain temple," he said, spitting betel juice at our feet. There was something oddly solemn in his tone, in his use of the present continuous, that made us pause. We stood beside him, laden with duffel bags, while our bus rumbled out of sight. Then, when a proper interval seemed to have passed, we said a polite thanks and headed for the dharamsala in search of a room.

When we inquired at the booking desk, a willowy Jain nun, wrapped in white from head to foot and holding a swath of sari across her mouth to prevent the inhalation and death of any small insects, told us that we had arrived in the middle of a religious festival. All the dorms were full, and the kitchen was short of supplies. I asked about a low building on the other side of the temple that looked promisingly like a hotel.

"Ah, that is the Shilpi Tourist Bungalow. Those rooms have been booked for many months." She punctuated the word *many* with an outward wave of her hand, as if to sweep away any last hope for accommodation. The cloth fell away from her face to reveal a supple, generous smile. Then she covered her mouth, and bent over the ledger she had been tallying when we arrived.

Back out in the compound, Nitzan began studying the guidebook. This was mainly an evasion, since we were six hours from the nearest town, but he liked to preserve the illusion that he was in charge. We had been on tenterhooks from the first moments we met, bickering over matters of comfort, finance, and the like. Loneliness makes strange bedfellows.

As a rule, Nitzan chose to walk instead of taking rickshaws, allowed himself a room with hot water only once a month, and favored overnight bus rides because they saved a night's hotel costs. I lobbied for comfort and a taste of the subcontinent's small luxuries: a dinner buffet at a maharaja's palace, a hotel room with pressed-tin sunflowers on the ceiling. Of course, I admired Nitzan's restraint — he had a competence and calm that matched his economy — but on a few things I refused to budge.

Overnight bus rides were one of them; I couldn't sleep sitting up. The first time I gave in to all-night travel, I spent the ride bolt upright on the bench — grain sacks under my feet, two snoring women slumped on my shoulders. I seemed to be the only witness to our bus driver's nocturnal habits: long detours down gutted dirt roads for what appeared to be impromptu visits with relatives, or the practice, when another vehicle approached at full speed, of turning off his headlights so as not to blind them. I passed the night clutching the seat in front of me, feeding peanuts to the goat tethered in the aisle, and casting the evil eye on Nitzan's lolling head.

Perhaps life on the kibbutz had given my friend a taste for

hardship. He had stories of boyhood trials that rivaled Jim's
4 A.M. paper route: waking in the dark to harvest bananas before school, riding on a tractor, dust billowing around him, and
nicking the bunches free with a small knife. He told these stories with a flat voice and a shrug. When I got worked up over
some trivial matter, he always had a ready phrase: "Hey, Lis,
don't take it so hard."

So a night without lodging or food didn't faze my friend. He
snapped the guidebook shut, as if something had been solved,
and suggested we take a look at the temple.

When we got closer, I had to say he was right: it was worth it
to come. The temple, set in a cleft in the hills, was made of white
marble and had the high-flown beauty of a circus tent cast in
stone. A broad flight of steps led to a room cut open to the
desert: carved columns held up the upper floor, and set among
the columns were marble sculptures — a bull on its haunches
surveying the desert, an elaborately carved wheel. Above us
were domes worked into filigree, delicate as inverted wedding
cakes.

We wandered up a narrow stairway that led to the roof, and
there all the detail dropped away: smooth domes and spires
and pyramids, as stark as an astronomical observatory, an abstract plane hovering over the ornate. Jim would have loved
that place. He would have snapped off half a roll of film, after
waiting politely for the man in khaki and a crimson turban to
move out of the frame.

I went back downstairs and sat cross-legged on the steps.
Someone nearby was murmuring in Hindi, and the smell of
jasmine and sandalwood wove a cowl about my head. The
courtyard was like a ballroom, cool and luminous, the light
echoing from wall to wall without losing incandescence. I
imagined it was like the light inside an egg, when the roost was
empty and a shaft of sun hit the shell.

That sense of transportation, peculiar to traveling, often felt
like the prelude to some profound event. It was an old confusion, not unlike the one I felt on the rooftop at Kerckoff Hall. I
mistook that first sensory flush for information, as if the body
were a gateway to knowledge. But those moments didn't give

way to anything else. They *were* the event, and then they were gone. The light changed, my feet chafed on the sun-baked floors, and still the carvings looked like no more than giant souvenirs. I liked beginnings, the first wondering glance, the first breaths of incense in the inner sanctum. I didn't have patience for anything else.

When I first arrived in India, I met a couple trying to see the country in two weeks — only the highlights — taking short Air India flights between stops. They were miserable. I kept running into them, and each time they seemed more haggard and crazed. The woman looked as if she were considering a murder. She would swing her eyes around in search of a victim — the waiter who brought her rice studded with rocks; her husband, who was herding her through this whirlwind tour. Every time I crossed their path, I was reminded of my own useless railings against the interminable waits, the ennui of the dusty southern villages.

Stranded there in Ranakpur, it seemed foolish to fight our fate. There was nothing to do but follow the festival we had stumbled on. When we wound back around to the front of the temple, a group of devotees had formed a circle at the door to the inner sanctum. On a small raised platform, musicians played tabla and sarod, while, at random, men and women came forward and danced — shy, lumbering, happy — in the center of the ring. Nitzan and I had just taken a seat a polite distance from the group when an Indian man, dressed in white slacks and shirt, suddenly stepped from behind a pillar. "You are Americans, no?" He grinned broadly.

His appearance was so abrupt we could say nothing at first. He must have used the columns as blinds, approaching sideways like a novice private eye.

Nitzan was the first to answer: "I am Israeli. Lis, here, is from the United States." I heard a note of irritation in my friend's voice. He disliked being taken for an American. He figured his kibbutznik's sandals and extended beard should read as clearly as the Israeli flag. In fact, his beard, which could have housed a nest of small birds, attracted considerable attention. Once, a group of children, chasing cows to gather manure for kitchen fuel, stopped and ogled the blond tuft. When he smiled, they came closer, gesturing at it with their sticky hands. Still, no one had heard of Israel, and it was beginning to wound him.

"Oh, United States, very fine," said the man. "And you are staying at the dharamsala?" He leaned jauntily against a pillar, stroking his chin.

Nitzan explained our predicament.

The man seemed thrilled. "I am Sanjit Mehta," he said, extending his hand to Nitzan, "and you must be my guests. My wife and I are staying at the tourist bungalow with our friend. He must go on to Udaipur tonight on some business. You can stay in his room."

We protested vaguely, just for show, then thanked him for his offer.

"I assure you, the pleasure is completely mine," Mr. Mehta said, as he led us to the low building we had seen upon our arrival and showed us to our room. "When you are properly settled, you must share some lunch. Last door on the left."

Sanjit's room faced a small courtyard. The walls were chalky blue and the furnishings simple: a wood-frame bed made with madras sheets, a long-stemmed ceiling fan, a few straight-back chairs. When we arrived, Sanjit's wife was washing clothes in the bathroom and seemed embarrassed to have been caught indisposed. She wiped her hands quickly and dipped her head as we were introduced.

"This is Nitzan, an Israeli gentleman, and his wife, Lisa." Sanjit gestured to us grandly. "My wife, Pune."

I saw Nitzan open his mouth to explain that we were not, in fact, married, and just as quickly watched him close it. We had already lied about our relationship on several occasions, and since Sanjit had made this declaration of his own accord, it didn't seem prudent to set him straight. Our room for the night may have depended on it.

"They have just arrived and are lacking accommodations," he told his wife. "I have insisted they stay in Gupta's room while he is taking the photos to Udaipur."

There was a subtle officiousness in Mr. Mehta that was beginning to bother me. The man didn't talk; he made pronouncements. Soon he launched into a soliloquy about the Jains, puffing out his chest and dropping his chin like a third-rate Shakespearean actor. While he talked, Pune began laying out small tins on the bed. Curried vegetables and rice, crispy nan. Nitzan and Sanjit chatted about camera equipment and Sanjit's hardware business in Jaipur. I asked him how he felt about India's trade embargo, but he behaved as if I hadn't spoken, fixing his attentions on my friend. Pune and I ate slowly and smiled when our eyes met.

I was having less enjoyment of the actual interlude than I was from the *idea* of it. As Pune proffered more curry and the men's conversation droned on, I consoled myself with the thought that I was getting a glimpse of the Indian business class. I felt guilty about this attitude, this hoarding of exotica. Even as I was in the middle of an experience, I was calculating its value on some scale of authenticity, oddness, the absurd.

Then the conversation took a promising turn. We learned that the Mehtas had traveled to Ranakpur to visit their guru, Anil, a businessman who had given up his fortune in order to live the life of an ascetic.

"He reads faces," Sanjit informed us. "You must come to see him. He is always looking for new types to study."

As Sanjit pressed this idea, I began to get the feeling that he had taken us under his wing to satisfy the appetites of his mentor, but we agreed to make a visit. The swami was staying nearby, and Sanjit seemed to relish the chance to drive us there in his new minivan. He opened the side door with a flourish for Pune and me, then let Nitzan into the passenger seat and slid behind the wheel.

I spent the short drive staring at the unforgiving scenery. Other than an occasional gnarled tree, the landscape was quite barren. Out the back window, the domes of the temple rose like tiny lumps of sugar above the coffee-colored ground.

We were met at the gates of another low-walled compound by two Jain monks, dressed in the usual white robes. They seemed to know Sanjit well and, after eyeing us carefully, laughed with him and clasped his hands. Pune looked off into the distance, appearing for the moment to understand little of

her native Hindi. My impression that we were to be offered as
prey to a holy man in training seemed confirmed. Nitzan, un-
troubled by the exchange, checked out the compound through
the viewfinder of his camera. As I saw it, there was not much
worth photographing: a tamped-dirt courtyard bounded by
concrete walls, and in the center a low blue building with a
spindly bougainvillea inching over the doorway. The monks
led us into a cool, darkened room where a third monk watched
the news on a television mounted on the wall, then out the back
door to a patio, set on the edge of a hill. When my eyes adjusted
to the light, I saw a round-shouldered man in a faded peach
robe, seated with his back toward us, and four chairs arranged
in front of him. Sanjit hadn't been anywhere near a phone since
we met him, but the swami seemed to be expecting us.

We settled into the assembled chairs, and Sanjit made introductions. "This is Mr. and Mrs. Yarmar," he said, sweeping a
hand in our direction with a modest dip of his head.

The swami said nothing. He stared at our faces, first Nitzan's,
then mine, then Nitzan's again. A faint smile played about his
lips. "But of course you are not married," he said.

"No," Nitzan answered. "We're not."

Sanjit looked shocked, but the swami gave him a dismissive
wave. He was already scanning our faces — devouring them.
Then he closed his eyes and tipped back his head, as if he had
just sampled a rare wine and was savoring the finish. After a
moment, his head snapped forward and his eyes flew open.
He stared at Nitzan with an alarming intensity. I looked over,
trying to judge my friend with fresh eyes. Blond corkscrew
curls burst from his head; his beard jutted forward like an
enormous chin. He returned the guru's stare with an impassive
expression.

The swami took a deep breath through his nostrils and
spoke: "He is not a king, but a maker of kings. He cannot tell
the lie. He does not have the forkèd tongue."

No one spoke after these pronouncements, and I had time
to consider their accuracy. Nitzan was often selfless, always
loyal. In the beginning, I had been jarred by his blunt speech,
but his frankness was predictable, and like all reliable traits in a

friend, it began to seem like a virtue. He looked amused by the swami's flattery.

"Note the development of the brow," the swami said, moving one finger in an arc in front of Nitzan's face as if smoothing out roughness in a clay bust. He seemed to be slipping into some kind of trance. "He is like the lion. He takes only from need, never pleasure. Consider the fullness of the lips . . ." The swami let this last comment trail off and made a grunt of pleasure under his breath.

By this time my friend was beginning to glow like the well-fed beast to which the swami had likened him. I looked over at Sanjit and Pune. They looked radiant. Suddenly, a wave of envy broke over me. This was the last of a load of irritating trifles I'd put up with since we crossed the Mehtas' path. I looked down at the swami's feet, hoping my fury wouldn't show. He was wearing a type of sandal I'd seen on other holy men: a flat wooden sole, with a single peg between the toes. Minimalist footgear — it must have been some kind of penance to walk in them. For a moment, I considered seizing one of his shoes and braining him with it.

Then the swami turned to me and spoke. "You," he said, his eyes bugging wide, then narrowing, "have a lot of aggression."

I worked to smooth my face.

"You have intelligence, but little patience, little patience." He sighed. "Someday you will meet a teacher and your life will be changed."

I thought of my crusty high school math teachers; of Professor Howe at UCLA, chasing Descartes. I couldn't imagine myself falling under a teacher's sway. The swami leaned forward and whispered to Sanjit, as if he were tutoring an apprentice: "Please notice the difference in the eyes." Then to the group, without preamble: "People have forgotten — om is the sound of air entering the body." His head wobbled back and forth, as if held by a weakening spring, and he folded his hands in his lap.

It appeared that he was through with me. I held out hope for a few more predictions, since he'd spent such a long time fawning over Nitzan's bone structure, and no sooner had this thought crossed my mind than the swami gave me a desultory glance. He wore the expression of a man checking his plate for a few last morsels.

"Everything is possible," he said. "If one man can achieve a thing, any man can do it. He has the curly hair." He gestured in Nitzan's direction. "Just think of it, sing the name of Ram, and you will have this hair."

Then the swami closed up shop before our eyes. The bones of his shoulders sank into their cloaking flesh. His chin dropped to his chest and he gusted gently.

"The reading is exhausting for him," Mr. Mehta whispered, ushering us back through the compound.

Before we boarded the van for the drive back to Ranakpur, our host had us pose against a sun-bleached wall. "A photo for Anil," he told us from behind the lens. "He keeps an album of the faces he's read. Something to browse over in the evenings."

When we returned to our rooms, Mr. Mehta asked Nitzan if he would enjoy a massage; he had been receiving one daily from a man at the dharamsala, and insisted on treating his new friend to the experience. Perhaps I might enjoy the company of his wife, who planned to spend the afternoon doing laundry.

Nitzan took little note of our parting of paths. He even asked, in the most innocent tones, if I would mind scrubbing a few of his shirts — I was so good at it. I had begun to notice a subtle imperiousness in him since Anil's reading, a certain noblesse oblige in the way he handed out coins to the boys crying "One rupee, one rupee" near the bungalow, but this was the trump. While he was getting his massage, I went to the tea stall by the road and inquired about the next bus to Jodhpur.

It was a night bus, but I was determined to be on it. When Nitzan returned from his rubdown, pink cheeked and in terrific spirits, I told him he was free to stay on with the Mehtas if he liked, but I was heading for Jodhpur. He claimed he needed to think it over, but when I walked to the bus stop at two in the morning, he was striding along several paces ahead of me. A few devotees were conducting a tabla marathon in the court-yard, their elastic rhythms bouncing off the walls. The bus stop was deserted except for a few conductors eating melon in the yellow light from the tea stall. They tossed the rinds at their feet, then shared a smoke. The night air turned sweet with fruit and tobacco.

Nitzan and I settled at a table and ordered chapatis and tea. I fell asleep and woke later to the sound of pots clanking in time to the radio. The tea had not come. In the kitchen doorway, I caught sight of the flashing pant leg of the tea wallah. A foot appeared and did a little wild circling in the dust. I felt as if I hadn't slept for days, and before me stretched the seven-hour ride to Jodhpur. Then I caught sight of a line in writhing script on my menu — "A little patience will enjoy you a majestic service and the superior food" — and I thought of Anil bent over his album on a quiet evening years hence, devouring like a bitter delicacy my impatience, my quicksilver greed.

thirteen

I HAD BEEN LUCKY in India thus far. All my fears of typhoid and theft and drugged cookies proffered on trains had been for naught. Then in Jodhpur, I got violent food poisoning from a bowl of corn flakes and milk and spent most of the night vomiting in a communal hotel bathroom. It was a good eighty degrees in the middle of the night, and when an episode passed, I rinsed myself with a bucket, rinsed the floor, then went back to bed to lie for a few minutes in peace before I had to head down the hall again.

Nitzan woke off and on through the night and stroked my hair.

"Could I be dying?" I asked him at one point. It seemed like a real possibility.

He muttered something soothing in Hebrew — a feat, since most times his language sounded like someone gargling stones.

At last, after twenty or more trips, the pain ceased, and I lay on the mattress while the first honks and revvings of traffic pierced the window. It was almost cool, just before dawn. I curled up under the sheet and slept.

When I woke, even the bottoms of my feet hurt. Nitzan went out to buy bottled water, and while he was gone, I stood at the window watching a woman making chapatis on a nearby rooftop. She squatted under the shade of a tarp, licked her fingers, and flipped the bread on a rickety griddle. In the folds of her sari was a tiny child, suckling at her breast. Just the thought of that milk made a wave of nausea rise up my throat, but I was touched by her persistence, out there in the heat. I backed into the room. Lumpy bed. Light branding the walls. Nowhere to go and no one to marvel that I'd survived the night.

I decided to place a call to my mother. Always an imprecise science. Only some hotels even made an attempt. I gave the number to the desk clerk, then went upstairs to wait. An hour later a rap came at the door.

"Madam, call is going through."

I went downstairs, palming the wall for support, and picked up the receiver. Clicking and fuzz. The vast humming of distance. Then, miracles, my mother's voice.

I told her I'd been sick, that I was going to Nepal soon.

"Be! Safe!" my mother said, as if shouting across a canyon.

I rummaged my head for news, anything to keep her on the line. Hearing her voice was a kind of banquet; I felt I had to come bearing gifts. "I might buy a roll of silk for a friend back home. She knows the name of a dealer in Delhi and says we could get twice —"

Our voices crossed somewhere over the Pacific.

"Think! About! Smugglers!"

My mother never got the knack of those calls, the bounce and delay. She talked like a telegram, her message boiled down to the bones. When I was a little girl and the visits to my father's house made me lonely, she made up a ritual to keep us linked. "We're both under the same moon," she told me. "You can look up at the moon and think of me." We had no moon in common now, no shared weather or landscape or stars. I hung up the phone feeling lost.

"Do you know, madam, you are talking twenty minutes total?" the desk clerk asked me when he saw I was through. This would cost a pile of rupees. He seemed to admire the extravagance.

Not long after that, I headed for Nepal. Nitzan, who'd already been there, would travel north, into the Indian Himalayas. I think he would have gone with me if I hadn't asked him not to. We were in our hotel room in Jodhpur when it came up, sipping glasses of cold tea. I was mending the hem of my favorite shirt — worn paper-thin from scrubbing — making tiny stitches and trying to measure my words.

"So how are you thinking about this Nepal thing?" Nitzan asked me. The subject had been raised before.

"I don't know. I want to try to get there before the rains."

He gave me a bare look. "I don't mean weather."

Nitzan had never pulled a punch with me, so I figured I owed him the truth. "I'm scared to go there alone, to be by myself again, but that's why I came here." What I didn't say: that I'd begun to chafe at his company, the way he considered himself in charge. I feared I was missing the instructive grit of solitude.

"I understand," he said.

"I'm going to miss you," I told him, but he held up his hand.

"Not so much, you won't." He kept his face light. "You'll be staying in some fancy hotels now for sure."

A week later, when Nitzan came with me to the train station in Delhi to say goodbye, I wept like a baby. That stubborn, bearded lunk looked like the best friend I'd ever had. The platform was packed, a river of bodies, and his was the only familiar face. We sat down against a wall, waiting for the last call aboard. I gave him an electronic address book, which I bought back home as a gift for some potential host, and which he had often admired.

"That's really something special," he said, fingering the tiny keypad. He put an arm around me. "I'll for sure remember my crazy American girl. Always weeping about some sad thing. You can tell your friends back home about me."

I wiped my face. "I'll tell them, 'He was not a king, but a maker of kings.'"

Nitzan laughed. "Yeah, that's good."

Then he helped me lock my bag under the bottom berth, and walked down the platform as the train picked up speed, waving through the window until he couldn't keep up.

When I arrived in Kathmandu, I went straight to the GPO to check for mail. A crowd of travelers gathered outside the door, and when the office opened we were directed into a dusty side room. Kathmandu, the only sizable city in Nepal, got so much mail for foreigners that a whole room had been devoted to its distribution. A long table ran the length of this room, its surface covered with shoebox-sized troughs, one for each letter of the alphabet. A clerk unlocked a heavy cabinet and pulled out the bundles of mail, each tied with string and marked with a letter, and dropped them into the bins. I took a seat in front of the Ms and flipped through two feet of thin air-mail letters, searching for a familiar hand. All down the table there were crowds in front of the popular consonants, and several people leaned over my shoulders for a glimpse of the flashing envelopes. We were like a pack of starved animals. Now and then someone shouted with delight. "Morton! That's me." I passed postcards and fat packets back to Miles and Milford and Masterson, and began to lose hope. Only a few inches left and not a single letter. Then, at the very end of the pile, four months after I left home, I found a letter from Mau.

I went out to the stone steps and tore it open. He seemed to have forgotten how much I drove him crazy. He was staying in a shack in Venezuela surrounded by wild calla lilies and was thinking about settling there to raise bees. Did I want to join him? The letter went on in this vein, full of plans. Then it came to a breezy close. "Before I decide whether to stay in Merida, I want to tour around for a while. Don't know where I'm going next. Argentina, Bolivia, Ecuador, maybe Chile and Peru?"

I wrote a ten-page reply on tissue-thin paper, not worrying until the end that I had no place to send it. Yes, I wanted to raise bees. Yes, I still loved him. On the back of my journal from those months is a list of South American countries. Far from an atlas, my sixth-grade geography strained, I resorted to querying strangers in cafés: "Pardon me, do you know the capital of Bolivia?"

When I had the names, I cycled through Kathmandu in search of a copy machine, finally coming across one in a dusty shop near the bus station. I made five copies of my letter and mailed one each to Buenos Aires, La Paz, Quito, Santiago, and Lima, hoping one might find its mark.

I had come to Nepal for the trekking, and when I met an Englishwoman who had a guide lined up and a trip planned, I decided to accompany her. Sarah was planning to hike up a small valley called Langtang, home to many Tibetans, then over a high pass and back down into the Kathmandu Valley.

We took an eight-hour bus ride to the point where the paved road ended, and spent the first few days hiking comfortably along wide forested trails, sleeping at night in small huts along the way. Sarah, a plucky Oxford graduate, who'd been teaching English in Kathmandu, wasn't big on exertion, but she managed to haul herself from one hut to the next in a day's time. Our guide, Shiva, a slim, fox-faced man from Kathmandu, coaxed us along by exhortation and example. "Good going, Sarah," he'd say, pausing by the side of the trail. Then he'd sprint ahead, unable to check his natural stride, and wait for us at the next fork in the road.

By the tenth day, the trail had risen above the tree line and angled through massive granite terraces. At fourteen thousand feet Sarah and I were both beginning to drag a bit, and Shiva quickly climbed out of sight. We followed slowly, stopping to catch our breath and look down at the quilt of firs below, then starting again only to be winded within a few steps. We were both getting a bit delirious. Sarah turned pink and wheezy, and leaned back on a large slab to rest. "That's it. We've been left for the jackals," she said. The sight of her, collapsed under her canvas baggage, blotches of red in her cheeks, made me laugh, which was a bad idea. It felt like I was breathing through a straw, and soon I was hunched over, hands on my knees, gasping for air. Sarah started to snicker. "Bloody Shiva!" she said, wiping tears from her cheeks. "He knows we're not fit."

We were both relieved when we saw the peaked roof of a lodge up ahead. We dropped our packs at the door and stood on the hillside, looking down at the way we'd come. A level bank of clouds had rolled in while we climbed, covering the valley and the lower wooded slopes. Punching up through the clouds were the snowcapped peaks of Annapurna and Everest. We appeared to stand at the edge of a vast empty dance floor, plumped white by a fog machine, and I was tempted to step onto that white expanse for a waltz. A last waltz, it would have been, ending several thousand feet in the valley below.

That night, I slept in every stitch of clothing I had, including gloves and a hat, and still woke in the night from cold. The couple who ran the lodge pulled down heavy batted blankets and slept near the dying fire. Still, I heard them rustling in the blackness at 4 A.M., when the cold took over the rooms.

The next morning, the clouds had disappeared. The deep green cleft of the valley opened below us, wet with mist. Shiva had gone off on a prebreakfast hike, and Sarah was late in rising. I ducked into the hut to check on her. She was sleeping soundly, but her breathing was rough.

I asked the lodge owner if I could have some lemon tea. She stirred the coals under a dented kettle and pointed to a seat by the fire. At times like this, I cursed my poor Nepali. I could ask how far a certain town was, count to five, say thank you and please, and order food in butchered phrases. But this morning, I longed to ask this woman if she was cold at night, if she had ever been to Kathmandu, if she was happy.

Sarah finally rose and stumbled out of the sleeping room. "Tell me, do I have a pickax between my eyes?" she asked, leaning against the door frame and looking wan. She seemed to have all the signs of altitude sickness: headache, listlessness, disorientation. We both decided that she should rest for a day. Shiva would wait with her, in case she needed to descend in a hurry, and I would go on to the next lodge with a young Australian couple, Ron and Juliet, who had arrived late the night before. When Sarah got acclimatized, we could cross over the Gosaikund saddle together.

The day's walk was easy, a traverse across a bald hillside dusted with snow. When we reached the crest, we looked down on a pair of glacial lakes. Robin's-egg blue and ringed with ice, the upper lake fed into the lower, which then ran off into a wide, rushing stream headed downslope toward the valley. We skirted the lakes, and in the shelter of some small hills on the south shore came to a lodge — rock walls, a sheet-metal roof, a prayer flag braced in a pile of boulders near the door.

We were the only guests at the hut. The lodge owner, a twenty-four-year-old who spoke some skeletal English, seemed lonely, and so we sat inside drinking tea and listening to Radio Nepal's English news broadcast. China and the USSR had established diplomatic relations after thirty years. I wondered what my father would have thought of that.

The lodge owner, we learned, lived most of the year alone by the lake, waiting for tourists to pass through. In the monsoon months, when the rains were too heavy for trekkers, he lived with his family in the lower valley. I sat next to him on a low bench near the fire, taking sidelong looks at his face, trying to imagine how he weathered the cold and the solitude. When he caught me staring, he turned, a little shy and surprised, and busied himself with the coals.

Ron and Juliet and I tucked into our sleeping bags early — the sun left the lake basin long before dark, and we were too cold to sit still without blankets — and ordered food in rotating order to keep the low fire warming the room. I asked the lodge owner if I could borrow an extra blanket, and he pulled a heavy straw-filled tick from a pile of batting in the corner and laid it over my sleeping bag.

That night I dreamt I was in a cathedral of ice, where a choir, set deep in the apse, sang mournful chants. The pews were cold, but I stayed, transfixed by the voices. Sometime before morning, I woke in the dark and heard the young lodge owner singing from his pallet near the fire. It was a lonely song, with no verse or refrain, and it warbled on like whalesong until the sun rose.

Over breakfast I asked him about it.

He shrugged and set bread to toast on the coals. "I sing keeping warm," he said, taking a quick glance at my borrowed blanket.

After tea and bread with honey, Ron and Juliet set out for Ghopte, a small village on the far side of the pass. God, how I hated to be left behind. I watched them move up the snow-packed peak until they looked like ants crawling across a white wall. I barely knew these people, and yet the sight of their tiny retreating figures made my throat catch. It was a relief when they broke the horizon and sank out of sight. I walked over the smooth hillside beside the lake and sat on a rock, trying to warm myself in the thin sun. I felt ashamed of having deprived our host of his extra blanket the night before, and decided that I would use up no more firewood before I left. Squirrels popped up from their burrows and skittered across the grass, dodging this way and that, not a shrub or tree to hide them from the hawks. It was a gorgeous, godforsaken place. I didn't see how that young man could stand it. I hoped that Sarah would come along quickly, so we could cross the pass in time to reach Ghopte before sundown.

By midmorning, Shiva came running over the crest of the hill. When he reached me, barely winded, he said that Sarah was no better and had decided to walk back down to our starting point and take the bus to Kathmandu. I could gather my things and make the return trip with them, or continue on, trying to catch Ron and Juliet. I worried over this for a few minutes, but it wasn't hard to make up my mind. Sarah would be safe with Shiva, and it seemed a pity to retrace my steps. I could see Ron's and Juliet's tracks leading away from the lodge in the hard-packed snow. I decided to follow them. Shiva assured me that I could make my way alone, and he wrote down the names of the villages I should pass through on my way down to Kathmandu: Ghopte, Tarepati, Kutomsom, Chisapani, Sundarijal. The trail was wide and well marked, he said, and I would run into Nepalese who would point the way if I gestured and looked sufficiently lost. I said goodbye to Shiva, wrote a note to Sarah explaining my plans, and set out.

It was a perfect day, the sky a flat, cobalt blue, the trail rising gently up the peak north of the lake. I walked quickly, breathless from my unexpected bravado, heart thumping under my ribs. Up ahead, the trail rose to the low point in a saddle, then disappeared over the other side. I had heard tales of people who became delirious and wandered off into the snow just yards from the crest, or those caught in sudden blizzards who were forced to turn back on their hands and knees, using the slope to guide them back to the lake. I had imagined that the pass would be a chink between peaks, a narrow windswept slot. But in daylight, following the tracks of Ron's and Juliet's boots, the crossing looked wide and benign.

Only my breath, shallow and ragged, gave a hint of how high I had climbed. I moved slowly, holding on to the straps of my backpack, surprised at my fortitude and foolhardiness. When I reached the crest, a vast bowl opened below me — snow and dark outcroppings, mist gathering lower down, a white amphitheater of cold. Through this basin threaded the faint depression of a trail. From my vantage, I could see where my friends had veered off, then found their way to the tamped rut again. I ran down the hill, glad to be on their heels.

After walking for half an hour or so at a fast clip, the snow turned patchy. I felt sure that my choice to go on was a good one. The trail was clearly visible, the good weather was holding. I even felt a little pride — pride I would later regret — that I hadn't suffered much from the altitude. I came over a rise and there, in a broad hollow of snow and dead grass, was a hut. It looked out of place, perched in the center of that stark space. When I came closer, I saw that the builder had been short of supplies; a grown person couldn't stand up inside. I bent over and ducked my head in the door, which faced downwind. A man sat inside mending a garment, his head nearly brushing the ceiling. He gave me one brief, indifferent look and turned back to his work.

"Ghopte, how far?" I asked in my pidgin Nepali.

"Far," he replied.

I pointed to the trail I was following. "Ghopte?" The man nodded and said nothing more.

Back on the trail, I swung my mittened hands and whistled to fill the silence. I knew it was childish, but that man took some of the wind out of my sails, preferring, as he did, solitude to the scarcest company. It didn't help that the landscape was desolate. In places where the snow thinned I could see the trail, but though I gained a sure sense of heading in those sections, I lost Ron's and Juliet's tracks, their comforting precedent. At one point I could see where it seemed they had stopped and turned around a bit, then stepped over a line of large rocks crossing the trail. I paused for a swig of water, then followed them.

The path contoured along a hillside for a while, curving around small ridges, then tucking into drainages between them, keeping a level course. It was easy going, but after an hour or so, I turned a corner and found the trail buried under a snowslide.

I walked to the edge to take a look. It was old snow, packed by wind to the stiffness of Styrofoam. It rose sharply above me — I couldn't hike upward to cross it at a flatter expanse — and below me the sheet angled down for a few hundred feet before ending in a pile of boulders.

I was ready to turn back, and then I saw a line of boot prints crossing the snow. It seemed my friends had continued. It must have been a small slide brought on by the warming temperatures. I cinched my pack tightly and stepped out on the angled crust, using their prints as footholds, laying my body flat to the slope and digging in with my gloved fingertips. I crossed without a mishap, hit the solid trail, and set out again.

About a mile farther on, I came to another iced-over section. Again the boot prints crossed and so did I. But there was another after that, and then two more. At each crossing I came close to slipping into the ravines below; when I reached the opposite side I ran down the trail, sure I had passed the last obstacle, only to turn a corner and find another.

On one sheet, about halfway across, one of the boot prints broke under my weight and I began sliding. I dug my fingers into the snow, listening to the scrape of my pack and shoes over the frozen crust, helpless to brake myself. The slope must have leveled off, because I came to a shuddering stop, crawled to the opposite edge, and sat on the trail, panting, till I recovered my breath.

I was convinced then that something was wrong. Shiva had never mentioned such difficult terrain. In my mind I retraced my route up to that point. Unless the man in the hut had lied, I must have gone astray after I stopped for directions. Then I remembered the line of rocks. They were no doubt the Nepali equivalent of a highway sign: road closed.

I tried to stay calm and consider my options. I didn't have a watch. As I walked, the mist had settled around me, muffling the light, but it seemed to be past midday. There was a chance I could make it back to the lone hut before nightfall, but I couldn't be sure. Then again, given the occupant's sour disposition, I couldn't be sure he would invite me in. And between me and that cold comfort were the ice slopes, one after another, a white gauntlet.

It might have been a wise decision to retreat, but something made me go on, and I wonder sometimes what steeled me. When I was in high school, I didn't keep a diary, but I used to record each day's events on my wall calendar: "Stayed home. Cleaned house. Burned my face with sun lamp." "Got a great watch from Grandpa . . . broke it." The notes were full of code, which my mother could have deciphered had she been nosy and a bit suspicious (she was neither). Tiny scissors marked the days I cut class, a torpedo shape with dots issuing from the end signaled the days I smoked dope. I crammed those squares with a record of my days, as if it might keep them from unraveling behind me. It never worked. At the end of the year, I took the calendar down and paged through the months, feeling an inexplicable loneliness, even as I remembered days when I knew myself to have been happy. The past collapsed behind me like an old sock. I couldn't recover its fullness.

So perhaps this had something to do with it. I couldn't stand the thought of heading back over the trail I had covered. Knowing exactly what I faced left me dry in the mouth. I could just see it: my body in a heap at the bottom of a gully — cheery, useless yellow slicker, limbs twisted this way and that. I wouldn't rot — it was too cold for that — but the snow and ice would cover over my body, and far away, on the back side of the globe, a handful of people would sicken with worry. So I might say that fear of the past made me go forward. A random thing, a character quirk. Someone else might have liked the idea of return. I opted for the future. Perhaps I had passed the last patch of ice, and just around the corner the trail tended downward. It seemed more of a heartbreak to imagine myself coming within a half mile of safety and turning back, than to plod deeper into the snow.

I made a quick check of my provisions. I had on light cotton pants and long underwear, a cotton shirt and wool sweater, tennis shoes and cotton gloves. Except for the wool sweater, all foolish. What was that phrase that Mau once used? "Cotton kills." In my pack I had a down sleeping bag (useless once wet), one quart of water, and a bag of dried chickpeas. If I didn't find shelter before nightfall, I'd most likely freeze.

I forced myself to chew some of the peas — sour, chalky little pellets. (They're a fad now in health-food stores, and I've tried to eat them once or twice, but it's no use: they taste of desperation.) I tried to think of good things: how I would catch up with Juliet and Ron, how they would turn around on the trail when I shouted, shocked to see me. How we would laugh at our stupidity and help each other out of this place. The two of them seemed more capable than I was, calmer, less prone to dread. It was toward their imaginary companionship that I set out.

It's difficult to build suspense in a tale of peril in the first person. The story survives, so it gives up its ending. But as I went through that day, I didn't know how it would end. That was the terror. (Or I could say, that *is* the terror, for all of us live with this ignorance of our fates, though we manage to submerge that fact for long stretches.) The trail continued on, neither rising nor falling. I had not crossed the last ice field; I came to one after another, and all the while the mist grew thicker, until finally I could see only a few yards.

Fog has a peculiar, dual nature: it's both a comfort and a blot. When I'm tucked inside with a comforter and tea, I like the way it pillows at the windows, and I like to go out into it, bundled, and let it wet my face. But then again it shuts down the view. I walked that day with the trail always blunted off before me. Beyond that mist, there might have been a forest or a cliff or a valley opening gently away, but I would never know it. I could have only one chunk at a time, and I had to make of it what I could.

The footprints continued, but I never heard or saw any other signs of my friends, and after a while I began to believe that I wouldn't survive. I'd had a few brushes with disaster before — one foot off the curb and a truck barreled past, lifting my jacket lapels. I stood there, shaking, on the lee side of my death; but it was over before I could even call out, and there was nothing to do but cross the street with the rest of the preoccupied foot traffic.

Midway through that day in the snow, I understood that I had made a fatal error, that I had stepped over that line of rocks like a pedestrian stepping off the curb, but I stayed in that canyon of time: the truck bearing down, no way to turn back. That hair-trigger terror lasted and lasted. I stopped on the trail and shook my head, stomped up and down, yelped. I couldn't believe it — this was real. Perhaps this is why we never dream our deaths. When the dream becomes too dire, and the dreaming mind believes in its plight, it scans for exits, just as the waking do when they face the gun, the long fall, the room filling with fire. The sleeper thinks, *Perhaps I don't have to suffer this*, and the mind lets go of the nightmare and wakes. But there was no trap door from that trail to my sheet-tossed bed. I was awake and lost, and I had arrived in that spot out of carelessness.

But it seems to me now that it wasn't only inattention that got me in trouble. It was more than that. It was my idea that fear had to be conquered. I believed, at twenty-two, that I had to force myself toward whatever filled me with dread, and along the way I'd lost the idea that fear was a useful gauge of risk. I was anxious sometimes, but I mistrusted my anxiety, thought it unfounded and overwrought, so I didn't heed my own instincts. In those days, I didn't know how to filter out the real news from the static. It was only a matter of time till I lost my way.

Nonetheless I kept walking, scrambling over more snowslides, sometimes leaving the trail and hiking down below the snow, then climbing up to the path again. What frightened me more than my actual death was the loneliness just before slipping off. I thought of Mau at a café in Bolivia, watching pigeons forage in the square; my mother at her kitchen table, correcting school papers in the glow of the skylight; and my sisters, in Los Angeles, making slow work of cleaning their rooms. How grim to die in this unlikely place. I decided to take a photo of myself, smiling into the camera for all of them. I would snap the shutter and then write a letter about the birds, how along the way I startled them out of the rocks: blue tails, red breasts, a bright dash of color on my starved eye. Or how the rocks piled in prayer mounds beside the trail looked like houses through the mist, how I ran to them, already phrasing my tale of survival, and found only wet stones, an old pennant snapping in the wind.

My mother, in particular, would have understood how the dimness wore on me. Her stories always described what the light was like. Often in my childhood she had recalled the view from the delivery room on the twelfth floor of Beth Israel Hospital, Newark, New Jersey, the room where I was born. She began the story like that, with all the particulars, the names and stats of a vital occasion. She was twenty-two, the same age I was then, and she labored alone. The nurses, knowing she had hours to go, checked her in and went on to more pressing things, and once the contractions got strong, my father became too frightened to stay with her.

That labor room had a pair of narrow windows that gave onto the Hudson River and Manhattan. The skyline, a winking stencil when she arrived, slowly hardened into gray stacks and spires in the daylight. The way she described that view, I knew my mother had looked at it often as the hours passed, perhaps nearly all the time, and for years I didn't understand that — her minute recollection of the horizon, the way the sun fell into the room like the tines of a tuning fork. She would run her thumb and forefinger down through the air, always off to the right, and squint, as if she were looking again through those panes. Now I know what held her. That window — the choppy glitter of the river, the skyscrapers where people lifted from floor to floor — offered her a way out, the long view, something to fasten on that didn't heave or sway.

She had told the doctor in advance that she didn't want anesthetics, but as the labor wore on, he came in every hour with a needle. "You've got a long way to go," he said. "I could give you some scop." When she said no, he went out again, closing the door behind him.

It was full noon when they finally held me up — the fat palpable sun of midday. They wheeled me to her side in a plastic bassinet — a little bundled comma with black hair — and told her she wasn't to touch me. Then they left her alone.

"And did you?" I asked once, sure that she had.

She was slow to answer, lost in the memory. "Oh, no. They said don't, so I didn't. I just looked at you and kept saying, 'I have a baby! I have a baby! Oh, my god, I have a baby!'"

She laughed and went quiet, sifting back to those hours in the delivery room: "Right at the end, when you were crowning, I had my hands out like this, flexing them, and the nurse said to me, 'If you can't keep your hands under the sterile sheet, we'll have to strap you down.'" She whispered this last line, her lips pressed together on all she would like to say to those people, thirty years later. Then she looked at me with a glint in her eye, and I stared back at her, both of us stoppered by helpless fury, for both of us had been there and neither of us could go back and change any of it.

Time just keeps moving, past scenes of devastation and sweetness, and I wonder sometimes how much we choose what we carry with us. From my mother's story, it was the light that I saved — not my father's fear or the doctor's pitiful brusqueness, but my mother's stamina and unlikely courage and her memory of the way the sun fell across the river and into her room. In the midst of that pain, she kept her eyes open and took note of the light.

As I walked, I cast my mind like that, over people half a world distant, and at times it seemed that they were never more fully with me than in those hours, that I carried in my head the whole story of who they were and how I had loved them, that they were presences within me — my mother, my father, Jim and Leslie, my sisters, my brother, Mau. Loving them could take place in their absence, a conjuring up of their specific dearness, which for the moment of its conjuring changed me in some unnamable way.

The mist deepened into a thick cocoon, and, wrapped in that cold, I got lonelier. Memory was a thin soup, nothing close to companionship. There I was, swamped by tenderness, by feelings that sprung up *between* people, feelings that were meant to reach their mark. It seemed to me then that the only things that mattered were the things that got said and done, the places where we struck up against one another and changed course. For that, I would have to make it back.

I made that vow and then I rounded a bend and saw the path
blocked by a wall of ice. A rock outcropping hung over the trail,
and a stream seemed to have spilled over it in warmer weather.
Now the water had frozen in a solid sheet that continued — a
long, slick chute — down the drainage into the mist below. The
lost section of trail was short, perhaps twenty feet, and beyond
this impassable gate the path continued, muddy but clear. I
squinted to see if I could make out footprints on the other side.
In places, the path looked trampled, but I couldn't be sure. I
looked down into the mist, roiling like steam from a teacup. If
Ron and Juliet had fallen, the drop would have killed them.

I called out anyway.

"Hello?"

The sound, and the quiet that came after, made fear lift
through me in waves. I paced back and forth on the ledge, and
considered leaping. It did have a kind of definitive appeal — to
hurl yourself toward one sure consequence, your hair blown
upward like flame.

But under my terror was an odd kernel of calm, and I fixed
on this, and waited for the panic to pass. I remember surprise at
this coldness. After all, I was known as a weeper. Mau would
turn from the most foolishly sentimental film and catch me
wiping tears from my eyes. I used to say it felt like my skin was
gone, but that wasn't the truth. I wept because I couldn't bridge
the gap between myself and those who suffered. I wept because
I was safe.

There on that blocked trail, caught in my own predicament, I
was too shocked to cry — a dry, fixated state. If I felt any sadness, it was for my parents, for the grief that was in store for
them. My father told me once that freezing to death terrified
him. He loves the desert, that dry enveloping heat, and has a
primal mistrust of the cold. If I had asked him why, late at night
after a brandy and a bath, I imagine he might have said something about the New York winters, when it became clear his
father had left for good, trudging up the snow-lined walk to an
empty house. To see me like that, lost in the snow, he might
have thought fate knew his heart, its exact fissures.

But if my body was found, I figured he would be the one to

come claim it. My mother, the practical one, couldn't bear it. Pragmatism was her smokescreen: she had no time for grief, no opening, not even a rib slot in her armor. She made a decision at twenty-three, alone in a flat with a daughter in diapers: she was sick of sorrow; she had had her fill, and wouldn't sit under its eaves any longer. What a strange gift then from my father, to have him make such a pilgrimage. She had once clung to the idea that he couldn't be trusted. But my father's not afraid of life's mire. He wades in, weeps and shines, somehow returned to a territory he knows.

But there I was, wasting time on life beyond the grave, when I should have been deciding how to save myself. I went closer to the ice fall and saw that the upper edge had melted away from the rock, leaving a gap the width of a sneaker. If I stood on the narrow crest and held on to the outcrop, I might be able to inch across. The rock was pitted, sharp, and full of handholds. I slid my foot into the crack and pulled myself upright. When I had two good grips, I advanced my right foot, then brought my left beside it, found two new handholds, and began again. I was nearly across, when I stepped to the right and the ice gave way beneath me. It made a sickening sound, like the grinding of teeth. I lost hold of the rock and slid downward. Then just as quickly I stopped. I had sunk straight into the ice, like a sword into its sheath, and when the ice reached my hips, my backpack, jutting out behind me, stopped my fall.

Not a molecule of air seemed left in my lungs; it had all gone out in one terror-struck howl. I was buried to the waist at the tip of a two-hundred-foot column of ice, and right in front of me, at my new eye level, was a small flower blooming in the rock. It had blue petals, thick as flaps of callus, with splashes of yellow in the center. Each petal was covered with fine hairs, and I was so close I could see tiny drops of mist balanced on their loft. The flower looked like the pansies my mother planted in great rafts along the path to the river. "Frivolous," she called them, because they were expensive and lasted only one season. This one was a gardener's dream: able to withstand freezing temperatures and rare sun.

This was some kind of shock-induced botanical swoon, but I

got over it and found two good handholds in the rock. I pulled
one leg out of the ice and laid it along the crest, then I dug my
fingers into a crack and heaved, letting my weight settle on the
free leg. Another leg free, another step, another handhold. Then
the blessed firm mud on the far side.

When I hit that path, I decided to run. I would run until the
sun went down, which it seemed near to doing, and then I
would turn on my flashlight and walk by its light until the
batteries went dead, and then I would crawl in the dark. I
started to jog, found a steady pace I could maintain uphill or
down, and gave in to its rhythm. After a while, the trail seemed
to tend downward, and the snow lightened on the slopes, but I
refused to take hope. When I passed the first rhododendron, I
didn't even pause. I took that mark of lower altitude like a
runner grabs a drink midstride, without thanks or hesitation. I
was sailing down the trail, no sound but the heavy thunk of my
sneakers and my ragged breath. Trees appeared between the
rocks, and then I turned a corner and saw a hut — a real hut this
time, not the rock piles that had tantalized me, but four sturdy
walls and roof. I walked up to it slowly and stuck my head
inside. It was empty, no bed or blanket, but I could sleep there
out of the rain, and I would not freeze. It would buy me a night.
In the morning I would begin again.

Then I smelled wood smoke on the wind. I can't say how that
first whiff wrenched me. I walked out the doorway and over a
small rise, and there, on the lee side of the hill, was a collection
of huts, each chimney expelling a thread of smoke. A small boy
stepped out of a doorway and came toward me, holding his
hand up in greeting.

"*Namaste*," he said, as if I had just stepped away for a moment, and he had been expecting me.

At first, my awkward sobs seemed to confuse him. He stood
in front of me, in a small peaked cap and a tattered windbreaker, furrowing his brow.

Then he recovered his poise. "Come," he said, pointing toward the huts. He started toward them, and when I didn't
follow, he came back again. I didn't think I could move, and I
didn't want to, so we stood there for a while, as the mist fell

apart and at last I could see where I was. Below us was a scallop
of hillside, and below that a deep valley, thick with pines. I quit
crying and wiped my face, and the boy nodded, but he didn't
move. We waited together a while longer, as steam lifted from
the roofs of the huts, and watched a pair of goats chewing their
way across the tough mountain grass.

Once we were inside, the boy set about stoking the coals for tea.
As the room filled with smoke and the sun went down, I mimed
and gestured at the way I had come. The boy spoke quickly to
his father, who sat on the doorstep puffing on a long pipe.

The man turned and gave me a surprised look. "Road no
good," he said. He waved his pipe in the direction I had come,
clicking his tongue. "Three men lost." So it wasn't Ron and
Juliet I had been following after all. It seems that three other
trekkers had made the wrong turn the day before, and it was
their boot prints that had led me astray. The man squatted on
the mud floor beside his son, nodding encouragement while I
gulped down some broth. The boy made lemon tea and bread,
which puffed up on the fading coals. Then he showed me to a
bed — a pile of hay wrapped in a cloth. I lay awake for hours
listening to the snap of the fire and the rustle of beetles in the
straw. Brief flashes of the afternoon returned with a clarity that
made my heart thud. Then I slept without warning, as if I'd
fallen into a black slot.

It took me three days to hike back down to Kathmandu. My
knees were like jelly. Every morning I ate four aspirin with my
tea and picked out a stout walking stick from the scrub. The
trail cut back and forth across the hillsides, through terraced
fields of rice and wheat. As far as I could see in the hazy sunshine, the hills were banded with bright green and gold, and
children passed by with scythes on their backs.

On the third day, I arrived at a dirt turnout with a few houses
and a store: Sundarijal. Here the bus would come to take me to
Kathmandu. The turnout was filled with schoolchildren in blue
cotton uniforms and villagers who had trekked down from the
mountains. I half expected some kind of reception, some ac-

knowledgment that I had finally hit flat ground. I did get a few long looks, mostly for my green backpack and running shoes. But no one knew or cared where I had been.

I stepped into the store and bought myself a Hershey bar. The proprietor told me I had just missed a bus. The next one would come in three hours. I didn't mind. I laid my pack against a low rock wall and turned my face up to the cold mountain sun, eating chocolate and dozing.

When the bus came, a crowd suddenly appeared and I was lucky to get a seat. The man who wedged himself in beside me was a businessman, an English speaker, and we chatted a little as the driver revved the engine and turned the bus around. Just as we were pulling out onto the road, a woman came running beside the door, cradling a bundle against her chest. The driver stopped and she got on, dipping her head in thanks. Something in her bundle moved, and then a small foot pushed out of the cloth. The woman edged her way down the aisle, protecting the child's head from bags and elbows, and squeezed onto the bench across from me. She turned then, and adjusted the drape, and I saw a face I will never forget. It was the face of a girl, a one-year-old with round cheeks and a button nose, but her eyes were ancient, and her whole scalp from forehead to nape was a raised blister, ruddy and crusted with matter.

The mother held the cloth gingerly away from the burn, and the child didn't once shift or whimper. Her stillness sent ripples out into the crowded seats, all of us turning and murmuring, a few of the mothers touching the woman's shoulders and arms. Someone asked what had happened, and the man beside me translated her story. The baby had pulled a kettle of hot dahl onto her head. The mother had carried her for two days to the bus.

"Where will they go?" I asked the man.

"To a clinic. They might have to wait a day or two, but someone will see them."

"Can't they afford a doctor?"

"Probably not," he said.

No one near me spoke for the three-hour ride into Kathmandu. The bus jolted over deep ruts, and at first I would glance over to see how the baby was faring, but her expression never changed, and after a while I couldn't look. When the bus stopped at the terminal, I asked the man how much a doctor would cost. He shrugged and named an amount. On the concourse, I found the mother and pushed a wad of rupees into her hand. She looked blank, and turned to the man for an explanation. "For the baby," I said, pointing to the child's head.

I looked at this woman, her face drawn tight with pain and now softened by confusion, and felt ridiculous. I wanted to rescue this child, as I had wished to be rescued from the snow, but she was already in competent hands. This mother had walked two days to Sundarijal, probably leaving other children behind. I remembered her courtesy, the way she paused in the foot well to give a word of thanks to the driver.

The businessman tapped my arm. "She says many thanks," he said. And then he was gone, and the baby was gone, and I walked toward Durbar Square in search of a room.

I spent the next week wandering through the streets of Kathmandu, not caring whom I spoke to or if I spoke at all, browsing through the bookstores, drinking hot chocolate in the sunlit cafes. I can't remember when I felt so content over simple things. In the afternoon, I went back to my single room — narrow, with a narrow bed — and washed my clothes in the concrete bathroom. The days were warm, and I went through everything in my backpack, welcoming the chill of cotton, the heft of soaked shirts. From the window came the sullen clop of cattle, whistles and laughter of schoolchildren let out for the day. I stripped down and piled the clothes against the wall, soaped and rinsed them under the rusty tap, then strung a line across my room and hung them under the ceiling fan. At the end of the week, I booked a flight to Bangkok, and from there I would go to Hong Kong, but in my mind I had reached the farthest point of my travels. I was already turning toward home.

On my last morning in Nepal, I woke at first light, put on earphones, and rode off on a rented bike — a rickety one-speed with bent rims — toward a temple on the outskirts of town. The sun broke across the peaks, and in the cobbled streets and down the short alleys a gray predawn mist still held, pale as tufts of cotton wool. A few elderly women walked at the edges of the road, swinging prayer wheels. I came clattering up behind them, sounding my bell in warning as the bike-rental boy had instructed, and none of them turned or flinched. The tape hissed in my ear, then a song began. It was the opening cut from Joni Mitchell's *Blue*, borrowed from a man in my hotel, and from the first bars her voice conjured up Alan Sarkissian's living room, in that valley were I grew up, the smell of gear oil and the polished wood of his sarod. But this was a song I had never heard. "I am on a lonely road and I am traveling, traveling, traveling . . ." The words made my blood ring. There was the unmistakable presence of a person in those lines — in the bell-clear soprano, the strumming, the wit. I swooped downhill in my skirt and sandals, dodging potholes.

In a trough at the bottom of the hill, a catch basin for the last bit of moonlight, I passed two boys carrying sacks of saffron on their backs. They were bent double by the heavy loads, stepping quickly over the wet cobblestones, hands braced on their head straps. Who knows how far they had come? Far enough that the spice had sifted through the burlap and over their arms and shoulders so their bodies glowed yellow in the phosphorescent light. Perhaps it was coarse to see such beauty in their labor, but I couldn't help it. I was glad I had lived until then.

epilogue

MAU FOUND A COPY of my letter in Bolivia, and when I made it home from India we moved into an apartment together. He enrolled in a Ph.D. program in zoology at U.C. Berkeley, which he stuck with until he tired of studying a rare epiphyte that only thirty people in the country could call by name and went into medicine. I wrote a letter to Michigan (the only school that accepted me) saying thanks but no thanks, and spent a few years doing scut work at a software company and trying to write poetry. And in time the swami's prophecy came true, in a manner of speaking. But that's another story.

This one seems to have arced down a few years ago, when Mau and I decided that ten years was a sufficient test drive and set a date to be married. We gathered for that event at an old hall in the Berkeley hills, where nine of our parents walked down the aisle, mothers and stepmothers and ex-stepmothers, the accumulation of seven marriages, my ring having been handed down from a union that petered out in Mexico City circa 1974. Hope springs eternal.

Once we made it out to the huppah, and the rabbi had ascertained that, pale as he looked, Mau was in fact not going to faint, our parents got up and made a series of speeches. Mau had gone through a brief but passionate return to his Jewish roots in the months before the wedding, and so the speeches were supposed to correspond loosely to the seven blessings of the Jewish marriage ceremony. We could have used the originals, which were lines of general praise and hosanna — except "Thank you, God, for making the barren woman fruitful" stuck in my throat.

My mother got up that day and talked about particle physics. "In the search for a unified field theory which would explain the mysteries of the universe, we've learned that tiny subatomic particles behave in unison across vast distances, in the absence of time, sharing their state and maintaining their relationship." She was holding a slip of paper, her voice shaking, but her face was as calm as it had been on those days when she stood at the head of a classroom. "I am Ann. My blessing today is for the field that structured the lives of Fanny and Bush and Carl and me, bringing us together for a while to send these good sweet children, Lisa and Mau, out of the void and into the future, drawing them together and toward this moment, from their births at almost the same time, a continent apart."

The blessers were offered a sip of ceremonial wine at the close of their speeches, but Jim made a show of taking a slug before he began, doing a vaudeville tremble to cover his nerves. Then he read a poem that I had recited to my mother during our mail-truck days.

Leslie was next, and she — who often took a role behind the scenes — surprised everyone by telling a story. "With the phrase 'Dare to struggle, dare to win,' little Lisa, in 1975, read the words of the Chinese communist Chairman Mao Tse-tung to bond her father and new stepmother in marriage." She looked elegant in a long black dress, a hat and high heels, and grasped my hand as she talked. "Little did we know then, another Mau would come on the scene . . ."

Leslie had been my consultant on the wedding dress — a long sheath with appliqué straps — which turned out to be an easy buy, compared to what went underneath it. She and I drove all over Los Angeles in search of the right bra, which was finally unearthed at Olga's Corsetorium, a dusty shop off Fairfax where the mustachioed Olga presided and the bras stood up by themselves.

My father got up and spoke of ethics, the closest he came to religion. "In the best tradition of ethical Judaism, of the laying on of hands and the laying down of words, I wish you happiness and love." My father's brevity was a measure of the ease between us. He had thrown himself into the wedding with sentiment and gusto, hosting the rehearsal dinner, handpicking the wines, flying up to Berkeley to plan the menu, the flowers, the music. By the time he stood up under the huppah, nothing much more needed to be said.

Then Mau's mother and stepfather said words of good luck, and his father sang a blessing in Hebrew and dissolved into tears. I wept. Mau wept. The rabbi wept. My sisters, who held the huppah poles, were — in the words of one of my friends — "wrecked," makeup moving down their faces in streams.

The night before, after hours of tossing and turning, I had risen to stare out the hotel window. The city glittered away below me, and beyond it I could see headlights moving over the Bay Bridge. Those lights calmed me. I was getting married in the morning. Someone else was headed for the night shift. Life went on.

I pried a banana from the fruit basket, went into the bathroom, plunked down on a nest of towels, and wrote my vows. In the other room, Mau was sleeping soundly, but he'd already passed through his own moment of anxiety. The day before, I'd gone down to the pool to nap under an umbrella, and when I came back to the room he was frantic.

"I'm so glad you're here," he said, pulling me into the room and shutting the door. His face was wild. "I was watching this nature show, it was about rats, and they were writhing around in their little dens, squeaking and squeaking."

Normally Mau loved a nature show. But this time it failed to have its usual calming effect. He was pacing around the hotel room.

"So, what happened?" I asked, following him back and forth.

"I don't know, I just lost it."

During the year the wedding was in the works, Mau had behaved as if he would be a guest at the party, albeit a special guest with special privileges. When I was trying to pick a caterer and decide between seven fixed menus — each one preplanned from hors d'oeuvre to entrée — I asked him if he

wanted input. "Look, I can either explain all the choices," I said, the menus in a jumble before me, "or I can just make a decision without you."

"Oh, no," he said, "I want to have input."

I had to admit I was relieved.

"I'd like a green salad to start," he said, cocking his head to the side as he imagined the plate, "with a vinaigrette, a simple pasta, maybe pasta primavera, a fruit salad (fresh, no syrup), nice bread." He waved a hand in the air, animated by his order, then caught sight of my face. "What? What's that look?"

That look — blanched, slack jawed — was: my god, I'm going to live with this man for the rest of my life.

But under the huppah, I managed to remember the things I'd scribbled on hotel stationery during the night, and I held on to his hand and said them to him.

Then the glass was stomped, and we went into the hall to dance, limp with relief and amazed to see all the people that we loved, together for a night under one roof. Mau's mother and stepfather pushed aside their plates and did a tango in a corner before the dinner was finished. My father was roused to some vintage disco moves by the Commodores' "Brick House," and when I joined him the guests opened into a ring. At first I felt embarrassed, but my father, who never disappointed a crowd, got some superhuman burst of energy and started doing floor taps and scraps of the hustle. His shirt was soaked through. He was ecstatic. I tried to keep up, laughing so hard I could scarcely breathe, and as I spun I caught flashes of my friends' faces. Wendy, in particular, was hysterical with delight to see those gestures, which I had tried to render during our college days, performed by the true original.

My little brother, by then ten, had been assigned to videotape the occasion, based on a piece of roving video reportage he made for fourth-grade show-and-tell. In the end he was too discouraged to bring it to class, but I thought it was a hoot: a cinéma vérité tour of the family medicine chest and the graffiti on my sister's bedroom wall, complete with doleful voice-over. But as a wedding videographer, he was a disaster. The tape, when we watched it later, was mostly black, as Little Jim,

soured by the party for which there had been so much buildup
and which turned out to be a loud occasion for grownups,
toured the patio and the far reaches of the lawn, beyond the
reach of the lights.

"I really can't see much out here," you could hear him mum-
bling. "There are some people out by the trees. There — if I
press Backlight I can kinda get a bead on them." Once in a while
he would make a quick pass through the party. There was a
blurred glimpse of Jim Senior against a wall, smiling and mum.
Mia and me dancing to some tinny Caribbean music — "I know
how to make 'em dance," the DJ said — filmed before my father
gave the man guidance.

At one point my cousin thrust his face into the frame, baring
his teeth and flipping his eyelids inside out. "Hey, Danny," my
brother said, snickering from behind the lens. "We can watch
this when we get back to the hotel."

When I first saw my brother's tape, I wanted to throttle him.
But after a while it seemed just as well. I had wanted to fix that
day down to its particulars, wanted to revisit the whirl from a
fresh angle, but it couldn't be fixed. That was the poignancy of
arriving at a moment of such completed feeling; half our delight came from the knowledge that we couldn't linger, that
time would keep carrying us away.

Toward the end of the evening, I went to the bathroom to cool
off and dry my face, and when I returned I caught sight of my
mother and father across the room. They were lost in conversation, seated at a table with their heads bent together, my
Grandma Leila between them. Someone spoke — I was too far
off to make it out — and they all threw their heads back and
laughed.

Over the years, my mother and father had held terse phone
conversations, brief exchanges in motel parking lots, and
shared five stiff minutes on the sidewalk at my college graduation, but I had never seen them together like this. I could tell
from across the room it was an exchange of another order.

When I walked over, my mother turned toward me and
smiled, a smile that seemed to reach through me, to some ap-

preciation of a glad hour. My father leaned back in his chair, surveying the room — my sisters bent over a table of my college friends, Leslie talking to Mau's great-grandmother, and finding out, we would later learn, that she hailed from a Polish village much like the one my great-grandmother had left a century before. My father has a nose for social phoniness, but I could see from his expression that it came up real. Or at least that's how it seemed to me then. I don't know why I should be any authority on them, these people who raised me. I come to them with such expectations.

"Look, here's the bride," my grandmother said, waving me to a chair. "I was just telling your mother she should write a book. You know, I still remember her letters?" She twirled the stem of her water glass. "She could take a casual day and make it interesting."

I smiled at her. I had heard this before, enough times to wonder how far the thread traveled. "What about you, Grandma, did you ever want to write?"

"Who, me?" She squinted slightly and looked away. "I was never any good at writing."

My father leaned forward and covered his mother's hand. "How could you have been a writer, Ma? No one encouraged you."

We sat for a moment in silence, the party whirling around us: my mother, my father, my grandmother, and me. Sometimes, we are peopled by our gratitude. Just then it seemed that I'd become what they — that sleek couple from the Grand Central photo booth, posed here together after thirty years — had given me, a girl with enough wild days to fill a story, and the faith to think I could tell it.